THE PASTOR

THE PASTOR

READINGS FROM THE PATRISTIC PERIOD

Edited by
Philip L. Culbertson
and
Arthur Bradford Shippee

FORTRESS PRESS   MINNEAPOLIS

THE PASTOR
Readings from the Patristic Period

Scripture quotations, outside the selections, unless otherwise noted are from the Revised Standard Version of the Bible, copyright © 1946, 1952, and 1971 by the Division of Christian Education of the National Council of Churches.

In the selections, scripture quotations follow the original publication, often the King James Version.

The editors gratefully acknowledge that:
Harvard University Press has given permission to reprint selections from Ignatius and Basil found in the Loeb Classical Library.
Paulist Press has given permission to reprint selections from Cyprian, Ep. 11; John Cassian; and Gregory the Great.
The Society for the Promotion of Christian Knowledge has given permission to reprint selections from Origen.
Westminster Press has given permission to reprint selections from O. Chadwick, *Western Asceticism*.

Interior and cover design: Publishers' WorkGroup
Cover art: Scala/Art Resource, N.Y. K 15634 Ravenna, Galla Placidia,
          Lunette with the Good Shepherd
Maps: C. Kim Pickering

Library of Congress Cataloging-in-Publication Data

Culbertson, Philip Leroy, 1944–
    The pastor : readings from the patristic period / Philip L.
  Culbertson and Arthur Bradford Shippee, editors.
      p. cm.
    Includes bibliographical references.
    ISBN 0-8006-2429-7 (alk. paper)
    1. Clergy—Office—History—Sources. 2. Pastoral theology—
History of doctrines—Early church, ca. 30–600—Sources.
I. Shippee, Arthur Bradford, 1957–   . II. Title.
BR195.P36C84   1990
253'.09'015—dc20   90-32823
                                                                  CIP

The paper used in this publication meets the minimum requirements of American National Standard for Information Sciences—Permanence of Paper for Printed Library Materials, ANSI Z329.48-1984.   ∞™

Manufactured in the U.S.A.   AF 1-2429
  94   93   92   91   90   1   2   3   4   5   6   7   8   9   10

———

Parentibus adiuvantibus
Magistris optimis
Amicis duobus carissimis
Deoque omnitenenti.

CONTENTS

CONTENTS

PREFACE

Pastoral theology is for the most part a field without a clear definition: its precise meaning and component parts seem to vary widely from one denomination to the next and from one seminary to the next. The how-to of pastoral care and the component elements in the process of clergy character formation seem to be equally slippery. In all three fields, however, constitutive material seems to be taught either from a strictly scriptural base, or from a base of modern psychological and sociological theory as it has been appropriated by the church, or through a combination of scripture and modern scientific insight—but rarely does the teaching of pastoral formation make direct reference to the fascinating history and tradition of the early church.

Instruction in pastoral theology and care may make reference to Jeremiah, John, and Jung, but rarely to Jerome; to Psalms, Philippians, and Freud, but rarely to Polycarp; to Amos, Acts, and Adler, but rarely to Athanasius; to Micah, Mark, and Maslow, but rarely to Mother Syncletice. This omission is due in part to a lack of familiarity with the vast library of writings from the early church. Even denominations that pride themselves on their sensitivity to the apostolic tradition include far too little time in their seminary curricula for reading source documents from the patristic period. A second reason for this omission is the attractiveness of modernity: the sophisticated ring of modern psychotherapeutic and sociological theory seduces us into granting a validity to Clinical Pastoral Education that we are reluctant to grant to the life experience of, for example, the desert ascetics. It is as if somehow the continuity of the human condition from Eden forward underwent a total and radical transformation in nineteenth-century Vienna. Yet as we read the pastoral literature of the early church, we find many of the same reasons for joy and for anger, the same elations and disappointments, the same rewards and struggles that face clergy and other professionals in ministry today; they are simply couched in a pre-Enlightenment frame of reference. A third reason for the omission is surely a sad reflection of the present age in which Christians struggle for identity: the major religions of the West— Christianity, Judaism, and Islam—are so deeply gripped by the threat of scriptural fundamentalism that we have all but lost our traditional balance of the trialogue of revelation among scripture *and* reason *and* tradition.

A more accurate balance will be found in our materials here. The writers we have chosen appeal to scripture on occasion, to their teachers and forebears on other occasions, and to their own contemporary reason and common sense on still other occasions. They understand God to be revealed in all three areas of authority, and to be revealed with particular clarity when two or three sources of authority are brought into conversation with one another. Tradition is the bridge that spans scripture and contemporary scientific insight, and pastoral theory and praxis are impoverished by having lost touch with the church's valuable heritage of tradition and time-hallowed practical experience.

The genesis of this book is worth noting. Some years ago, I was asked to teach a course, in the seminary where I am professor of the theory and practice of ministry, on "Source Documents in Pastoral Care." Searching for an appropriate textbook for the course, I discovered that most of the material from the patristic and medieval periods was available only scattered within large collections of documents, and that no readily accessible sourcebook in the field existed. The present collection, then, provides a sampling of documents in pastoral care and priestly formation, drawing on selected materials from the first six centuries of the history of the church. The selection is necessarily limited in scope and chosen subjectively; whatever consistency it has is not due to any comprehensive expertise of mine in the field of patristics, but rather to that of my friend and colleague Arthur Shippee, with whom this book is coedited. Although this book can be read on its own, it can also complement textbooks in early church history and in pastoral care, such as the now nearly classic *Pastoral Theology: Essentials of Ministry* by Thomas Oden.

Our texts have been chosen according to certain specific criteria. First, we sought texts that address how the character of a pastor is

formed and how it is kept on the right track in the midst of both
worldly temptation and ecclesiastical strife. Second, we chose texts
that address the way pastors nourish their personal spirituality and
then act it out in Christian service. Finally, we chose texts that
reveal the early church's absorption in worship and pastoral care.
Standard historical accounts of early church history tend to portray
the period as one long string of theological and christological
disputes. Yet even these theological points sprang initially from
some thorny pastoral complication. The Christian community
spent its time trying to be a community, and it was aspects of
pastoral care, then as now, that chiefly occupied the attention of
laity and clergy. For these reasons, the texts have a compelling
character that transcends the words themselves.

In the introductions to our various texts, secondary sources are
cited by author and date; full citations are given in the bibliography.
We have provided paragraph and verse numbers where they are
standard, but not all texts have standard divisions. Unless otherwise credited, the translations here are in the public domain.
Some, indeed, are well over a century old. We have generally not
tampered with these translations, but have simply reproduced
them. Where necessary, however, and feasible, the texts have been
modified to reflect a more inclusive style of English. In a few
instances, for Clement, Origen, the Elviran canons, Ps.-Basil, and
occasionally elsewhere, Mr. Shippee has provided corrections or
translations.

Our appreciation is extended to those who made this volume
possible: to the National Conference of Christians and Jews and to
the Shalom Hartman Institute in Jerusalem, under whose auspices
we originally met; to the School of Theology of the University of
the South in Sewanee, Tennessee, and its dean, the Very Rev.
Robert Giannini, for making travel funds available, and to its li-
brarians Ed Camp and Don Haymes for their help in locating texts
and for creating the environment in which to enjoy them; to research assistants Lyndon Harris and Darlene Ehinger for proof-
reading and indexing; to Jim Jones for computer formatting; to our
editors Hal Rast and Michael West for their warm professional
support and encouragement, and to our book designers Publishers' WorkGroup for gifts of felicity and style.

Philip L. Culbertson
Arthur Bradford Shippee

ABBREVIATIONS

ACW   *Ancient Christian Writers*
ANF   *Ante-Nicene Fathers*
CCSL   *Corpus Christianorum. Series Latina.*
Clem.   Clement
CSCO   *Corpus Scriptorum Christianorum Orientalium*
Ep.   epistle
FoC   Fathers of the Church
HE   *Historia Ecclesiastica*
Hom.   homily
LXX   Septuagint, Greek version of Old Testament
NPNF   *Nicene and Post-Nicene Fathers*
ODCC   *Oxford Dictionary of the Christian Church*
Ps.   pseudo

Standard abbreviations of biblical books are used.

INTRODUCTION

THE PASTOR IN HISTORY

Paul or Athanasius or Augustine: They are usually presented as writers defending or attacking rival theologies, steadfastly opposing Gnosticism, Arianism, or other heresies. But if we were to examine their job descriptions, if we could peruse their time sheets, we would find something different. They spent most of their time being pastors.

This simple observation should interest the church historian and the pastoral theologian. The historian will want to know what the church and all its various members did from day to day, and what they thought about it. The pastoral theologian, trying to articulate a coherent, modern, Christian pastoral theology, is faced today with the quickly changing pastoral roles of numerous communions within a wide variety of cultures across the world. Early Christianity was decentralized, its pastoral roles grew and shifted continuously, and it spread within a multicultural world in flux. It is clearly a relevant field of study.

The pastor, too, will find concrete suggestions and the challenge of intriguing alternative understandings of the pastor's job.

Because of this observation, we present the pastors of the early church doing their jobs and talking about their roles. This book is their book. Like any traveler to another land, however, the modern reader may need a guidebook and a phrase book, so we have added introductions and annotations to help the reader experience these authors as directly as possible. The following pages begin the introduction of readers to writers, first from a historian's perspective and then from a pastoral theologian's perspective.

Definition

While collecting the texts for this work, we used a broad understanding of what pastoral care involves. This is called practical theology, when pastoral and practical theologies are distinguished. In the course of our research into the early church we found not a single system of pastoral thought and action but instead an odd jumble of duties and ideologies variously interrelated, with different emphases in different times and places. It looked quite modern in its undisciplined plurality. We chose texts that we found were, above all, representative, but also representative of the better traditions—and interesting too.

Historiography: How to View the Past

In the past quarter century, certain pastoral theologians have felt that Christian pastoral theology was losing its peculiarly Christian voice and becoming a mute stepchild within the psychotherapeutic world. Part of their strategy to reformulate a vital Christian pastoral theology was to reclaim the hard-gained insights of the Christian tradition. These ancient insights turned out to be workable in the modern world, often even prefiguring supposedly modern advances.

These writers, however, were educated primarily in modern psychology, and the methodology they applied in their quest reflects their background. It is no accident that psychology has studied mythology very fruitfully, because the two points of view are similar in many ways. Both are profoundly ahistorical, presenting a schema of eternal truth peopled by more or less ideal and characteristic types. Their discussions of the history of pastoral theology fit this idealizing mode. These are generally schematic and reductionistic, attempting to distill a particular trait of a period, a trait so dominant and pervasive that it could represent the entire period. Idiosyncrasies are pared away to arrive at an essence, an essence not meant to help organize and relate the mass of data from a certain period, but to replace the data and to be the proxy of the period. And so the first one-and-a-half centuries of Christianity become the daily awaiting of the end of the world, and the next century and one-half become the persecuted life under the daily threat of martyrdom. As representative types functioning within a Christian psychological mythos, these are interesting to ponder. As historical statements, however, they are manifestly absurd.

Our book presupposes a different historiography. Our realm of discourse is one historical period, clothed in all its particularities. The first principle of our hermeneutic is to avoid a rush to relevance, but instead to gain a strong or significant irrelevance, since relevance and significance are not the same. Relevance here means relevance to modern questions. The questions emerge from the modern discussion, and so they exist as *a priori* guides in the historical search, telling us beforehand what to see. How can we judge whether these questions are good guides? Are they well formulated? Are there deeper questions?

A historical approach that patiently attends to a thick description of the individuality of a subject will let its questions emerge naturally from the data observed. Since our texts were written fifteen centuries ago, and over 5,000 miles away, the emergent questions may well be irrelevant. But for this very reason they will also be independent of the modern discussion. As independent voices, they can cross-examine and critique the presuppositions of our modern concerns. The historian's task in this program then is to help establish a strong, independent voice and, as far as possible, to keep it true to itself so that it can speak not only to our questions but also against them. Such a program is more difficult, more dangerous, and more interesting.

Diagnosis or Healing

I will risk an example of what one can gain from this approach. We moderns tend to look at our world in terms of coherent predictive theory: not only in physics, but also in psychology, economics, medicine, and so on. In fact, the lack of such a theoretical framework might be seen to indicate a lack of seriousness or a naïvete. Construing the world around them as a series of theoretical constructs was almost wholly foreign to the culture of late antiquity. A few topics, among them rhetoric and dream interpretation, were fairly well systematized, but most were not, and people then were rarely concerned with developing theoretical systems. This is an important difference between us.

In important ways, we moderns have a distinct advantage. One need only look at the field of health care. We have the ability first to

analyze the difficulties found to be common to a certain group of
people, such as adult children of alcoholics, and then to develop
therapies based on the analysis. This is clearly an intellectual gain,
and it is a pastoral gain as well: more practical steps may be de-
signed to deal with more thoroughly understood problems.

Modernity has a darker side, however. The theories that can
organize our observations and therefore increase our knowledge
can also replace our observations and knowledge with mere framework. This framework, abstracted from knowledge and observation, can then be used to oppress people.

The evil power of diagnosis is found in labeling a person, because that person may from then on be safely ignored. The diagnosis of AIDS functions this way; a human being becomes a
P.W.A.—a person with AIDS—to be blamed or avoided. The cate-
gory of madness has a long similar history, as Michel Foucault has
powerfully described. The penitentiaries, the eugenics movement,
cancer scares: all these provide disastrous examples of the wrong
application of diagnosis and theory.

We should listen to our forebears, partly along the lines that
Greer (1986 and 1989) has sketched out. Doing without such theories, our authors had to treat the person before them, and they took
seriously the ability of that person to be healed. Their seeming
naïvete saved them from trivializing a human being into an anony-
mous exemplum of the aggregate. When a theory is the preferred
goal, diagnosis can actually become a hindrance to healing a person. Chrysostom's final lines in chapter 9, for example, remind us
that the pastor's duty is not to understand, but to heal.

Exploring the Historical
Background

Turning from theory to our proper subject, we have sought to
provide texts and notes clear enough to be picked up and read as
is, which we encourage. At every turn, however, are points that
will be more interesting and suggestive as the reader learns more.
Beyond the particular points noted in the chapters, we will also
propose tools that can help fill in the general background more
richly. Do not be intimidated by the specter of extra work. Read the
texts themselves. You may find that they invite further reflection or
study, and we have tried to help you accept the invitation.

General Aids

The most helpful tools to have close by are the encyclopedic ones, such as Cross and Livingstone's ODCC (1974²) or Ferguson, et al. (1990) and the patrologies of Quasten (1983) and DiBerardino (1986). From them one can quickly gain an individual portrait or find a definition or bibliography. Comby (1985) and Ramsey (1985) give basic introductions to how to read early Christian literature. The Messages of the Fathers of the Church series, under Thomas Halton's direction, covers separately many aspects discussed in these chapters.

Our book is organized within a historical framework, and a good church history will clarify the interrelationships and general significance of its writers. H. Chadwick's Pelican history (1967) is standard and easily accessible; Walker et al. (1985⁴) packs much wisdom into a short compass. Fuller and more detailed pictures are given in Lietzmann's four volumes (1961); although Frend (1984) is newer, its numerous drawbacks counterbalance its advantages. Von Campenhausen (1959 and 1964) paints vivid pictures of most of the writers used herein.

Late Antique Setting

1. Greco-Roman Society

Our texts and their authors were products of their culture, and it is important to see them within late antique society at large. One might start with Lane Fox (1987), a large, accessible volume full of information and descriptive and methodological insight. Jones (1964) is a vast storehouse of *realia* presented with wit and insight. What was a religion? MacMullen (1981) will help one to understand the types of and expectations from religion(s) in that society. Mac-Mullen (1984) examines the growth of Christianity amidst those expectations.

Pastoral or practical theology had its non-Christian counterparts, then as now. Let us note some of the specific tasks.

Healings and other magic or wonder working were accepted and often prominent pastoral tools in the early church, and, with regret, we have had to pass them by for the most part, since we could not give them the careful treatment they deserve. MacMullen's books show the cultural importance of healing and magic; Garrett

(1989) for the first century, and Greer (1989) for the fourth, show how Christian miracle workers appeared within their cultural backgrounds and how they functioned within Christian ideology and self-definition. Greer describes a gap "between the social and institutional development of the church and dominant themes in Christian theology during [this] period." The miraculous functioned in the building and preservation of the community, while theology developed within "a Christianized version of the late antique quest for virtue. The deeper issue, then, has to do not so much with miracles in and of themselves, but with the tension between the realities of the Christian community and attempts to articulate the Gospel that constitutes it." So Greer (p. 119) sets up his analysis. This issue emerges in several of our chapters.

A leader's presiding at cultic functions constitutes an integral but vast topic. One can begin with Beard and North (1989) for the pagan backgrounds, and with the ODCC articles, for example, "Priest," and with C. Jones et al. (1978) and Bradshaw (1983) for Christian origins. (Pueblo Publishing of New York publishes a number of relevant works.) The early Christian paradigms of leading worship most closely followed synagogal models, but the details are cloudy and variety seems the rule. The relationships of Christian liturgies to their myriad counterparts and predecessors are so complex that it is difficult to formulate adequate questions to define them. Pagan priesthoods usually functioned with little articulated ideology, but one might read the relevant parts of Plutarch's *Moralia*, in the Loeb Plutarch, volume 5, and the emperor Julian's attempts to formulate a standard pagan philosophic-cultic ideology in the fourth century.

Julian's attempts were consciously formulated over against Christian practices and so are quite relevant for us. In the Loeb Julian, one might read the long fragment called *Letter to a Priest* (Loeb 2.293–339; 288A–305D), and the letters to the high priests Theodorus (Loeb 3.54–61; 452A–454B) and Arsacius (Loeb 3.66–73; 429C–432A). Sozomen, HE 5.16, preserved the latter, with pertinent comments. Gregory Nazianzen, in Oration 3 *Against Julian*, discussed Julian's program. The aspect of Christian pastoral care that Julian envied most and wanted imitated was the liberality of Christian philanthropy.

Almsgiving and support of the poor were Christian characteristics that grew largely from Jewish roots; see Amos, the Sabbath

Year requirements, and the extensive legislations on tithing in the Mishna and the Talmud. In the cities, the general mechanism of support for the poor, both for feeding and public works, was the patronage system. P. Brown (1978) gives an elegant description of how it worked—and broke down; see Hands (1968) for a general picture and Jones (1964) for documentation. Christian support grew around the bureaucracy of the bishop and deacons. Bobertz (1988) shows how models of the episcopate and diaconate grew out of the existing patronage system.

The heart of our book covers aspects of moral formation and reformation, which were vital commonplace topics for the moral philosophers. Excellent introductions to the Greco-Roman framework of these tasks are given in Malherbe (1986) and Meeks (1986). (The other volumes in the Library of Early Christianity series are also helpful.) These books can introduce as well the ancient backgrounds of the preaching ministry, of which Hunter (1989) shows the next steps. Many of the moralists are available in the Loeb series.

2. Jewish Traditions

Besides the influences of the Greco-Roman society at large, there were, of course, significant influences on the development of the pastoral roles that came from specifically Jewish sources. First among these is obviously the Bible: Proverbs and Wisdom of Solomon, Isaiah and Amos. Heroes such as Abraham, Moses, and Job were looked to as models of righteous behavior. Later Jewish literatures, those called intertestamental, Hellenistic, and rabbinic, present difficulties in classification and excerpting for our purposes. The Talmud, for instance, is entirely relevant, but because of its form and genre does not easily provide selections to fit a plan like ours. It must be taken more on its own terms. We can now only offer a few pointers and a warning.

The warning is to be careful. Even when one is rid of silly prejudices, of which too many survive even in scholarly works, it is easy to misread these texts, especially the rabbinic, by imposing on them forms of thought and expectations that are really quite foreign to them. The first tool that is needed is patient discernment. The history of these difficult topics is well set out in Kraft and Nickelsburg (1986).

Among earlier Jewish works, often classed as the Pseudepigra-
pha, relevant parallel material can be found in the Wisdom material, like the *Sentences* of Phocylides, and in the testamentary literature. The texts discussed and quoted in Nickelsburg and Stone
(1983, see chapters 2 and 3) and in Collins (1986, see chapter 4)
cover a wide range. Philo was immensely influential on the church,
and many of his treatises are helpful, if a bit theoretical and one
step removed. There are ten volumes in Loeb; Winston (1981) has
The Contemplative Life, and his selections in the sections of chapter
11, "Ethical Theory," will help guide one into the corpus. From the
Qumran material, the *Manual of Discipline* and the *Damascus Rule*
provide a mixture of historico-theological ethical theory and specific, practical advice. The rabbinic midrashim and talmudic texts
are full of delightful material; some easily accessible works are
Pirqei Avoth (Chapters of the Fathers), found in many translations,
Herford's edition (1945) having helpful commentary; the minor
tractate *Derekh Eretz* (a phrase denoting correct social behavior or
comportment); and the tractate *Semahoth (Mourning;* the Hebrew
title is euphemistic), best consulted in Zlotnick (1966).

3. New Testament

It ought not surprise anyone to find that among ancient texts
the New Testament has attracted the most detailed study of pastoral practice, not only as "scripture" but in large part because it is
such a good source for social historical information. Foundational
to this study is Meeks (1983). Social-historical study has brought us
to recognize that the New Testament gives witness to a wide
variety of responses to a wide variety of situations, pastoral as well
as theological.

Various offices began to develop from the earliest times.
Thurston (1989) describes a vital clerical order often overlooked.
The new study on *diaconia* in early Christian writings by Collins
(1990) claims to challenge standard views. Faivre (1990) reverses
the question: The most innovative change was not the creation of
officers, but the creation of the laity, people *not* set apart. Until the
third century the entire community was commonly considered
elect.

The Pauline communities have attracted the most notice. Malherbe (1987) examines the fascinating picture of the initial formation of a Christian community given by the earliest document in

the New Testament. Other views of Paul are given in Best (1988) and Meeks (1988), a very provocative article. Kruse (1985) covers a number of exegetical issues solidly but lacks flair. For the Johannine communities one can begin with R. Brown (1979) and Malherbe (1983²). The differing perspectives of John Elliott and David Balch (in Talbert, 1986) help us see First Peter's pastoral concerns. Matthew, James, and Revelation: pastoral concerns are constant in the New Testament.

The New Testament was also, obviously, a primary pastoral guide to our authors. The writings of Paul, including the deutero-Pauline letters, were particularly influential. As Augustine and John Chrysostom were the pastors of the Latin and Greek churches, so Paul was their pastor.

4. Patristic or Early Church Period

Volz (1990) now provides a fine synthesis of a number of aspects of early Christian pastoral practice, under various rubrics. His topical approach should complement our presentation well.

A great number of studies on particular texts or situations illuminating pastoral practice and thought are available, some of which are noted in our chapter introductions. A sensitive and fruitful step toward synthesizing these concerns and material is Greer (1986). McNeill (1951) gives the big picture. It has held up relatively well, with exceptions: for example, his knowledge of Judaism is skewed, and his focus on penitence is too narrow. Concerning our authors, we offer a caveat: Gregory the Great and perhaps Cyprian were from the senatorial class, Ambrose from the equestrian, one step below; the Cappadocians were landed and accustomed to patronage; and so on. They represent a very narrow social range, coming from a group that constitutes but a small percentage of the population. Only one of our authors was not male, Syncletice, preserved among the *Verba Seniorum*, often called the "Sayings of the Desert Fathers." One does well to keep this limitation in mind: how representative of the "common life" were our authors? Yet being part of a social stratum does not utterly prevent one from transcending its boundaries. We must not overlook the facts that our authors in a variety of ways usually rejected the assumptions and social prerogatives of their class and explicitly stated their pastoral concern for the people they served, and that our authors were beloved by those people.

Most of our material comes from the late fourth century. In part, this represents the quality of the period's authors—but only in part. Before Constantine there were fewer Christian writers, of course, and many of their works are lost. The following centuries could easily supply their share of pastoral theology, "had we but world enough, and time" to include another book's worth of material.

Donatism: A Case Study

To conclude, a historical example may help suggest how one can integrate a pastoral dimension into the study of church history. All modern Western churches, Protestant and Roman Catholic, spring from medieval European roots. The medieval church was Latin based. The greatest Latin patristic writer was Augustine; the two earliest major Latin Christian writers were Tertullian and Cyprian. All three were North Africans, and the careers of all three were deeply involved in fundamentally the same issue, ecclesiology. The debate over ecclesiology focused most sharply on what status gross sinners had in the church, especially those who lapsed in persecution. It involved how and even if they could ever be received back into communion, and by whose authority. The lapsed, because of their vast numbers and circumstances, served as a test case for the wider problem of the church's response and responsibility towards believers caught in sin.

Although plain old party politics usually exacerbated the situation, the two polar positions in the debate on church membership are easily if roughly summed up: laxists, for whom the reintegration of the sinner was the first goal; and rigorists, for whom the purity of the sinner was primary. In cosmopolitan Rome, both aspects had long histories. The rigorist tradition is represented by the Epistle to the Hebrews, Tatian, Hippolytus, and Novatian; the laxist, by Hermas, Callistus, Stephen, and, later, Leo and Gregory. Carthage, more parochial than Rome, remained more consistently rigorist, as the examples of Tertullian and Cyprian show.

Ecclesiology and its pastoral dimensions can be studied in detail in the history of Donatism. Donatism is usually presented as a social-historical topic or as a theological topic dealing with the theory of penance and priesthood. The controversy that grew from it, however, raised a multitude of practical pastoral concerns. Some are "minister's nightmares." The rich Lucilla, rebuked by a priest for ostentatiously flaunting and kissing a martyr's bone during mass, was offended and decided to bankroll the opposing side. One side brought a civil suit against the other to the emperor, only to end up convicted itself. Then this faction began to oppose Roman civil authority. Which side was the schismatic side? Was it the Donatists, who had the loyalty of the great majority and who were much closer to the traditional position of Tertullian and Cyprian, or the Catholics, who had international and imperial support? Were the Circumcellions theological and nationalist freedom fighters, or terrorists? How does one evaluate Augustine's pastoral strategy in dealing with the Donatists, for instance, his use of Imperial troops?

Donatism provides a wide range of pastoral issues, and since there is relatively much primary evidence and secondary study available, it provides a rich source for case studies with pastoral analysis. Briefly, here are some places to begin. The chief ancient literary sources are Optatus, Augustine, and Eusebius. They preserve many original documents, from both sides and from the court actions. A fair number of these are given in Ayer, 1913, §§61, 62, 67, and in Kidd, 1920–41, §§190–93, 196–201, 214–19 (note chronology). The only full-length treatment of Donatism is Frend (1971); many of his articles are relevant. P. Brown (1967) is vital for understanding the chief player of the later stages of the controversy, and the perspective of Greer (1989) helps. Besides these, see the relevant sections of ODCC and DiBerardino (1986) for further bibliography. Be sensitive to the biases, mainly anti-Donatist, in the presentations in the various handbooks.

Keep asking questions about pastoral practice, and listen attentively. The attentive, open listener will gain many new answers and, more valuable, new questions.

PASTORAL THEOLOGY AND PASTORAL TRADITION

Remembrance

Early Christian pastoral practices are open not only to historical analysis. The familiarity we often feel when reading ancient texts on pastoral care comes in part from their continued influence on writers through the centuries, and it comes as well from the fact that they deal with situations basic to the human condition. This continuity of tradition and condition has to a great extent formed modern society.

Anamnesis, the refusal to forget, has always been highly prized in Judaism and Christianity. The Torah repeatedly instructs the Jewish people to teach the tradition to their children, and the Oral Torah has been cherished with the same fervor as the Written Torah. In Christianity, community memory has played a central role, from the eucharistic words of Jesus, "Do this in memory of me," through centuries of catechetical traditions and credal statements, to the centrality of Sunday school instruction and the keeping of genealogical records in local congregations. A people without a memory is a people without a history, and a people without a history is a people without an identity: if we do not know where we came from, then we cannot know where we are now, nor where we are going. Without a history and a memory, pastors risk repeating endlessly the mistakes of history, but without the benefit of the solutions of history. If we have no sense of identity, whether the church's historical identity or our own, then we are of little use to the lost and suffering who seek our pastoral care.

The Fruits of Remembrance

The documents of tradition are a written record of our memory, which is a prerequisite for our present Christian identity. Much of the material in this book has a ring of familiarity about it because we are facing the same issues, and making the same mistakes, in the church today as our pastoral forebears did some twelve to twenty centuries ago. If we can allow our own historical tradition to instruct us in the present, perhaps the elusive goals of church unity and effective pastoring will move closer to our grasp and our church communities will find themselves less fractured and less at odds with their own pastoral leadership.

How well we recognize ourselves in the pastoral literature of the early church! Although the writers here presented span a period of five centuries, and the entire geography of the Mediterranean world, specific issues arise repeatedly, issues all too like those faced by the church today.

Clergy

One of the observations most often repeated, as in the words of Origen, Athanasius, Pseudo-Clement's *Homilies,* the *Apostolic Con-*

stitutions, Aphrahat, Ambrose, Chrysostom, and Gregory, was that the best candidates for the clergy were those who did not volunteer with easy zeal, who did not approach the church assured of a personal call to ministry. It is likely, said our writers, that people who volunteer, or approach the church unbidden in assurance of a call, sought the ministry in order to satisfy a personal need, such as praise or power or status. Preferred candidates were those who had a proven record of public service and lay ministry and who were chosen for ordination by some form of popular election, subject to confirmation by the bishop.

In general, our writers subjected the clergy to grave criticism. Almost all of them spoke of the temptations of ordained ministry, such as pride, ego gratification, abuse of authority and power, destructive competition with other clergy, gossiping and meddling in the affairs of others, and sexual misconduct. Cyprian, Pseudo-Clement, Basil, Ambrose, Jerome, Leo, and Gregory all bewailed the clergy's overwhelming failure to exercise personal discipline, in everything from their penmanship to their gait, from their eating habits to their verbosity. Ambrose, Jerome, Chrysostom, and Leo deplored the ignorance of the clergy; Ignatius, Cyprian, Athanasius, Pseudo-Clement, Jerome, and Leo emphasized the responsibility of both clergy and laity to maintain obedience to the bishop, even when the character or the decisions of the bishop might have been in doubt.

Authority

The structures of ecclesiastical authority, discipline, and obedience were in flux. Responding to a troublesome and widespread lack of personal discipline among both clergy and laity, various conciliar canons, as well as St. Basil and others, struggled to solidify a hierarchical structure of patriarchal authority and church discipline. The laity apparently did not often respect the clergy, the clergy did not respect the bishops, and all repeatedly needed to be called to task. In the meantime, Origen, Cyprian, Chrysostom, and others observed that leaders of whatever rank were themselves held responsible for the sins of those over whom they exercised authority. In other words, a given incidence of sin or disobedience might not simply be the fault of the sinner, but blame might also be traced to the failure of ecclesiastical superiors to provide proper guidance, exhortation, and example. The laity, however, were as much to blame for the continuing problems of the church as were the clergy; Origen, Basil, and Chrysostom, as well as various ecclesiastical canons, attested to the general lack of self-control throughout the church membership. For example, problems with marriage, adultery, and remarriage appeared again and again. It was not clear within the tradition whether marriage or celibacy was the higher calling for the laity. Remarriage was absolutely never allowed for clergy, and occasionally celibacy seemed to be preferred for all clergy as "a higher state." Adultery was generally classed as the primary sin in which both clergy and laity were engaged.

Duties and Identity

Clergy have struggled with the problems of adequate compensation since before the period of the Pastoral Epistles. Basil, Augustine, and Jerome warned how clergy were tempted to maintain lucrative businesses on the side, in order to prosper by worldly standards, and were even tempted to usury. Clergy were cautioned not to amass any sort of financial security, and the laity were charged to compensate clergy to a sufficient degree that the ordained were at least distinguishable from beggars.

Preaching was clearly not of a consistently good quality. Jerome, Chrysostom, and Gregory all commented on the generally poor quality of preaching heard in churches and the need for clergy to provide more solid content, more sophistication, more variety, and less dramatic flair in their sermons. The art of pastoral counseling was still developing. Origen, Nazianzen, Chrysostom, and Gregory were all aware that effective counseling demanded an advanced degree of discernment and a developed sensitivity to the appropriate "diet" needed by each of the wide variety of persons who came to the clergy for counsel. Neither pat answers nor strictly standardized techniques were proper to pastoral care; instead, "while we hold a single doctrine," that single center of faith must be mediated in a variety of languages and manners to many diverse adherents.

In the midst of theological heresy and repeated dysfunction at every level, our authors continued their calls for church unity. Although discipline and obedience were clearly marks of this unity, it was not to be so narrow a uniformity as to rule out the diversity of, say, ancient liturgical practices inherited within the larger Mediterranean tradition. For example, both marriage and celibacy were approved, and discrepancies in setting the date of Easter were not seen as contrary to the tradition. In general, we find the church still struggling to articulate its identity, both in terms of its own community boundaries and in its relation to the secular world. Origen, various canons, Nazianzen, and Leo all cautioned the church against working too closely with the secular authorities, although *The Teaching of the Apostles* allowed the monarch to join the clergy at the altar as a sort of concelebrant. The community of the church was clearly to be in the world but not of it. Christians were cautioned against close relationships with non-Christians. Temporary or permanent exclusion from the community itself, in the forms of deposition and excommunication, very real threats, was the discipline enforced in the case of several specified sins. The dogma of *extra ecclesiam non salus* emerged clearly in these earliest centuries of the church, and yet the boundaries of the Christian community often seemed fuzzy and indefinable.

In the church, as in society, rules are made because someone is already breaking them, and as soon as rules are made people will find ways around them. As Clebsch and Jaekle (1964) have so admirably pointed out, the church in both its theology and its institutional structure has been reactive rather than proactive. Society at large or existing life styles and thought patterns of the laity and clergy set the standard, and then the church busies itself with responding to that standard. So, between the lines of our texts, we can read that rules about clergy adultery would not be necessary if the clergy were not already committing adultery; rules about episcopal elections would not be necessary if the elections were not already tainted. This reactive stance of the church could produce contradictions as well. Since the agenda of Syrian society in the third century hardly matched that of Italian society in the sixth century, when "the church" responded to two different situations, at times it appeared to speak out of both sides of its mouth. This is one of the fascinations of history. From its origins, the tradition of the church has been broader and more fluid than popular views of dogmatic conservatism would prefer to recognize.

Hermeneutics

Finally, we are faced with the question of how these texts might be reclaimed in our present age. An immediate stumbling block is, of course, the sexism frequent in the texts. The status of women in both society and the church of this period contrasts significantly with the freedom and equality that the church attempts to offer women today. In trying to represent the tradition accurately, we deemed it important to leave in some particularly heinous observations, for example, about women's inferior character, as a point of historical reference.

We learn the truth of Ecclesiastes: there is nothing new under the sun. Apparently from the start clergy have been bucking the authority of the bishop, laity have been complaining about the scandalous behavior of the clergy, remarriage has been an option opposed by the church, salaries and educational levels of clergy have been too low, and the leadership of the church has insisted that all would be well if only we could (a) achieve church unity or (b) go back to the good old days when things were the way they were supposed to be or (c) convince people to take their baptismal vows more seriously or (d) all of the above. Our texts help us to understand that there never were halcyon days of the church, nor will there be until the advent of the long-delayed *parousia.* So our ancient texts help us critique our romantic and unfounded notions of an ecclesiastical "golden age," as much as our modern advances help us correct the foibles of the past.

We also learn that pastoral care is not always gentle, nor does the loving God rule out harshness and censure within the counsel of the church. Pastoral care is blunt when necessary, and God is an authority to be feared as well as a loving benefactor. Above all, we learn how difficult and complicated it is to be a member of the cloth. Perhaps our forebears were right; those who seek the position too readily have something wrong with them, a hidden agenda. Being a pastor is often a thankless job, surrounded by competitive peers while struggling to do ministry among a rebellious and rejecting laity. All the old problems seem to be still with us, and a new set of problems have been added in our troubled age. A remarkable sophistication is demanded of the clergy, more now than ever before. An inner vocation is not enough; indeed, as in the early centuries of the church, vocation would seem often to lead either to pride or to bitter disappointment. It is the institution that forms and sustains the clergy in its midst, and ministry is effected through the support and challenge of the church community. The age-old irony is that the same institution that frustrates the pastor so regularly and against which the pastor is almost compelled to rebel is that very institution that teaches, encourages, and enables one to take up the pastor's calling.

1

THE SECOND CENTURY:
ALREADY IN FULL SWING

Ignatius of Antioch
To Polycarp 1–6; To the Ephesians 4–6, 15

The epistles, Ignatius's only surviving work, can be found in any collection of the Apostolic Fathers, for example, as here, Lake (1912). See also his Magnesians 3, 6, 7; Philadelphians 1–4; Trallians 2. Schoedel (1985) provides background and helpful commentary; Brown and Meier (1983) give suggestive context.

An early bishop of Antioch, Ignatius was arrested, for unknown reasons, during some church crisis there. All seven letters were written on his slow trip to Rome, where he was martyred, probably late in Trajan's reign, ca. 115.

A vibrant personality steeped in Christianity, writing in a time of crisis, Ignatius gives us a vivid and individual snapshot of Christian developments. Ignatius had definite views about the episcopate, but one might ask by what authority he taught other communities, and how secure his own position had been in Antioch. Often it seems he didst protest too much. Development of the episcopal office was not uniform or linear: for contrast, see the Didache, perhaps fifty years later and perhaps coming from around Antioch.

Polycarp of Smyrna
To the Philippians 4–8

Of Polycarp's writings, only this letter survives, but the *Martyrdom of Polycarp* (along with the letter, in the Apostolic Fathers), a letter from the church of Smyrna, written soon after Polycarp's death ca.

155, is largely or wholly authentic. The selection here is from ANF, volume 1.

The language and thought of Polycarp, as of Ignatius, show a synthesis of the Synoptic tradition, John, and especially Paul, whereas the Hebrew Bible is not prominent. Contrast this with 1 Clem. to see the interaction of hermeneutics and pastoral theology.

Dionysius, Polycrates, and Irenaeus

These three late second-century epistles are preserved in Eusebius's *Historia Ecclesiastica* (HE 4.23.9–10 and 5.24.1–18, respectively). On these historical figures see Quasten, volume 1, and ODCC. These selections are taken from NPNF, series 2, volume 4.

Dionysius to Soter

Dionysius was bishop of Corinth around 170, and a collection of his letters circulated in Eusebius's time.

The Christian duty to the poor and its diligent performance are witnessed again and again from the earliest Christian writings. Even an opponent, the pagan emperor Julian, complimented Christian benevolence towards Christians and non-Christians alike by urging a pagan high priest to imitate it (Epistle 22, dated 362). The frequent founding of hospitals and orphanages was more or less a Christian innovation. Great liberality was a constant element. In the West, besides the examples of Leo and Gregory the Great, see Eugippius's *Life of Severin* (died 482) ch. 17; in the East, see the *Life of John the Almsgiver*, Patriarch of Alexandria (early seventh century, in Dawes and Baynes [1948] [a delightful book] and selections of Geanakoplos [1984] sec. 119). Hands (1968) and Constantelos (1968) provide analysis. Earlier in the second century, the *Shepherd* of Hermas, written in Rome, is another good example of liberality; for the mid-third century, Cyprian's career stands out; for the mid-fourth, see Gregory Nazianzen, pp. 125f., and Jerome, pp. 160f. For background, see Bolkestein (1939).

Polycrates to Victor and Irenaeus to Victor (HE 5.24.1–18)

Polycrates was bishop of Ephesus, and Victor was bishop of Rome, 189–198. Irenaeus was bishop of Lyons, after the fierce local

persecution, from ca. 180 to ca. 200, although he grew up in Asia
Minor and knew Polycarp of Smyrna. Better known for his *Against
Heresies* and *Demonstration of the Apostolic Preaching*, Irenaeus is
shown here to have worked for an irenic solution to the Quartodeciman conflict.

Christian worship, following analogously Jewish tradition, was
first the weekly Lord's Day service; next, yearly celebrations such as
Easter took shape, differently in different areas. In question between Victor and Polycrates is the Quartodeciman ("fourteen")
practice, which is the celebration of Easter actually on the Jewish
Passover, the Fourteenth of Nissan, regardless of the day of the
week. Elsewhere, Easter was always observed on a Sunday. These
practices represent different theologies of the feast.

Theological logic, however, was not the only one operating.
Tradition, in fact, and respect were the main points of Polycrates
and Irenaeus: the antiquity of the practice, the tradition of peaceful
union, and the tradition of diversity of practice. On Quartodeci-
manism, see ODCC, s.v.

IGNATIUS OF ANTIOCH, LETTER TO POLYCARP

1–6

Ignatius, who is also called Theophorus, to Polycarp, who is bishop of
the Church of the Smyrnaeans, or rather, who has for his bishop God the
Father and the Lord Jesus Christ, abundant greeting.

1.1. Welcoming your godly mind which is fixed as if on immovable
rock, I glory exceedingly that it was granted me to see your blameless face
wherein I would fain have pleasure in God. 2. I exhort you to press
forward on your course, in the grace wherewith you are endued, and to
exhort all to gain salvation. Vindicate your office with all diligence, both of
the flesh and spirit. Care for unity, for there is nothing better. Help all, as
the Lord also helps you; suffer all in love,[1] as you indeed do. 3. Be diligent
with unceasing prayer. Entreat for wisdom greater than you have, be
watchful and keep the spirit from slumbering. Speak to each individually
after the manner of God. Bear the sicknesses[2] of all as a perfect athlete.
Where the toil is greatest, is the gain great.

---

1. Cf. Eph. 4:2.
2. Cf. Matt. 8:17.

2.1. If you love good disciples, it is no credit to you; rather bring to subjection by your gentleness the more troublesome. Not all wounds are healed by the same plaster. Relieve convulsions by fomentations. 2. "Be prudent as the serpent" in all things "and pure as the dove" forever.[3] For this reason you consist of flesh and spirit, that you may deal tenderly with the things which appear visibly; but pray that the invisible things may be revealed to you, that you may lack nothing and abound in every gift. 3. The time calls on you to attain unto God, just as pilots require wind, and the storm-tossed sailor seeks a harbor. Be sober as God's athlete. The prize[4] is immortality and eternal life, of which you have been persuaded. In all things I am devoted to you—I and my bonds, which you loved.

3.1. Let not those that appear to be plausible, but teach strange doctrine, overthrow you. Stand firm as an anvil which is smitten. The task of great athletes is to suffer punishment and yet conquer. But especially must we endure all things for the sake of God, that God also may endure us. 2. Be more diligent than you are. Mark the seasons. Wait for him who is above seasons, timeless, invisible, who for our sakes became visible, who cannot be touched, who cannot suffer, who for our sakes accepted suffering, who in every way endured for our sakes.

4.1. Let not the widows be neglected. Be yourself their protector after the Lord. Let nothing be done without your approval, and do nothing yourself without God, as indeed you do nothing; stand fast. 2. Let the meetings be more numerous. Seek all by their name. 3. Do not be haughty to slaves, either men or women; yet do not let them be puffed up, but let them rather endure slavery to the glory of God, that they may obtain a better freedom from God. Let them not desire to be set free at the church's expense, that they be not found the slaves of yearning.

5.1. Flee from evil arts, but rather preach against them. Speak to my sisters that they love the Lord and be content with their husbands in flesh and in spirit. In the same way enjoin my brothers in the name of Jesus Christ to love their wives as the Lord loved the church.[5] 2. If anyone can remain in continence to the honor of the flesh of the Lord, let him do so without boasting. If one boast one is lost, and if it be made known except to the bishop, one is polluted. But it is right for men and women who marry to be united with the consent of the bishop, that the marriage be according to the Lord and not according to lust. Let all things be done to the honor of God.

---

3. Matt. 10:16.
4. 1 Cor. 9:19-27.
5. Cf. Eph. 5:25, 28-29.

6.1. Give heed to the bishop, that God may also give heed to you. I am devoted to those who are subject to the bishop, presbyters, and deacons; and may it be mine to have my lot with them in God. Labor with one another, struggle together, run together, suffer together, rest together, rise up together as God's stewards and assessors and servants. 2. Be pleasing to God in whose ranks[6] you serve, from whom you receive your pay—let none of you be found a deserter. Let your baptism remain as your arms, your faith as a helmet, your love as a spear, your endurance as your panoply; let your works be your deposits that you may receive the back pay due to you. Be therefore longsuffering with one another in gentleness, as God is with you. May I have joy in you always.

IGNATIUS OF ANTIOCH, LETTER TO THE EPHESIANS

4–6, 15

4.1. Therefore it is fitting that you should live in harmony with the will of the bishop, as indeed you do. For your justly famous presbytery, worthy of God, is attuned to the bishop as the strings to a harp. Therefore by your concord and harmonious love Jesus Christ is being sung. 2. Now do each of you join in this choir, that being harmoniously in concord you may receive the musical key of God in unison, and sing with one voice through Jesus Christ to the Father, that God may both hear you and may recognize, through your good works, that you are members of the Son. It is therefore profitable for you to be in blameless unity, in order that you may always commune with God.

5.1. For if I in a short time gained such fellowship with your bishop as was not human but spiritual, how much more do I count you blessed who are so united with him as the church is with Jesus Christ, and as Jesus Christ is with God, that all things may sound together in unison! 2. Let no one be deceived: unless a man be within the sanctuary he lacks the bread of God, for if the prayer of one or two has such might, how much more has that of the bishop and of the whole church? 3. So then he who does not join in the common assembly is already haughty and has separated

---

6. *To Polycarp* 6:2 is full of military imagery, some of it very specific. A Roman soldier "deposited" half his pay with the regiment, which was paid to him upon honorable discharge. Military imagery was used by Christian authors from the earliest documents (see 1 Thess. 5:8; 2 Cor. 6:7; Eph. 6:11; 2 Tim. 2:3-4; 1 Clem. 37), but then the Roman army amazed many people in antiquity and was proverbial for organization and power. See Jaeger (1961, p. 19) and Jerome, Ep. 52.1, p. 153.

himself. For it is written, "God resisteth the proud":[7] let us then be careful not to oppose the bishop, that we may be subject to God.

6.1. And the more anyone sees that the bishop is silent, the more let him fear. For everyone whom the master of the house sends to do business ought we to receive as the one who sent him. Therefore it is clear that we must regard the bishop as the Lord. 2. Indeed, Onesimus himself gives great praise to your good order in God, for you all live according to truth, and no heresy dwells among you; nay, you do not even listen to any unless he speak concerning Jesus Christ in truth.

15.1. It is better to be silent and be real, than to talk and to be unreal. Teaching is good, if the teacher does what he says. There is then one teacher who spoke and it came to pass, and what Christ has done even in silence is worthy of the Father. 2. He who has the work of Jesus for a true possession can also hear Jesus' silence, that he may be perfect, that he may act through his speech, and be understood through his silence.[8] 3. Nothing is hid from the Lord, but even our secret things are near him. Let us therefore do all things as though he were dwelling in us, that we may be his temples, and that he may be our God in us.[9] This indeed is so, and will appear clearly before our face by the love which we justly have to him.

POLYCARP OF SMYRNA, LETTER TO THE PHILIPPIANS

4–8

4. "But the love of money is the root of all evils."[10] Knowing, therefore, that "as we brought nothing into the world, so we can carry nothing out,"[11] let us arm ourselves with the armor of righteousness; and let us teach, first of all, ourselves to walk in the commandments of the Lord. Next, [teach] your wives [to walk] in the faith given to them, and in love and purity tenderly loving their own husbands in all truth, and loving all [others] equally in all chastity; and to train up their children in the

---

7. Prov. 3:34; James 4:6; 1 Pet. 5:5.

8. On speaking and doing, see Gen. 1 and John 1, also Ps. 33:9 = 148:5 and Jth. 16:14. Jesus' silence was a powerful image of Christ's true authority; see Matt. 27:11-14, John 19:8-11; specifically on the silent Lamb, from Isa. 53:7, see Barnabas 5; Melito, *On Passover* 64, 71, 104; fragment 13. The exact meaning of the bishop's silence is hard to gauge. Schoedel thinks the silence suggests a laconic person, but perhaps it shows a more mystical understanding of bishop as icon or image of Christ. In any event, the bishop's centrality appears more liturgical and symbolic than administrative. See also p. 139.

9. Cf. 1 Cor. 3:16.

10. Cf. 1 Tim. 6:10.

11. 1 Tim. 6:7.

knowledge and fear of God. Teach the widows to be discreet as respects the faith of the Lord, praying continually[12] for all, being far from all slandering, evil speaking, false witnessing, love of money, and every kind of evil; knowing that they are the altar of God, that God clearly perceives all things, and that nothing is hid from God, neither reasonings, nor reflections, nor any one of the secret things of the heart.[13]

5. Knowing, then, that "God is not mocked,"[14] we ought to walk worthy of his commandment and glory. In like manner should the deacons be blameless before the face of his righteousness, as being the servants of God and Christ, and not of human beings. They must not be slanderers, double tongued,[15] or lovers of money, but temperate in all things, compassionate, industrious, walking according to the truth of the Lord, who was the servant[16] of all. If we please Christ in this present world, we shall receive also the future world, according as Christ has promised to us that he will raise us again from the dead, and that if we live[17] worthily of him, "we shall also reign together with him,"[18] provided only we believe. In like manner, let the young also be blameless in all things, being especially careful to preserve purity, and keeping themselves in, as with a bridle, from every kind of evil. For it is well that they should be cut off from the lusts that are in the world, since "every lust warreth against the spirit";[19] and "neither fornicators, nor effeminate, nor abusers of themselves with humankind, shall inherit the kingdom of God,"[20] nor those who do things inconsistent and unbecoming. Wherefore, it is needful to abstain from all these things, being subject to the presbyters and deacons, as unto God and Christ.

6. And let the presbyters be compassionate and merciful to all, bringing back those that wander, visiting all the sick, and not neglecting the widow, the orphan, or the poor, but always "providing for that which is becoming in the sight of God and humanity";[21] abstaining from all wrath, respect of persons, and unjust judgment; keeping far off from all covetousness, not quickly crediting an evil report against anyone, not severe in judgment, as knowing that we are all under a debt of sin. If then we entreat the Lord to

---

12. Cf. 1 Thess. 5:17; 1 Tim. 5:5.
13. Cf. 1 Cor. 14:25; Sus. 42.
14. Gal. 6:7.
15. Cf. 1 Tim. 3:8.
16. Cf. Matt. 20:28.
17. Cf. Phil. 1:27.
18. 2 Tim. 2:12; cf. Rom. 8:17.
19. 1 Pet. 2:11; cf. 1 John 2:16.
20. 1 Cor. 6:9, 10.
21. Cf. Prov. 3:4; Rom. 12:17; 2 Cor. 8:21.

forgive us, we ought also ourselves to forgive;[22] for we are before the eyes of our Lord and God, and "we must all appear at the judgment seat of Christ, and must every one give an account of himself."[23] Let us then serve God in fear, and with all reverence, even as the Lord has commanded us, and as the apostles who preached the gospel unto us, and the prophets who proclaimed beforehand the coming of the Lord have alike taught us. Let us be zealous in the pursuit of that which is good, keeping ourselves from causes of offense, from false believers, and from those who in hypocrisy bear the name of the Lord, and draw away vain persons into error.

7. "For whosoever does not confess that Jesus Christ has come in the flesh, is antichrist";[24] and whosoever does not confess the testimony of the cross, is of the devil; and whosoever perverts the oracles of the Lord to his own lusts, and says that there is neither a resurrection nor a judgment is the firstborn of Satan. Wherefore, forsaking the vanity of many, and their false doctrines, let us return to the word which has been handed down to us from the beginning; "watching unto prayer"[25] and persevering in fasting; beseeching in our supplications the all-seeing God "not to lead us into temptation,"[26] as the Lord has said: "The spirit truly is willing, but the flesh is weak."[27]

8. Let us then continually persevere in our hope, and the earnest of our righteousness, which is Jesus Christ, "who bore our sins in his own body on the tree,"[28] "who did no sin, neither was guile found in his mouth,"[29] but endured all things for us, that we might live in him.[30] Let us then be imitators of his patience; and if we suffer[31] for his name's sake, let us glorify him. For he has set us this example[32] in himself, and we have believed that such is the case.

DIONYSIUS OF CORINTH, LETTER TO SOTER

4.23.9. There is extant also another epistle written by Dionysius to the Romans, and addressed to Soter, who was bishop at that time. We cannot

---

22. Matt. 6:12-14.
23. Rom. 14:10-12; 2 Cor. 5:10.
24. Cf. 1 John 4:2-3; 2 John 7.
25. 1 Pet. 4:7.
26. Matt. 6:13.
27. Matt. 26:41; Mark 14:38.
28. 1 Pet. 2:24.
29. 1 Pet. 2:22.
30. Cf. 1 John 4:9.
31. Cf. Acts 5:41; 1 Pet. 4:16.
32. Cf. 1 Pet. 2:21.

do better than to subjoin some passages from this epistle, in which he commends the practice of the Romans which has been retained down to the persecution in our own days.

10. "For from the beginning it has been your practice to do good to all the saints in various ways, and to send contributions to many churches in every city. Thus relieving the want of the needy, and making provision for the faithful in the mines by the gifts which you have sent from the beginning, you Romans keep up the hereditary customs of the Romans, which your blessed bishop Soter has not only maintained, but also added to, furnishing an abundance of supplies to the saints, and encouraging the faithful from abroad with blessed words, as a loving father his children."

POLYCRATES AND IRENAEUS,
LETTERS TO VICTOR OF ROME

5.24.1–18. But the bishops of Asia, led by Polycrates, decided to hold to the old custom handed down to them. He himself, in a letter which he addressed to Victor and the church of Rome, set forth in the following words the tradition which had come down to him: "We observe the exact day; neither adding, nor taking away. For in Asia also great lights have fallen asleep, which shall rise again on the day of the Lord's coming, when Christ shall come with glory from heaven, and shall seek out all the saints. Among these are Philip, one of the twelve apostles, who fell asleep in Hierapolis; and his two aged virgin daughters, and another daughter, who lived in the Holy Spirit and now rests at Ephesus; and, moreover, John, who was both a witness and a teacher, who reclined upon the bosom of the Lord, and, being a priest, wore the sacerdotal plate. He fell asleep at Ephesus. And Polycarp in Smyrna, who was a bishop and martyr; and Thraseas, bishop and martyr from Eumenia, who fell asleep in Smyrna. Why need I mention the bishop and martyr Sagaris who fell asleep in Laodicea, or the blessed Papirius, or Melito, the eunuch who lived altogether in the Holy Spirit, and who lies in Sardis, awaiting the visitation from heaven, when he shall rise from the dead? All these observed the fourteenth day of the Passover according to the Gospel, deviating in no respect, but following the rule of faith. And I also, Polycrates, the least of you all, do according to the tradition of my relatives, some of whom I have closely followed. For seven of my relatives were bishops; and I am the eighth. And my relatives always observed the day when the people put away the leaven. I, therefore, who have lived sixty-five years in the Lord, and have met with the saints throughout the world, and have gone through every holy scripture, am not affrighted by terrifying words. For those greater than I have said, 'We ought to obey God rather than people.'"[33]

"I could mention the bishops who were present, whom I summoned at your desire; whose names, should I write them, would constitute a great multitude. And they, beholding my littleness, gave their consent to the letter, knowing that I did not bear my gray hairs in vain, but had always governed my life by the Lord Jesus."

Thereupon Victor, who presided over the church at Rome, immediately attempted to cut off from the common unity the parishes of all Asia, with the churches that agreed with them, as heterodox; and he wrote letters and declared all the faithful there wholly excommunicate. But this did not please all the bishops. And they besought him to consider the things of peace, and of neighborly unity and love. Words of theirs are extant, sharply rebuking Victor. Among them was Irenaeus, who, sending letters in the name of the church in Gaul over whom he presided, maintained that the mystery of the resurrection of the Lord should be observed only on the Lord's day. He fittingly admonishes Victor that he should not cut off whole churches of God which observed the tradition of an ancient custom, and after many other words he proceeds as follows: "For the controversy is not only concerning the day, but also concerning the very manner of the fast. For some think that they should fast one day, others two, yet others more; some, moreover, count their day as consisting of forty hours day and night. And this variety in its observance has not originated in our time, but long before in that of our ancestors. It is likely that they did not hold to strict accuracy, and thus formed a custom for their posterity according to their own simplicity and individual mode. Yet all of these lived nonetheless in peace, and we also live in peace with one another; and the disagreement in regard to the fast confirms the agreement in the faith. . . .

"Among these were the presbyters before Soter, who presided over the church which you now rule. . . . They neither observed it themselves, nor did they permit those after them to do so. And yet though not observing it, they were nonetheless at peace with those who came to them from the parishes in which it was observed. . . . None were ever cast out on account of this form, but the presbyters before you who did not observe it, sent the eucharist to those of other parishes who observed it. And when the blessed Polycarp was at Rome in the time of Anicetus, and they disagreed a little about certain other things, they immediately made peace with one another, not caring to quarrel over this matter. For neither could Anicetus persuade Polycarp not to observe what he had always observed with John

---

33. Acts 5:29.

the disciple of our Lord, and the other apostles with whom he had associated; nor could Polycarp persuade Anicetus to observe it, as he said that he ought to follow the customs of the presbyters that had preceded him. But though matters were in this shape, they communed together, and Anicetus conceded the administration of the eucharist in the church to Polycarp, manifestly as a mark of respect. And they parted from each other in peace, both those who observed, and those who did not, maintaining the peace of the whole church."

Thus Irenaeus, who truly was well named, became a peacemaker in this matter, exhorting and negotiating in this way in behalf of the peace of the churches.

2

ALEXANDRIA:
THE ERUDITE PASTOR

Clement
Who Is the Rich Person Who Will Be Saved? (ch. 34–36)

This portion is from ANF 2.591ff., with corrections; one might also read the story of St. John and the Robber, ch. 42. *The Exhortation to the Greeks (Protrepticus); The Pedagogue,* or *Tutor* (see books 1, 3); and the *Stromateis* (see books 1, 2, 7) are also in ANF 2. A good appreciation of Clement and Origen is H. Chadwick (1966).

Clement was born ca. 150 in Athens, where he was first educated. After his conversion he traveled, visiting Christian teachers. He joined Pantaenus, the first head of Alexandria's famous catechetical school, and succeeded him in the 190s (the third head later would be Origen). In 202 he fled persecution in Alexandria and died ca. 215. All his writings are from Alexandria.

Clement was cultured, that is, he had leisure, learning, and taste. The common purpose of his writings was to articulate a fully cultured Christianity. He worked towards a synthesis of theology and philosophy, but that was only part of his program. In the *Exhortation to the Greeks,* for instance, he argued for conversion to Christianity, yet by means of frequent quotation of the classics, namely Homer and the tragedians.

Who Is the Rich Person . . . ? (Quis dives salvetur?) beginning from Mark 10:17-31, was written to the cultured to show that those who are materially well off can play a positive role in the Christian community. Notice the logic of inversion: the wealthy tend the worldly needs of those who are truly important to God and who will plead for them to God. Similarly, Hermas, *Similitude* 2: the poor support the rich like an elm the vine. A different situation can lead to a different analysis; see Cyprian, *On the Lapsed* (ANF 5.437ff.), written just after the Decian persecution, 251.

Origen
Homilies 11.6; 13.3 on Ex.; 20.4; 27.1 on Num.;
6.1 on Isa.; 14.1-5 on Jer.

The selections are from R. Tollinton (1929), all except Hom. in Ex. 13.3 (Shippee). Other relevant Origen is easily found in ACW 19, 26; FoC 71; H. Chadwick, *Origen: Contra Celsum*; and Greer (1979). In addition to Chadwick (1966), see Daniélou (1955), and especially Crouzel (1989). Eusebius, HE 6, is the chief ancient source; Gregory Thaumaturge's Panegyric, ANF 6.21–39, shows us Origen's educational practices and goals.

Origen was born in 185 to a Christian family in Alexandria, where he was educated in Christian and classical subjects by his father. In 202 his father was martyred, and Origen became the third head of the catechetical school. In 231, after continued problems with his bishop, he continued his teaching in Caesarea. Having suffered in the persecution there, he died in 254.

Origen is one of the most fascinating and attractive figures of Christian antiquity. Not only tremendously learned in Christian and classical topics, and among the best biblical scholars of any age, he was also a tremendously creative theologian. His fusion of theology and philosophy was deeper than any before and was the foundation to the great syntheses of the next centuries. Yet all this work was done to serve the Christian life: the life of the church and the life of the believer. Origen constantly emphasized that the faith is open not only to an elite, intellectual or spiritual, but to all (cf. *Contra Celsum* 3.44–49, against elitism). In works such as *On Prayer,* and throughout his homilies, we see the intimacy and immediacy of the natural pastor.

Our passages show two of Origen's concerns: that the needs of all Christians, especially the simple, be met; and that scripture, God's word, be central to Christian formation.

CLEMENT, WHO IS THE RICH PERSON WHO WILL BE SAVED?

34–36

34. This visible appearance cheats death and the devil; for the wealth within, the beauty, is unseen by them. And they rave about the carcass,

which they despise as weak, being blind to the wealth within; knowing not what a "treasure in an earthen vessel"[1] we bear, protected as it is by the power of God the Father, and the blood of God the Son, and the dew of the Holy Spirit. But be not deceived, you who have tasted of the truth, and been reckoned worthy of the great redemption. Contrary to what is the case with the rest of humanity, collect for yourself an unarmed, an unwarlike, a bloodless, a passionless, a stainless host, pious old folk, orphans dear to God, widows armed with meekness, people adorned with love. Obtain with your money such guards, for body and for soul, for whose sake a sinking ship is made buoyant, when steered by the prayers of the saints alone; and disease at its height is subdued, put to flight by the laying on of hands; and the attack of robbers is disarmed, spoiled by pious prayers; and the might of demons is crushed, put to shame in its operations by strenuous commands.

35. All these warriors and guards are trusty. No one is idle, no one is useless. One can obtain your pardon from God, another comfort you when sick, another weep and groan in sympathy for you to the Lord of all, another teach some of the things useful for salvation, another admonish with confidence, another counsel with kindness. And all can love truly, without guile, without fear, without hypocrisy, without flattery, without pretense. O sweet nurture of the affectionate! O blessed service of the courageous! O pure faith of those who fear only God! O truth of the words of those unable to lie! O beauty of the works of those who resolve to serve God, to petition God, to satisfy God. They do not intend to affect your body only, but each one of them his own soul, nor to speak to a brother or sister only, but to the king of eternity dwelling in you.

36. All the faithful, then, are good and godlike, and worthy of the name by which they are encircled as with a diadem. There are, besides, some, the elect of the elect, and so much more or less distinguished by drawing themselves, like ships to the strand, out of the surge of the world and bringing themselves to safety; not wishing to seem holy, and ashamed if one call them so; hiding in the depth of their mind the ineffable mysteries, and disdaining to let their nobleness be seen in the world; whom the Word calls "the light of the world, and the salt of the earth."[2] This [class] is the seed, the image and likeness of God, and God's true child and heir, sent here as it were for foreign service under the great plan and proportionment of the Father, on account of which also the visible and invisible things of the world were created: some for the seed's service, some for its discipline, and some for its instruction. And all things, while the seed should remain

---

1. 2 Cor. 4:7.
2. Matt. 5:13, 14.

here, hold together, and when it is gathered, all things will most quickly dissolve.

ORIGEN, SELECTIONS FROM THE HOMILIES

Homily 11.6 on Exodus

Indeed when I observe that Moses, a prophet filled with God, to whom God spoke face to face, received advice from Jethro, a priest of Midian, my mind grows bewildered, so great is my surprise. For the scripture says, "So Moses hearkened to the voice of his father-in-law and did all that he said unto him."[3] He did not say, "To me God speaks; what I am to do is told me by a voice from heaven; how shall I receive advice from a man, a man who is a Gentile, a stranger to the people of God?" No, he listens to his voice, and does all he says, and gives ear not to the speaker but to his words. This shows that we also, if we chance anytime to find something wisely said by the Gentiles, should not straightaway reject along with the status of the speaker also the things said; nor, because we have the law given by God, ought we to swell with pride and to reject the words of the wise, but rather to do as the Apostle says, "Proving all things, holding fast that which is good."[4]

Yet among those who have authority among the people today, who is there—I do not say if he has already some revelation from God, but even if he has any slight pretension through his knowledge of the law—that will condescend to receive advice from a priest of clearly lower standing, let alone from a layperson or a Gentile? But Moses, who was meek above all others, received advice from an inferior, so as to set an example of humility to the leaders of the peoples and present an emblem of a mystery of the future. He knew that at some future time the Gentiles would bring to Moses good advice, that they would apply good and spiritual interpretation to the law of God. He knew that law would hearken to them and do all as they say. For the law is not able to do as the Jews say, because the law is weak in the flesh, that is, in the letter, and can do nothing according to the letter; for the law brings nothing to perfection.[5] But according to the advice which we bring to the law, all things can be done in a spiritual sense. Even the sacrifices can be offered in a spiritual sense, which are now impossible according to the flesh. The law of leprosy too can be observed in the spirit, which is impossible according to the letter. Thus,

---

3. Ex. 18:24.
4. 1 Thess. 5:21. In general, that we should attend to the truth of the words, not the status of the speaker, is found in Seneca, *Epist. Morales* 12, and often elsewhere.
5. Rom. 8:3; Heb. 7:19.

then, according to our interpretation, according to our view and the advice that we give, the law accomplishes all things; according to the letter not all, but very few.[6]

Homily 13.3 on Exodus

What can we say about the rest of the text? There is so much, and if we took it point by point, it would turn out very long. But, in fact, if we did take so much trouble to examine the text, it would be slanderous if this were spurned by overly-busy listeners, who only stand for the Word of God barely a fraction of an hour and, when spurned, perish. "If the Lord does not build the house, the builders work in vain. . . . "[7]

"So as each can take it to heart."[8] See if you can take it in, see if you can hold it, so that what is said doesn't drip out and perish. I will admonish you by examples from your own religion: you who partake regularly of the Divine Mysteries know how, when you receive the body of the Lord, you watch with all care and veneration so that no piece falls off, and nothing of the consecrated host is lost. You think yourself culprits, and rightly so, if by neglect any piece should fall off. You who use so much care in conserving God's body, a meritorious care, how can you think it less a crime to neglect God's word than to neglect God's flesh?[9]

Homily 20.4 on Numbers

And the anger of the Lord was kindled against Israel, and the Lord said unto Moses, "Take all the chiefs of the people and expose them unto the Lord over against the sun, and the anger of the Lord shall be turned away from Israel."[10] It is possible that in discussing this passage we may give offense to some persons, but, even if we do, our obedience and service must be given to the words of the Lord rather than to the favor of people. Israel sinned, and the Lord told Moses to take all the chiefs and to expose them unto the Lord over against the sun. The people sins, and the chiefs are exposed over against the sun. They are led forth for investigation, so that they may be tested by the light.

See what is the lot of the leaders of the people; they are not only put on trial for their own offenses, they are also compelled to give account for the

---

6. Origen's view of the relative values of literal and spiritual senses is phrased differently in different contexts: contrast *On First Principles* 4.2 (Greer [1979], 178ff.) and Hom. in Lev. 14.2, "Both letter and spirit we defend."

7. Ps. 127:1.

8. Ex. 35:5; cf. Eph. 6:6.

9. That the word is fully equal to the sacrament is affirmed also by Jerome, *In Psalm.* 147 (CCSL 78.338), and later by Caesarius of Arles (died 542), Sermon 78 (FoC 31). People always stood in church then; there were no pews.

10. Num. 25:3-4.

sins of the people. Perhaps it is their fault that the people offends. Perhaps they did not teach, they did not warn, they did not take the trouble to convict those who had been the first to do wrong, so as to prevent the spread of the malady to others. The performance of these duties is laid upon leaders and teachers. If through their inaction, through their lack of care for the multitude, the people sins, it is they who are exposed, they who are led forth to judgment. Moses, that is the Torah of God, charges them with indolence and slackness; upon them shall the anger of the Lord be turned, and it shall cease from the people. If others thought of these things, they would never desire or intrigue for the leadership of the people. Enough for me to be tried for my own offenses; enough for me to give account for myself and for my sins. What occasion is there for me to be exposed for the sins of the people as well? To be exposed over against the sun, before which nothing can be hidden, nothing kept dark?

But perhaps there is also some hidden and secret meaning in the passage, with further teaching for us than the common interpretation seems to possess. Possibly this passage also has reference to those princes of the people of whom we spoke a little earlier. For the angels shall come to judgment together with us, and stand for us before the sun of righteousness; perhaps some responsibility for our sins lies with them; perhaps they failed to pay sufficient care and attention to us, so as to call us back from the disease of our sins. Unless there had been some defect in them, which seemed to deserve blame on our account, the language of scripture would never say to the angel of this or of that church, You have—for instance— some who hold the teaching of Balaam; or, You have left your first love, or your patience, or something else of the same kind, as we mentioned above, on account of which in the Apocalypse the angels of each church are blamed.[11] For if, let us say, the angel who has received me, marked with the sign, from God, looks for a reward for my good deeds, it is certain he will also look for censure for those deeds of mine which are not good. That is why they are said to be exposed over against the sun, doubtless to make it clear whether it was through my disobedience, or through the angel's carelessness, that sins were committed which led to my devotion to Baal-phegor, or to some other idol, according to the character of my sin. Now if my chief, I mean the angel assigned to me, did not fail but counseled me to right action, and spoke in my heart, as he did through conscience calling me back from sin; whereas I, despising his advice and scorning the restraint of conscience, rushed headlong into sin, for me there will be the double penalty, both for despising my adviser and for offending in my deed. Nor should you feel any surprise if we say that

---

11. Rev. 2:4.

angels come to judgment together with us, since scripture says, "The Lord will enter into judgment with the elders of his people and the princes thereof."[12] Thus the princes are exposed, and, if the fault be in them, God's anger ceases from the people. We should have the keener vigilance over our actions, now that we know that not ourselves alone shall stand before God's judgment seat for our deeds, but that the angels, as our chiefs and guides, shall also be brought into judgment on our account. Therefore it is that the scripture says, "Obey them that have the rule over you, and submit yourselves in all things. For they watch as those who shall give account for your souls."[13]

Homily 27.1 on Numbers

When God made the world, he created countless varieties of foods to correspond, I suppose, to the diversity in human appetites and in the natures of the animals. Thus not only does a person, when he sees the food of animals, know that it was not created for him but for the animals, but even the animals themselves recognize their own proper fare. The lion, for example, feeds on one kind of food; the stag, the ox, the bird, on different kinds. And even among human beings there are certain differences of appetite; one person, who is healthy and in sound condition, needs robust fare, confident and assured that he can eat anything. Such are the strongest athletes. But anyone who knows that he is ailing and delicate enjoys vegetables and declines robust fare on account of the infirmity of his body. And a little child, even though unable to express itself by speech, as a matter of fact needs no other nourishment than milk. Thus each one according to age or vigor or health of body seeks the nourishment that is fit for himself and proportionate to his powers.

If you have sufficiently examined the parallel case of the body, let us now leave that and come to the study of the spiritual meaning. Every

---

12. Isa. 3:14.

13. Heb. 13:17. Similar issues are raised in Hom. 6.1 on Isaiah. The dangers of spiritual office are noted again and again. Origen saw how priesthood could draw those ambitious for power or money (see Tollinton, p. 189, n. 2, adding Hom. 2 on Numbers, to Num. 1:1; in *On First Principles* 4.2.2 he insisted that the exegete be humble). Many others noticed also: see Jerome, Ep. 22:28 and 40 (in Loeb) for typically sharp observations, also Ambrose, *Duties* 2.24.121. below p. 146. That being a minister of God should fill with awe the one who is called is common among the great authors, e.g.: Athanasius, Ep. 49 (pp. 69, 71); Ps.-Clement, Hom. 3 (pp. 88f.); Leo, Ep. 19 and 167.2 (pp. 190-92); and Gregory the Great, *Pastoral Rule* (p. 197); and several times in the *Verba Seniorum*; also Chrysostom (*On the Priesthood*, e.g., 3.10, p. 169); and Nazianzen (Oration 2, NPNF 2.7.204ff.) defend at length their own reticence; Augustine, Sermon 78, is a moving meditation; later we have Sidonius (died 489) Ep., book 7.9 (cf. 5.3, 6.1); Caesarius, Sermon 230; Braulio of Saragossa (died 651), Ep. 13.

rational nature must be fed on food that is right and proper for it. Now the true food of a rational nature is the word of God. But just as we have shown a moment ago that there are many distinctions in the diet of the body, so too is it with our rational nature, which feeds as we have said upon the reason or word of God; every nature is not sustained by one and the same word. Thus, keeping up the comparison of the parallel of the body, some find in the word of God the food of milk. This is that plainer and simpler teaching, usual on moral subjects, which is normally supplied for those who are at the beginning of their divine studies and receive the early elements of rational instruction. Such persons, when there is read to them some passage from the divine books which is clearly free from obscurity, gladly receive it; for example, the book of Esther or of Judith, or even the story of Tobias, or the admonitions of Wisdom. But if the book of Leviticus is read to such a person, at once his mind is repelled, and he rejects it as not his proper fare. When one has come in order to learn how to honor God, and how to receive God's commandments of righteousness and piety, and instead hears orders given about sacrifices and instruction on the ritual of offerings, naturally he ceases at once to listen and rejects fare that is not convenient. Someone else, when the Gospels or the Apostle or a passage of the Psalms is read, receives it gladly and gives it cordial welcome and has the joy of deriving from it a cure for weakness. If the book of Numbers is read to him, more particularly these passages we are now dealing with,[14] he will regard it as quite unprofitable for any good purpose, either for the cure of his weakness or for the salvation of his soul. He will at once refuse and reject it, like heavy and oppressive food, beyond the powers of sick and ailing souls.

Yet, if we may revert again to the parallel of the body, if you could, shall we say, give intelligence to a lion, it will not because it feeds on raw flesh therefore find fault with the quantity of grass that exists, nor say that it has been needlessly supplied by the Creator, because it does not feed on it. Nor again should a person, because he eats bread and other suitable food, blame God because God has made serpents, which he sees God gives to the stags for food. Nor must, say, the sheep or the ox find fault because other animals are allowed to feed on flesh, while for themselves grass alone is sufficient fare. So is the case with rational food—I mean the holy volumes. One must not straightaway criticize or reject a scripture because it seems to be difficult or not clear in meaning, or to contain things of which a beginner or a child or one weak in understanding could make no use, or because he thinks he can derive nothing advantageous or salutary from it. You must bear in mind that just as a serpent, a sheep, an ox, a

---

14. Num. 23.

person, a bundle of hay, are all creatures of God; and this variety contributes to the praise and glory of the Creator, because these things afford or receive the nourishment that is appropriate and in season for each of those for whom they were made: in like manner all these things, which are words of God, containing diversity of food according to the capacity of souls, are appropriated by each individual according as he feels possessed of health and capacity. And yet, if we make careful examination, say, in a passage of the Gospel, or in some apostolic teaching, wherein you take evident delight and in which you find the food that is most fit and pleasant for you, how much there is that you fail to see, if you examine and investigate the commands of the Lord. If we are to reject and avoid right off whatever seems abstruse or difficult, you will find, even in passages where you are specially confident, so much that is abstruse and difficult that if you keep to this principle you will have to abandon even these. And yet there are many things in these passages expressed with sufficient openness and simplicity to instruct a hearer of even little intelligence.

So much we have said by way of preface, to arouse your attention, since the passage we have to deal with seems likely to appear difficult of understanding and unnecessary to read. But we cannot say of the words of the Holy Spirit that anything in them is useless or unnecessary, even though some find it obscure. This rather ought we to do, to turn the eyes of our mind to God who ordered these things to be written and to ask of him their meaning, that if there be weakness in our soul, God who heals all infirmities may heal us; or if we be of little understanding, the Lord who protects little ones may be with us and nourish us and bring us to humanity's full estate. Each is in our power: we may come from weakness to strength, from childhood to full grown maturity. Therefore it is in our power to ask these things of God. It is God's part to give to those who seek and to open to those who knock. But this introduction will be long enough.

Homily 6.1 on Isaiah

When Isaiah saw the Lord of Hosts sitting upon a throne, high and lifted up, when he saw also the seraphim standing round about the throne, and when he received forgiveness of sins through the fire which was brought from the altar and purged his lips by its touch, he tells us that he heard the voice of God not commanding but arousing him and saying, "Whom shall I send and who will go unto this people?" Then he says that he answered the Lord, "Behold, here am I, send me."[15] Being occupied with this passage and examining what is written, I find Moses did one thing, Isaiah

---

15. Isa. 6:8.

another. For Moses, when he was chosen to lead the people out of the land of Egypt, says, "Secure someone else to send."[16] He seems even to oppose God. Whereas Isaiah, not chosen, but hearing the words, "Whom shall I send and who will go?" says, "Here am I, send me." So is it worthwhile to compare spiritual things with spiritual, and to ask which of the two did better: Moses, who after being chosen, refused; or Isaiah who, without even being chosen, offered himself to be sent to the people. I do not think anyone observing the difference of procedure, which appears in the two cases, could say that Moses acted as Isaiah did. I have ventured to make comparison between two holy and blessed men, to point out a distinction, and to assert that Moses acted with more humility than Isaiah. I suppose Moses had in mind the great responsibility of taking command of the people to lead them out of the land of Egypt, and of opposing the incantations and curses of the Egyptians. Therefore he says, "Secure someone else to send." But the other, without waiting to hear what he might be bidden to say, or whether he was chosen, says, "Here am I, send me." On this account, because without knowing what he would be bidden to say, or whether he was chosen, he said, "Here am I, send me," he is bidden to say things which he had no desire to say. For was it not an undesirable task the moment he was bidden to prophesy to commence his words with curses: "You shall hear with the ear and not understand, and seeing you shall behold and not perceive, for the heart of this people is waxed fat,"[17] and so on? Perhaps—if indeed I ought to speak so boldly— he received the reward of his rashness and boldness in being bidden to utter prophecies which he disliked.

As we have compared Isaiah and Moses, let us make another similar comparison of Isaiah and Jonah. The latter is sent to foretell to the people of Nineveh its fall after three days, and he is reluctant to set out and become the unwilling cause of calamity to the city.[18] But Isaiah, without waiting to hear what he was bidden to say, answers, "Here am I, send me." It is a good thing not to rush eagerly to those honors, high positions, and ministries of the church which are from God, but to imitate Moses and with him to say, "Secure someone else to send." The one who wishes to be saved takes no steps to high position in the church, and, if appointed, takes office for the church's service. If we are to use also the words of the Gospel, "The princes of the Gentiles have lordship over them, and they that have authority over them are called officers. But it shall not be so with you. For your princes do not exercise lordship among you, but whoever of you wishes to be greater shall be least of all; the one who wishes to be first

16. Ex. 4:13.
17. Isa. 6:9-10.
18. Jon. 1.

shall be last of all."[19] The one then who is called to a bishop's office is not called to a prince's position but to the service of the whole church. If you seek scripture evidence for believing that in the church the one who rules is servant of all, our Lord and Savior himself may convince you, who in the midst of his disciples showed his nature and true greatness not by reclining at table but by ministering. For after he had laid aside his garments, he took a towel and girded himself and poured out water into a basin and began to wash the disciples' feet and to wipe them with the towel with which he was girded. Teaching us what character our leaders, as servants, ought to possess, he says, "You call me Master and Lord, and you say well, for so I am. If I then, your Lord and Master, have washed your feet, you also ought to wash one another's feet."[20]

Thus the prince of the church is called to service, that he may be able by such service to attain the throne of heaven, as it is written, "You shall sit upon thrones judging the twelve tribes of Israel."[21] And listen to Paul, wonderful man that he was, declaring himself the servant of all believers. "For I am the least," he says, "of the apostles; I am not worthy to be called an apostle, because I persecuted the church of God."[22] Further, if this seems only to show his humility and not his service, hear him say, "We were babes in the midst of you, as when a nurse cherishes her children, when we might have been burdensome as apostles of Christ."[23] We then should be followers of the lowly words and deeds of the Lord himself and of his apostles, and do as Moses did, so that if a person be called to leadership he will say, "Secure someone else to send." To God he says, "I am not worthy, neither yesterday nor the day before. I am feeble of speech and slow of tongue."[24] And because he spoke humbly to God—feeble of speech and slow of tongue—he hears God answer, "Who has made the mouth? or who made someone deaf or dumb or seeing or blind? Is it not I, the Lord God? Trust in God, sanctify yourself unto him. Feeble of voice, slow of tongue, commit yourself still to the Word of God. Later you shall say, 'I opened my mouth and drew in my breath.' "[25] So far on Isaiah's words, "Here am I, send me."

Homily 14.1–5 on Jeremiah

Concerning the passage, "Woe is me, my mother," down to, "Therefore thus says the Lord, If you return, then will I bring you again."[26] Physicians

---

19. Luke 22:25-26//Matt. 20:25-28.
20. John 13:13-14.
21. Matt. 19:28.
22. 1 Cor. 15:9.
23. 1 Thess. 2:6-7.
24. Ex. 4:10.
25. Ps. 119:131. On this selection, see note 13 above.
26. Jer. 15:10-19.

of the body spend their time with the sick and constantly devote themselves to the cure of their patients. According to the purpose of their profession they view the parts affected and handle repulsive cases. In the sufferings of other people they reap their own troubles, and their life is constantly at the mercy of circumstances. They never live with healthy persons but are continually with the disabled, with those who have spreading sores, with people full of discharges, fevers, various diseases. And if one decides to follow the physician's calling, he will not grumble nor neglect the purpose of the profession he has undertaken, when he finds himself in the situation we have described.

This introduction I have made, because in a sense the prophets are physicians of souls and ever spend their time among those who require treatment. For, "They that are whole have no need of a physician, but they that are sick."[27] What physicians undergo for the sake of patients who have no restraint, prophets and teachers also suffer at the hands of those who decline to be cured. They are disliked because their directions conflict with the preferences of their patients' desires, because they forbid delicacies and indulgences to people who even in illness crave to have what is unsuitable for their state of illness. So patients who are without self-control avoid physicians, frequently even abusing and vilifying them, treating them exactly as one enemy would treat another. These people forget that physicians come to them as friends; they look to the troublesome character of their regimen, to the pain caused by the incision of the surgeon's knife, not to the result that follows such pain. They detest them simply as the authors of suffering, not as of suffering which brings the patient to good health.

Now the ancient people had fallen sick. Various diseases existed in the people that was called the people of God. And God sent them prophets as physicians. Jeremiah was one of these physicians. He reproved sinners, endeavoring to convert those who did evil. When they should have listened to his words, they accused the prophet and accused him before judges like themselves. The prophet was continually on trial before those who, as regards his prophecy, were under treatment, but through their own disobedience remained uncured. At this he says in one place, "And I said, 'I will not speak, nor will I name the name of the Lord.' And it was as a burning fire, raging in my bones. I am altogether faint and unable to endure."[28] In another place, perceiving himself continually put on trial, vilified, accused, the victim of false witness, he says, "Woe is me, my mother, how have you borne me a man"—so run his words—"who

---

27. Luke 5:31.
28. Jer. 20:9.

endures not causes contest, who endures not causes strife, with all the earth."[29] And since the sick did not listen to his wise professional advice, "I have availed nothing," he says. He offered to lend them spiritual money, but they would not listen to his words, that they might be gainers by what they heard. Neither, says he, was anyone indebted to me, nor was I myself in debt.

This I have said by way of anticipation, before explaining the words "I was not in debt, neither was anyone indebted to me."[30] The text has two readings. In most copies it runs, "I was of no help, nor did anyone help me." But in the most correct, which agree with the Hebrew text, it stands, "I was not in debt, neither was anyone indebted to me." We must then both explain the text that is current and usually commented on in the churches, and also not leave unexplained the text based upon the Hebrew. The prophet then preached the word; no one attended to what he said. It is like a physician squandering his drugs upon patients who are without self-control and just satisfy their desires. It is as if he too should say, "I was of no help, neither did anyone help me." A reciprocity perhaps there is through the good will of the one who receives help towards his helper, so that the speaker too is in a position to receive advantage, for blessed is he that speaks to the ears of those that hear. In this way would a teacher receive help from hearers who made advance and improvement. He would be helped by having fruit in them. Failing to receive this from the Jews, Jeremiah says, "No one helped me." For if the speaker should have fruit in his hearers, but he who hears misunderstands and is beyond reach of what is said, the words "Nor did anyone help me" would apply. For the speaker has not received that help which he would have received through the hearer being himself helped and becoming a source of advance and blessedness to the one who gave him help. Besides, every teacher by his very teaching is helped in his teaching and his studies through the intelligence of his pupil. Lecturers become more competent in the very instruction they impart, when their hearers are intelligent and do not accept their words right off, but criticize them and ask questions and examine the meaning of the language used. "I was of no help, neither did anyone help me."

But a further interpretation also is necessary, because the most accurate copies read thus: "I was not in debt, neither was anyone indebted to me." Let us then interpret the passage in this form. One who pays to all their dues, fear to whom fear is due, tribute to whom tribute, custom to whom

29. Jer. 15:10-12.
30. Jer. 15:10.

custom, honor to whom honor,[31] and who renders to all their rights, so that he does not owe their rights to any, honoring, let us say, his parents as parents, siblings as siblings, children as children, bishops as bishops, presbyters as presbyters, deacons as deacons, believers as believers, catechumens as catechumens, if he pays all claims, is not in debt. But if he was under obligation to meet a claim and has not met it, he cannot say, "I was not in debt." For he owed but he did not pay. But how then am I to interpret "Neither was anyone indebted to me"? I indeed was ready to lend and willing to give spiritual wealth, but they turned away from my words, and did not show themselves receptive so as to be in my debt. Consequently, not one person was indebted to me. For who received what I said, so as through receiving it to become a debtor for what was heard and liable as a debtor to the claim for interest on my words? In this sense it is better for the hearer to receive rational money from the speaker and to be in debt, rather than by not receiving and not gaining to avoid indebtedness. For the phrase "No one was indebted to me" stands as a reproach.

The words follow, "Woe is me, my mother, how have you borne me a man of strife and of contention to the whole earth."[32] I do not think they can be so appropriately used of the other prophets as of Jeremiah. For most of the prophets, after time had gone by, after wickedness, after their sins, repented and began to prophesy. Whereas Jeremiah was a prophet from childhood. One might give an instance from the scriptures. Isaiah did not hear the words "Before I formed you in the belly, I knew you, and before you came forth out of the womb, I sanctified you. I have appointed you a prophet unto the nations." Nor did he say, "I cannot speak, for I am a child."[33] But when he beheld the vision recorded in his prophecy, he beheld it and said, "Woe is me, for I am undone; because I am a man of unclean lips, and I dwell in the midst of a people of unclean lips, and I have seen with my eyes the King, the Lord of Hosts. And there was sent unto me," he says, "one of the seraphim, and he touched my lips and said, 'Lo, I have taken away your iniquities and this shall cleanse your sins.' "[34] Thus after the sins he had previously committed, later on, Isaiah became worthy of the Holy Spirit and was a prophet. The same you would find also in the case of any other. But not so Jeremiah. He from his cradle was endowed with the prophetic spirit; he was a prophet from childhood. Hence he says, to take first the common interpretation, "Woe is me, my

---

31. Rom. 13:7.
32. Jer. 15:10.
33. Jer. 1:5-6.
34. Isa. 6:5-7.

mother, how have you borne me a man of strife and of contention to the whole earth."

But one of the teachers before my time made a comment on the passage and said that the prophet used these words not to the mother of his body but to the mother who bears prophets. But who is it bears prophets but the Wisdom of God? So what he said was, "Woe is me, my mother, how have you borne me, O Wisdom." There is a reference also in the gospel to the children of Wisdom:[35] "And Wisdom sends forth her children." The words are then, "Woe is me, my mother Wisdom, how have you borne me a man of strife." Who am I that I should have been born for this, to be a man of strife, a man of contest, through my rebukes, through my attacks, through my teaching, unto all who are on the earth? If it is Jeremiah who says, "How have you borne me a man of strife and of contention to the whole earth," I cannot interpret the words "to the whole earth." Jeremiah had no contest with the whole earth. Or are we to force ourselves to say that "the whole earth" stands for the whole of Judaea? For his prophecy, at the time he was a prophet, did not extend to the whole earth. But possibly, just as in a hundred other places we have shown that Jeremiah stands for our Lord Jesus Christ, so too shall we say of this passage. Originally I put a mark[36] against the words "See, I have set you over the nations and kingdoms, to pluck up and to break down, to destroy and to build and to plant." Jeremiah did not do this. But Jesus Christ plucked up the kingdoms of the land of sin, and broke down the edifices of wickedness, and in place of these kingdoms made righteousness and truth to have royal power in our souls. Just as then it was more appropriate to refer the earlier passage to Christ than to Jeremiah, so I think must we deal with many other passages and with these words.

---

35. Matt. 11:19; Luke 7:35.

36. A text critical mark, denoting that the passage was not original. His method in the Hexapla followed contemporary scholarly practice. The words are Jer. 1:10.

3

NORTH AFRICA:
A PURITANIC TENDENCY

Tertullian
From *To His Wife 1.3; 2.8; On Modesty 1, 21, 22;*
On Fleeing Persecution 2, 7, 8, 14

The first two portions are taken from Ayer; the last from ANF 4.
Further relevant works are described in Quasten 2.290–316, on
such issues as personal holiness, women's and men's roles in the
community, and Christianity's relationship to the surrounding
culture. The only complete translation of Tertullian's works is in
ANF 3–4, where all the problems of Tertullian's Latin style are
not solved. T. Barnes (1985[2]) is the only full-length treatment in
English.

Born after 150 of pagan parents, Tertullian became trained in
advocacy. In the 190s he converted, perhaps drawn by the example
of the martyrs, and settled in Carthage, where he applied his skills
in philosophy and especially rhetoric and advocacy to the defense
of true Christian life and doctrine. He allied himself with the
stricter Montanists ca. 207, and his last works date from ca. 220.

Although he was the first central figure in the translation of
Christian theology and philosophy into Latin, Tertullian's passionate focus on Christian ethics and ethos was classically North African (see Jaeger, 1961, p. 33). He was quite candid about himself
(see his confession in *On Patience* 1.1!) but expected the Christian to
take the duty of moral growth very seriously. If the church was to
be a "school for sinners," it was to offer an honors curriculum, not
just remedial courses.

Tertullian apparently did not enter the clergy. Compare the relationship of his work with his background (he was a legally trained

layman) to that of Cyprian (from the patron's class, later a bishop) and of Augustine (from a professional class, later a bishop).

On Modesty came from Tertullian's Montanist period, and here the conflict was over who had the authority to loose and bind sins. Both sides based their arguments on the promise to Peter; but Tertullian argued that it was extended to others, not formally or institutionally, but rather by analogy: one must be spiritual like Peter to have this authority. So neither bishop nor confessor attained to this authority by office alone. Contrast this position with Augustine's against the Donatists. There are two (perennial) problems here: who is the physician? and what is the cure for sin?

Cyprian
On the Dress of Virgins 1–5; Ep. 11, 67.1–4, 9; 68.8

On the Dress of Virgins and Ep. 67 are from ANF 5; Ep. 11 from Clarke (1984), and 68 from Ayer. ANF 5 contains much other relevant material, for example, *On the Unity of the Church, On the Lord's Prayer,* and *On Works and Alms.* Cyprian's letters are vitally important, since so much of his work had to be conducted through them: see now Clarke's well-annotated translations. Besides G. Walker (1968), Hinchliff (1974) gives a vivid portrait (the first paragraph is wonderful), but he is somewhat prone to anachronistic sensibilities. The forthcoming work of C. Bobertz will be fundamental to understand how the paradigm of the patron-client relationship guided Cyprian's understanding of the responsibilities of the episcopate. On Cyprian's two-part crisis, see Poschmann (1940) for early penitential process and R. Evans (1972) for ecclesiology. Ipse dixit: in *To Donatus* he described his entry into Christian life; in Ep. 81, a farewell to his clergy, he looked towards his martyrdom.

Nothing specific is known of Cyprian's early life, although placing his birth around 200 in Carthage is a reasonable guess. His family was wealthy, perhaps even senatorial, and Cyprian had rhetorical and administrative experience.

In about 246 Cyprian converted to Christianity. In his reflection *To Donatus* he describes his disgust with the immorality of the wealthy and the corruption of the legal system. Baptism (with its usual extensive benefaction to the poor) achieved for him a moral liberation. Cyprian was soon ordained, and in 248 (two years after his conversion) he was elected bishop by popular acclamation, although against the wishes of a group of deacons.

When the Decian persecution arose, Cyprian took the controversial step, not of fleeing, but of going into hiding and discharging his duties, chiefly of succor and relief, through letters and messengers. Almost the whole first half of his letters come from this period. When the persecution ended, with Decius's death, Cyprian faced a two-part crisis (see *On the Lapsed* and *On the Unity of the Church*). The practical part concerned how to treat the mass of Christians who had to greater or lesser degrees lapsed, balancing justice with mercy. His program included long, even life-long, penance. When persecution threatened again under Gallus, the program was changed. Those under penance were readmitted so that nourished in the church they might be strong enough to withstand the coming challenge (the logic in Leo, Ep. 167.3, question 9, below p. 195, is similar). The political part concerned the problem of how to treat his old opponents who had now formed schismatic communions: one group was centered on the confessors favoring quick readmission (see Tertullian; but after the Great Persecution, 303–311, the confessors sided with the rigorists!) and another, the more serious threat, was the Roman-based, rigorist movement named after its founder, Novatian. As so often happened both earlier and later the threat of internal fragmentation proved more dangerous than attacks from without. Cyprian's deepest insight was that the body of Christ must be one body, and that this implied that if one is outside this body at all, one is outside it absolutely.

This principle, along with an old-fashioned personality conflict, led to Cyprian's last crisis, that with Pope Stephen over the baptism of heretics. Roman Christianity had always been more of a federation of communities than one church, and it was accustomed to a factionalized situation. It is not odd that Stephen saw the propriety of baptism to lie in its correct theology and performance, and not in the baptizer's affiliation. Novatian's theology was orthodox, and his baptism was in the triune Name: hence his baptism was valid, for Stephen, and readmission to communion was through penance. But, for Cyprian, one body meant one body: Novatian, by leaving the church, could no longer impart through baptism the Holy Spirit. Hence, one baptized by Novatian was no more baptized than an initiate of Eleusis. Admission to communion must clearly be through baptism. At the heart of this dissension is where one locates the root of Christian identity. Both positions have compelling arguments, and the question remains divisive.

Stephen and Cyprian had little chance to solve the problem. Valerian began a new persecution, aimed first at destroying Christian leadership. Stephen died in 257. In September 258, Cyprian knew he had to take a stand: he was arrested, and his public condemnation and execution drew a huge crowd of Christians. Cyprian died nobly, in the bosom of his family.

One final aspect must be mentioned. After the Decian persecution, plague swept the empire, and in Carthage the people began to blame the Christians. Cyprian, however, was already mobilizing care for all the sick—Christian or not. Although Cyprian was simply following the gospel teachings, these precepts of liberality and love have often been lost from sight.

Cyprian's Christian career spanned a mere dozen years, yet he helped to shape the church of his day, and, because his works continued to be popular and widely read, he remained directly influential throughout the Middle Ages.

TERTULLIAN, TO HIS WIFE

1.3. There is no place at all where we read that marriages are prohibited; of course it is a "good thing."[1] What, however, is better than this "good," we learn from the Apostle in that he permits marriage, indeed, but prefers abstinence; the former on account of the insidiousness of temptations, the latter on account of the straits of the times.[2] Now by examining the reason for each statement it is easily seen that the permission to marry is conceded us as a necessity; but whatever necessity grants, it itself deprecates. In fact, inasmuch as it is written, "It is better to marry than to burn,"[3] what sort of "good" is this which is only commended by com-

---

1. I.e., because of God's institution; see Gen. 1:28; 2:21-22; Matt. 19:5-6.
2. Cf. 1 Cor. 7:26.
3. 1 Cor. 7:9. The Bible speaks equivocally about marriage. Tertullian based his remarks on Paul's rather negative view, which he modifed by reference to more positive comments and (Stoic?) moral commonplaces. (See the ambiguous attitude also in Gangra, Epilogue, p. 104, and Basil, canon 6, p. 106; Jerome Ep. 52.16, p. 160; and in Leo, Ep. 167 question 13, p. 196; but contrast Ps.-Clement Hom. 3, p. 90; Clement, *Stromateis* book 3, defends marriage at length, but a marriage, if not chaste, is to be for procreation.) Notice how different Tertullian's picture is from, e.g., America's "nuclear family." Family practice, largely a social construct, varies greatly from place to place and age to age. But, however changeable in fact, it is usually felt to be (1) permanent and (2) in need of defense. Christianity, by providing a parallel "family," was often seen as a threat to the family. See, e.g., *Martyrdom of Perpetua* or Origen's *Contra Celsum*. For the flip side, see canons 51–55 of Laodicea, where family events are seen as a threat to Christians.

parison with "evil," so that the reason that "marrying" is better, is merely that "burning" is worse? Nay; but how much better is it neither to marry nor to burn?

2.8. Whence are we to find adequate words to tell fully of the happiness of that marriage which the church cements and the oblation confirms, and the benediction seals; which the angels announce, and the Father holds for ratified? For even on earth children do not rightly and lawfully wed without their father's consent. What kind of yoke is that of two believers of one hope, one discipline, and the same service? The two are brother and sister, the two are fellow servants; no difference of spirit or flesh; nay, truly, two in one flesh; where there is one flesh the spirit is one.

TERTULLIAN, ON MODESTY

1. I hear that there has been an edict set forth, and, indeed, a peremptory one; namely, that the Pontifex Maximus,[4] the bishop of bishops, issues an edict: "I remit to such as have performed penance, the sins both of adultery and fornication."

21. "But," you say, "the church has the power of forgiving sins." This I acknowledge and adjudge more, I, who have the Paraclete himself in the person of the new prophets, saying: "The church has the power to forgive sins, but I will not do it, lest they commit still others." . . . I now inquire into your opinion, to discover from what source you usurp this power to the church.

If, because the Lord said to Peter, "Upon this rock I will build my church. . . . To you I have given the keys of the kingdom of heaven,"[5] or "Whatsoever you shall bind or loose on earth, shall be bound or loosed in heaven," you therefore presume that the power of binding and loosing has descended to you, that is, to every church akin to Peter; what sort of person, then, are you, subverting and wholly changing the manifest intention of the Lord, who conferred the gift personally upon Peter? "On you," he says, "I will build my church," and "I will give you the keys," not to the church; and "whatsoever you shall have loosed or bound," not what they shall have loosed or bound. For so the result actually teaches. In Peter the church was reared, that is, through Peter himself; he himself tried the key; you see what key: "People of Israel, let what I say sink into your ears; Jesus, the Nazarene, a man appointed of God for you,"[6] and so forth. Peter

---

4. The reference to Pontifex Maximus is satirical. It is the office of the Roman State High Priest, and a title held then by the (autocratic) emperor.

5. Matt. 16:18-19.

6. Acts 2:22.

himself, therefore, was the first to unbar, in Christ's baptism, the entrance to the kingdom of heaven, in which are loosed the sins that aforetime were bound. . . .

What, now, has this to do with the church and your church, indeed, O Psychic?[7] For in accordance with the person of Peter, it is to spiritual people that this power will correspondingly belong, either to an apostle or else to a prophet. . . . And accordingly the "church," it is true, will forgive sins; but it will be the church of the Spirit, by a spiritual person; not the church which consists of a number of bishops.

22. But you go so far as to lavish this power upon martyrs indeed; so that no sooner has anyone, acting on a preconceived arrangement, put on soft bonds in the nominal custody now in vogue,[8] than adulterers beset him, fornicators gain access to him; instantly prayers resound about him; instantly pools of tears of the polluted surround him; nor are there any who are more diligent in purchasing entrance to the prison than they who have lost the fellowship of the church. . . . Whatever authority, whatever reason, restores ecclesiastical peace to the adulterer and the fornicator, the same will be bound to come to the aid of the murderer and the idolater in their repentance.

TERTULLIAN, ON FLEEING PERSECUTION

2. If, because injustice is not from God, but from the devil, and persecution consists of injustice (for what more unjust than that the bishops of the true God and all the followers of the truth should be dealt with after the manner of the vilest criminals?), persecution therefore seems to proceed from the devil . . . we ought to know . . . that the injustice necessary for the trial of faith does not give a warrant for persecution, but supplies an agency; that in reality, in reference to the trial of faith, which is the reason of persecution, the will of God goes first, but that as the instrument of persecution, which is the way of trial, the injustice of the devil follows.

. . . So righteousness may be perfected in injustice, as strength is perfected in weakness.[9] For the weak things of the world have been chosen by

---

7. "Psychic" is Tertullian's sarcastic name for his Catholic opponents, perhaps related to Gnostic terminology. See the opening sentences of *On Monogamy* and *On Fasting* for other indications of Tertullian's estimation of his former allies.

8. Not all the confessors (those arrested in persecution but not killed) suffered all torment, as Tertullian mockingly describes. The first canon of Ancyra, p. 102, shows the possibility for fraud. *The Martyrdom of Perpetua* shows a different side: of her imprisonment the worst she can say is that it was dark and crowded. Even this hardship was alleviated when the prisoners got better quarters through payments to the jailers by the deacons.

See *Apos. Const.* 8.23, p. 93, for the quasi-office of confessor.

9. 2 Cor. 12:9.

God to confound the strong, and the foolish things of the world to confound its wisdom.[10] Thus even injustice is employed, that righteousness may be approved in putting unrighteousness to shame. Therefore, since the service is not of free will, but of subjection . . . we believe that persecution comes to pass, no question, by the devil's agency, but not by the devil's origination. Satan will not be at liberty to do anything against the servants of the living God unless the Lord grant leave, either that he may overthrow Satan himself by the faith of the elect which proves victorious in the trial, or to show the world that apostatizers to the devil's cause have been in reality his servants.

You have the case of Job, whom the devil, unless he had received authority from God, could not have visited with trial. . . . So he asked in the case of the apostles likewise an opportunity to tempt them, having it only by special allowance, since the Lord in the gospel says to Peter, "Behold, Satan asked that he might sift you as grain; but I have prayed for you, that your faith fail not";[11] . . . Whence it is manifest that both things belong to God, the shaking of faith as well as the shielding of it, when both are sought from God—the shaking by the devil, the shielding by the Son. And certainly, when the Son of God has faith's protection absolutely committed to him, . . . how entirely out of the question is it that the devil should have the assailing of it in *his* own power! But in the prayer prescribed to us, when we say to our Father, "Lead us not into temptation"[12] (now what greater temptation is there than persecution?) we acknowledge that temptation comes to pass by God's will whom we beseech to exempt us from it. For this is what follows, "But deliver us from the wicked one," that is, do not lead us into temptation by giving us up to the wicked one, for then are we delivered from the power of the devil, when we are not handed over to him to be tempted. Nor would the devil's legion have had power over the herd of swine[13] unless they had got it from God; so far are they from having power over the sheep of God. . . . Against those who belong to the household of God he may not do anything as by any right of his own, because the cases marked out in scripture show when—that is, for what reasons—he may touch them. . . . The sinner is handed over to him, as though he were an executioner to whom belonged the inflicting of punishment. . . . For the apostle . . . delivered Phygellus and Hermogenes over to Satan, that by chastening they might be taught not to blaspheme.[14] You see, then, that the devil receives more suitably power even from the servants of God; so far is he from having it by any right of his own. . . .

10. 1 Cor. 1:27, 28.
11. Luke 22:31, 32.
12. Matt. 6:13. The Greek can mean "evil" or "Evil One."
13. Mark 5:11-13.
14. 2 Tim. 1:15; see also 1 Tim. 1:20.

7. God wished us either to suffer persecution or to flee from it. If to flee, how to suffer? If to suffer, how to flee? In fact, what utter inconsistency in the decrees of One who commands to flee, and yet urges to suffer, which is the very opposite! . . . "Of him who shall be ashamed of me, will I also be ashamed before my Father."[15] If I avoid suffering, I am ashamed to confess. "Happy they who suffer persecution for my name's sake."[16] Unhappy, therefore, they who, by running away, will not suffer according to the divine command. . . .

But it is said, the Lord, providing for the weakness of some of his people, nevertheless, in his kindness, suggested also the haven of flight to them. For he was not able even without flight—a protection so base, and unworthy, and servile—to preserve in persecution such as he knew to be weak! Whereas in fact he does not cherish, but ever rejects the weak, teaching first, not that we are to fly from our persecutors, but rather that we are not to fear them. "Fear not them who are able to kill the body, but are unable to do ought against the soul; but fear him who can destroy both body and soul in hell."[17] And then what does he allot to the fearful? "One who will value life more than me, is not worthy of me; and one who takes not up the cross and follows me, cannot be my disciple."[18]

8. . . . He likewise acknowledged, it is true, that his "soul was troubled, even unto death,"[19] and the flesh weak; with the design, . . . that, by an exhibition of their states, you might be convinced that they have no power at all of themselves without the Spirit. And for this reason he puts first "the willing spirit,"[20] that . . . you may see that you have in you the Spirit's strength as well as the flesh's weakness; and . . . what to bring under what—the weak, namely, under the strong, that you may not, as is now your fashion, make excuses on the ground of the weakness of the flesh. . . . He also asked of his Father, that if it might be, the cup of suffering should pass from him.[21] So ask you the like favor; but as he did, . . . adding . . . the . . . words: "but not what I will, but what you will." But when you run away, how will you make this request? taking, in that case, into your own hands the removal of the cup from you, and instead of doing what your Father wishes, doing what you wish yourself.

14. But how shall we assemble together? say you. . . . To be sure, just as the apostles also did, who were protected by faith, not by money; which faith, if it can remove a mountain, can much more remove a soldier. Be

---

15. Mark 8:38; Luke 9:26.
16. Matt. 5:11.
17. Matt. 10:28.
18. Matt. 10:38; see also Luke 14:26.
19. Matt. 26:38.
20. Matt. 26:41.
21. Matt. 26:39.

your safeguard wisdom, not a bribe. For you will not have at once
complete security from the people also, should you buy off the inter-
ference of the soldiers. Therefore all you need for your protection is to
have both faith and wisdom: if you do not make use of these, you may lose
even the deliverance which you have purchased for yourself; while, if you
do employ them, you can have no need of any ransoming. Lastly, if you
cannot assemble by day, you have the night, the light of Christ luminous
against its darkness. You cannot run about among them one after another.
Be content with a church of threes. It is better that you sometimes should
not see your crowds, than subject yourselves. . . . Keep pure for Christ his
betrothed virgin; let no one make gain of her. These things, my brother
Fabius, seem to you perhaps harsh and not to be endured; but . . . who
fears to suffer, cannot belong to him who suffered. But one who does not
fear to suffer will be perfect in love—in the love, it is meant, of God; "for
perfect love casts out fear."[22] "And therefore many are called, but few
chosen."[23] It is not asked who is ready to follow the broad way, but who
the narrow. And therefore the Comforter is requisite, who guides into all
truth, and animates to all endurance. And they who have received him will
neither stoop to flee from persecution nor to buy it off, for they have the
Lord himself, one who will stand by us to aid us in suffering, as well as to
be our mouth when we are put to the question.

·CYPRIAN, ON THE DRESS OF VIRGINS[24]

1–5

1. Discipline,[25] the safeguard of hope, the bond of faith, the guide of the

---

22. 1 John 4:18.
23. Matt. 22:14.
24. Written before 251, this is based on Tertullian's tract, *On the Apparel of Women*,
advancing its literary style and pastoral sensibility. Augustine cited it as a model
work. A proper sobriety of dress was a classical topic soon discussed by Christians.
Clement's *Protrepticus* and *Who Is the Rich Person . . . ?* (see pp. 30f.) dealt with it at
length, as later Jerome did in his epistles. See Clark (1982). Virginity: the taking of
religious vows was ancient practice in Jewish and Greek traditions (see Acts 18:18);
the association of sexuality with ritual (not only moral) purity was also ancient; the
choice of a virgin continence was seen as gaining freedom from the vicissitudes and
"passions" of social life and convention (see Ps.-Basil, Ep. 366, p. 121). The issues
involved are myriad and vastly complex, as the 504 pages of P. Brown (1988) show;
some central points are summarized with bibliography in his 1985 essay. Reflection
on the many facets of this topic will be richly repaid.
25. Latin *disciplina* = Greek *paideia*, recalling the context of education, which always in classical thought would involve reproof and reward. Cyprian is melding
classical and biblical ideas.

way of salvation, the stimulus and nourishment of good dispositions, the teacher of virtue, causes us to abide always in Christ, and to live continually for God, and to attain to the heavenly promises and to the divine rewards. To follow discipline is wholesome, and to turn away from it and neglect it is deadly. The Holy Spirit says in the Psalms, "Keep discipline, lest perchance the Lord be angry, and you perish from the right way, when his wrath is quickly kindled against you."[26] And again: "But unto the ungodly says God, 'Why do you preach my laws, and take my covenant into your mouth? Whereas you hate discipline, and have cast my words behind you.' "[27] And again we read: "He that casts away discipline is miserable."[28] And from Solomon we have received the mandates of wisdom, warning us: "My child, despise not the discipline of the Lord, nor faint when you are rebuked of him: for whom the Lord loves he corrects."[29] But if God rebukes whom he loves and rebukes for the very purpose of amending, the faithful also, and especially priests, do not hate, but love those whom they rebuke, that they may amend them; since God also before predicted by Jeremiah, and pointed to our times, when he said, "And I will give you shepherds according to my heart: and they shall feed you with the food of discipline."[30]

2. But if in holy scripture discipline is frequently and everywhere prescribed, and the whole foundation of religion and of faith proceeds from obedience and fear, what is more fitting for us urgently to desire, what more to wish for and to hold fast, than to stand with roots strongly fixed, and with our houses based with solid mass upon the rock unshaken by the storms and whirlwinds of the world, so that we may come by the divine precepts to the rewards of God? considering as well as knowing that our members, when purged from all the filth of the old contagion by the sanctification of the laver of life [i.e., baptism], are God's temples, and must not be violated nor polluted, since one who does violence to them is himself injured. We are the worshipers and priests of those temples; let us obey him whose we have already begun to be. Paul tells us in his epistles, in which he has formed us to a course of living by divine teaching, "You are not your own, for you are bought with a great price; glorify and bear God in your body."[31] Let us glorify and bear God in a pure and chaste body, and with a more complete obedience; and since we have been redeemed by the blood of Christ, let us obey and give furtherance to the

---

26. Ps. 2:12 (LXX).
27. Ps. 50:16-17.
28. Wisd. 3:11.
29. Prov. 3:11-12.
30. Jer. 3:15 (LXX).
31. 1 Cor. 6:19-20.

empire of our Redeemer by all the obedience of service, that nothing impure or profane may be brought into the temple of God, lest he should be offended, and forsake the temple which he inhabits. The words of the Lord giving health and teaching, as well curing as warning, are: "Behold, you are made whole: sin no more, lest a worse thing come unto thee."[32] He gives the course of life, he gives the law of innocency after he has conferred health, nor allows anyone afterwards to wander with free and unchecked reins, but more severely threatens the one who is again enslaved by those same things of which he had been healed, because it is doubtless a smaller fault to have sinned before, while as yet you had not known God's discipline; but there is no further pardon for sinning after you have begun to know God. And, indeed, let as well men as women, as well boys as girls; let each sex and every age observe this, and take care in this respect, according to the religion and faith which they owe to God, that what is received holy and pure from the condescension of the Lord be preserved with a no less anxious fear.

3. My address is now to virgins, whose glory, as it is more eminent, excites the greater interest. This is the flower of the ecclesiastical seed, the grace and ornament of spiritual endowment, a joyous disposition, the wholesome and uncorrupted work of praise and honor, God's image answering to the holiness of the Lord, the more illustrious portion of Christ's flock. The glorious fruitfulness of Mother Church rejoices by their means, and in them abundantly flourishes; and in proportion as a copious virginity is added to her number, so much the more it increases the joy of the Mother. To these I speak, these I exhort with affection rather than with power; not that I would claim—last and least, and very conscious of my lowliness as I am—any right to censure, but because, being unceasingly careful even to solicitude, I fear more from the onset of Satan.

4. For that is not an empty carefulness nor a vain fear, which takes counsel for the way of salvation, which guards the commandments of the Lord and of life, so that they who have dedicated themselves to Christ, and who depart from carnal concupiscence, and have vowed themselves to God as well in the flesh as in the spirit, may consummate their work, destined as it is to a great reward, and may not study any longer to be adorned or to please anybody but their Lord, from whom also they expect the reward of virginity;[33] as he himself says: "All men cannot receive this

---

32. John 5:14.

33. *Study to please the Lord:* this extends the image of Christ the Bridegroom to involve the soul as the chaste bride. It was a very popular idea, often, but not at all universally, applied to women. A wonderful example is the story of Pelagia of Antioch, in Waddell (1957): a bishop mourns how this harlot will adorn herself more earnestly for men than he will for God. She soon converts. Brock and Harvey (1987) has other good examples.

word, but they to whom it is given. For there are some eunuchs, which were so born from their mother's womb; and there are some eunuchs, which were made eunuchs of men; and there are eunuchs which have made themselves eunuchs for the kingdom of heaven's sake."[34] Again, also by this word of the angel the gift of continency is set forth, and virginity is preached: "These are they which have not defiled themselves with women, for they have remained virgins; these are they which follow the Lamb whithersoever he goeth."[35] For not only thus does the Lord promise the grace of continency to men, and pass over women; but since the woman is a portion of the man, and is taken and formed from him, God in scripture almost always speaks to the protoplast, the first formed, because they are two in one flesh, and in the male is at the same time signified the woman also.[36]

5. But if continency follows Christ, and virginity is destined for the kingdom of God, what have they to do with earthly dress, and with ornaments, wherewith while they are striving to please people they offend God? Not considering that it is declared, "They who please people are put to confusion, because God has despised them";[37] and that Paul also has gloriously and sublimely uttered, "If I yet pleased people, I should not be the servant of Christ."[38] But continence and modesty consist not alone in purity of the flesh, but also in seemliness, as well as in modesty of dress and adornment;[39] so that, according to the apostle, she who is unmarried may be holy both in body and in spirit. Paul instructs and teaches us, saying, "He that is unmarried cares for the things of the Lord, how he may please God: but he who has contracted marriage cares for the things which are of this world, how he may please his wife. So both the virgin and the unmarried woman consider those things which are the Lord's, that they may be holy both in body and spirit."[40] A virgin ought not only to be so, but also to be perceived and believed to be so: no one on seeing a virgin should be in any doubt as to whether she is one. Perfectness should show itself equal in all things; nor should the dress of the body discredit the good of the mind. Why should she walk out adorned? Why with

---

34. Matt. 19:11-12.

35. Rev. 14:4.

36. *Protoplast:* the difficulties of "inclusive language" are not new: Cyprian, having cited two passages referring to males, needs to expand their relevance universally. What would result if Cyprian's principle of expanding male referents to all people were applied with full consistency?

37. Ps. 53:5 (LXX).

38. Gal. 1:10.

39. Similarly in Ps.-Basil, Ep. 366, below p. 122. A concern with overly-rich dress implies that there were those who could afford it, a small percentage of the population in antiquity. Ever since Paul wrote to Corinth, the place of wealthy Christians has been discussed.

40. 1 Cor. 7:32-34.

dressed hair, as if she either had, or sought for a husband? Rather let her dread to please if she is a virgin; and let her not invite her own risk, if she is keeping herself for better and divine things. They who have not a husband whom they profess that they please, should persevere, sound and pure not only in body, but also in spirit. For it is not right that a virgin should have her hair braided for the appearance of her beauty, or boast of her flesh and of its beauty, when she has no struggle greater than that against her flesh, and no contest more obstinate than that of conquering and subduing the body.

CYPRIAN, LETTERS 11; 67.1–4, 9; 68.8

Letter 11[41]

Cyprian sends greetings to his brothers, the presbyters and deacons.

1.1. I am aware, my dearly beloved brothers, that—such is the fear which all of us owe to God—you, too, in Carthage are urgent and importunate in constant prayer and earnest entreaty. Even so, notwithstanding your piety and solicitude, I send to you my personal exhortations as well that, in order to placate and appease our God, we should mourn not with voice only, but also with fasting and tears and every form of supplication.

1.2. For we must face the fact and acknowledge it that the raging devastation of this persecution which has ravaged the major part of our flock, and continues still to ravage it, has come upon us for our sins; we have not been keeping to the way of the Lord, we have not been observing the heavenly commandments given us for our salvation.[42] Our Lord has done the will of God, but for our part, we do not do the will of God. Instead, property and profit we strive for, pride we pursue, our time we devote to rivalry and dissension, innocence and faith we neglect, the world we renounce with words only, not deeds, each person pleasing himself alone and displeasing everyone else.

And so we are being given the thrashing which we deserve. As it is written, "The servant who recognizes the will of the master and has not obeyed that will, will be thrashed many times."[43]

---

41. This is the first letter from Cyprian's retreat during the Decian persecution, and his absence is the proximate cause.

42. The roots of understanding the cause of persecution to be the community's sin go back to the Prophetic literature, continue through Jewish martyr literature (2, 4 Macc.), and into Christian literature from the beginning (1 Clem.). The dangers of a false bravery were too well known.

43. Luke 12:47.

1.3. What blows, what flogging do we in fact not deserve when even confessors, who ought to have set an example of good conduct to others, fail to keep discipline. Hence, there being certain confessors swollen with immodest and insolent vainglory in their confession, the tortures have come, and tortures without any cessation of the torturer, without the release of condemnation, without the solace of death, tortures which do not readily let their victims go to their crown but which wrench for as long as it takes to break a person; the only exception being anyone who should have departed—through God's mercy taken away in the very midst of torments and gaining glory, not because the torturing had come to an end, but by the quickness of death.

2.1. These sufferings we are undergoing for our iniquities and our deserts, just as God forewarned with these words of stricture: "If they abandon my law and in my judgments they do not walk, if they violate my precepts and my ordinances they do not observe, I will visit their wicked deeds with the rod and with the lash their iniquities."[44] And that is why we are feeling these rods and lashes, for we neither please God by our good deeds nor render satisfaction to him for our sins.

2.2. From the depths of our heart and with our whole soul let us then ask for the mercy of God,[45] for he went on to say himself: "But my mercy I will not scatter away from them."[46] Let us seek, and we receive. And if we experience slowness and delay in receiving—our offenses are grave indeed—let us knock, because to one who knocks it is opened; that is, provided we knock at the door with our entreaties and cries and tears—we must be incessant and importunate in making them—and provided that we are united together in making our prayer.

3.1. You ought to know what has particularly induced, indeed driven, me to write this letter to you. The Lord thought fit to manifest and reveal a vision.[47] In it, these words were spoken: "Ask and you shall have." And then the congregation standing by was enjoined to ask on behalf of certain people pointed out to them, but in putting their request their voices were discordant, their wills conflicting; and he who had said "ask and you shall have" was exceedingly displeased at the fact that the people were divided and at variance, and that amongst the faithful there was no one, uniform agreement and harmonious concord. And this, despite the fact that it is written: "God who makes all dwell united together in a house,"[48] and

---

44. Ps. 89:30-32, q.v.!—notice the context and changes.
45. Cf. Matt. 7:7//Luke 11:10.
46. Ps. 89:33, q.v.!—again, notice the context and changes.
47. A contemporary vision, perhaps Cyprian's own. Visions were an accepted part of Carthaginian church life.
48. Ps. 68:6, here quoted after the Old Latin version, as always in Cyprian. It is a

even though we read in the Acts of the Apostles: "The multitude of those who believed were of one heart and mind."[49] Likewise the Lord has commanded with his own lips: "This is my commandment, that you love one another,"[50] and again: "But I say to you that if two of you are in agreement on earth in seeking any matter, it shall be granted to you by my Father who is in heaven."[51] Now, if two, united together, have such power, what could be accomplished if all should be united together?

3.2. Had there been agreement among all the faithful, in conformity with the peace which the Lord has given us,[52] we would long ago have gained from our merciful God what we are seeking, neither would we now have been tossed for so long on these waves which jeopardize our faith and our salvation. In fact, these evils would not have befallen our community had they all been of one mind together.

4.1. Now this was also revealed: the father of a household was seated, with a young man sitting on his right. This young man looked worried and somewhat aggrieved as well as distressed, as he sat mournfully holding his chin in his hand. But there was another person standing on the left side; he was carrying a net and he kept threatening to cast it and ensnare the crowd of bystanders.[53] And when the person who saw this vision wondered what this meant, he was told that the young man who was sitting like that on the right was grieving and sorrowful at the neglect of his precepts, whereas the one on the left was jubilant at being given the opportunity of obtaining from the father of the household leave to rage and destroy.

4.2. This revelation was made long ago before the present devastating storm arose. And we see now fulfilled what was then revealed: so long as we hold in scorn the precepts of the Lord, so long as we do not observe the saving ordinances of the law which God has given, the enemy gains power to do harm and with a cast of his net holds us enmeshed, too ill-armed and off-guard to repel him.

5.1. We must be urgent in prayer and raise our mournful cries with incessant supplication. For I must tell you, my very dear friends, that not so long ago in a vision this reproach was also made to us. We are slumbering

---

favorite maxim of his. The verse is interpreted in a variety of ways by ancient writers, both because of the textual variant (the Latin seems to have read a genitive singular for the accusative plural in the LXX) and because the Greek and Hebrew words have wide semantic ranges: from "single-minded" to "singular" to "solitary" to "lonely," and so on. Interpretations have been based on each of them. Cyprian's Bible text and interpretation are quite interesting to study.

49. Acts 4:32.
50. John 15:12.
51. Matt. 18:19.
52. Cf. John 14:27.
53. The imagery of the dream draws on stock figures of funeral sculpture.

in our supplications, I was told; we are not watchful in prayer. It is undoubtedly true that God loves the one whom he chastens. When he chastens, he chastens in order to improve us, and he improves us in order to save us. We must, therefore, cast off and burst the bonds of sleep and pray with urgency and watchfulness, as the apostle Paul enjoins us: "Be urgent and watchful in prayer."[54] Not only did the apostles never cease to pray day and night, but the Lord himself, too, the teacher of our rule of life, the Way for us to imitate, prayed often, and watchfully. As we read in the gospel: "He went out on to the mountain to pray and spent the whole night in prayer with God."[55]

5.2. There can be no doubt that when he prayed he was praying for us, for he was not a sinner himself, but he bore our sins. So earnestly did he seek to intercede for us, as we read in another passage: "And the Lord said to Peter: Behold Satan has demanded to sift all of you like wheat. But for you, Peter, I have pleaded that your faith fail not."[56]

Now if he goes to such pains for us and for our transgressions, watching and praying, it follows that we ought all the more to be urgent in prayer and supplication, firstly making our plea to the Lord himself, and then, through him, making our amends to God.

5.3. Jesus Christ our Lord and God we have as advocate and intercessor[57] for our sins, on condition that we are repentant of our sins in the past, that we confess and acknowledge our transgressions whereby at present we offend the Lord, that we pledge that for the future at least we will walk in his ways and fear his commandments.

The Father is both chastening and protecting us, if, that is, we stand steadfast in the faith, in spite of trials and tribulations, firmly clinging to his Christ—as it is written: "Who shall separate us from the love of Christ? Shall trial or tribulation or persecution or hunger or nakedness or peril or sword?"[58] None of these can separate those who believe, none can prize away those who cling to his body and blood. This persecution is a way of sifting and searching our sinfulness; God would have us threshed and tested as he has always tested his own. But it is nevertheless true to say that in his tests never has he failed to give support to those who believe.

6.1. Finally, even the least of his servants, set as they are in the midst of very many transgressions and undeserving of his favor, he favored nevertheless in his goodness towards us with these instructions: Tell them, he

---

54. Col. 4:2.
55. Luke 6:12.
56. Luke 22:31-32.
57. Cf. 1 John 2:1.
58. Rom. 8:35.

said, not to be anxious, for there is going to be peace, but there is, meantime, a short delay, for some are left still to be tested.

6.2. And further, through God's favor, we are admonished to be abstemious in diet and sober in drink. I have no doubt that this is to prevent hearts now uplifted with heavenly strength from being emasculated by worldly allurements or souls from being less watchful in prayer and petition by being weighed down with lavish feasting.

7.1. I had no right to keep these particular matters concealed or to confine knowledge of them to myself alone; for they can serve to govern and guide each one of us. In your turn, you ought not to keep this letter concealed among yourselves but you should make it available to others to read. To obstruct those things by which God has favored us with admonishment and instruction is the action of someone who would not have his own neighbor receive admonishment and instruction.

7.2. They must know that we are being put to the test by our Lord; they must not fall away, under the impact of the present persecution, from that faith whereby we once came to believe in him. Each person, recognizing his own faults, should even now put off the habits of the old self. "No one who looks back, once having put a hand to the plough, is fit for the kingdom of God."[59] And Lot's wife, on being freed, looked back in defiance of her instructions and forfeited her deliverance.[60] We must not turn towards the things which lie behind, to which the devil calls us back, but towards the things which lie ahead, to which Christ calls us. Let us lift up our eyes towards heaven lest we are beguiled by the delights and allurements of the earth.

7.3. Every one of us should pray to God not for self only, but for all his brothers and sisters, just as the Lord taught us to pray. His instructions are not for each of us to pray privately, but he bade that when we pray we should do so with united hearts in communal prayer for everyone. If the Lord shall observe that we are humble and peaceable, joined in union together, fearful of his wrath, chastened and amended by the present sufferings, he will make us safe from the assaults of the enemy. When discipline has led the way, forgiveness will follow.

8. What we must do is to beg the Lord with united and undivided hearts, without pause in our entreaty, with confidence that we shall receive, seeking to appease him with cries and tears as befits those who find themselves amidst the lamentations of the fallen and the trembling of the remnant still left, amidst the host of those who lie faint and savaged and the tiny band of those who stand firm. We must petition that peace be

59. Luke 9:62.
60. Luke 17:31ff.; cf. Gen. 19:17, 26.

promptly restored, that help be quickly brought to our places of concealment and peril, that those things be fulfilled which the Lord vouchsafes to
reveal to his servants—the restoration of his church, the certitude of our
salvation, bright skies after rain, after darkness light, after wild storms a
gentle calm. We must beg that the Father send his loving aid to his
children, that God in his majesty perform as so often, his wondrous works
whereby the blasphemy of the persecutors may be confounded, the
repentance of the fallen may be restored, and the courageous and un-
wavering faith of the persevering may be glorified.

I wish that you, my dearly beloved, may ever fare well and be mindful of
us. Greet the community in my name and urge them to be mindful of us.
Farewell.

Letter 67.1–4, 9

1. Cyprian, Caecilius, Primus, Polycarp, Nicomedes, Lucilianus, Suc-
cessus, Sedatus, Fortunatus, Januarius, Secundinus, Pomponius, Honor-
atus, Victor, Aurelius, Sattius, Petrus, another Januarius, Saturninus, another Aurelius, Venantius, Quietus, Rogatianus, Tenax, Felix, Faustinus,
Quintus, another Saturninus, Lucius, Vincentius, Libosus, Geminius, Mar-
cellus, Iambus, Adelphius, Victoricus, and Paulus, to Felix the presbyter,
and to the peoples abiding at Legio and Asturica, also to Laelius the
deacon, and the people abiding at Emerita,[61] brothers and sisters in the
Lord, greeting. When we had come together, dearly beloved, we read your
letters, which according to the integrity of your faith and your fear of God
you wrote to us by Felix and Sabinus our fellow bishops, signifying that
Basilides and Martial, being stained with the certificates of idolatry,[62] and
bound with the consciousness of wicked crimes, ought not to hold the
episcopate and administer the priesthood of God; and you desired an
answer to be written to you again concerning these things, and your
solicitude, no less just than needful, to be relieved either by the comfort or
by the help of our judgment. Nevertheless, it is not so much our counsels
as it is the divine precepts that reply to your desire, in which it is long since
bidden by the voice of heaven and prescribed by the law of God, who and
what sort of persons ought to serve the altar and to celebrate the divine
sacrifices. For in Exodus God speaks to Moses, and warns him, saying, "Let
the priests which come near to the Lord God sanctify themselves, lest the
Lord forsake them."[63] And again: "And when they come near to the altar of

---

61. Three towns in western Spain.
62. The *libelli*, which showed that they had fulfilled the legally required sacrifice.
See ODCC, s.v. Libellitici.
63. Ex. 19:22.

the Holy One to minister, they shall not bring sin upon them, lest they die."[64] Also in Leviticus the Lord commands, and says, "Whosoever has any spot or blemish shall not approach to offer gifts to God."[65]

2. Since these things are announced and are made plain to us, it is necessary that our obedience should wait upon the divine precepts; nor in matters of this kind can human indulgence accept anyone's person, or yield anything to anyone, when the divine prescription has interfered, and establishes a law. For we ought not to be forgetful what the Lord spoke to the Jews by Isaiah the prophet, rebuking, and indignant that they had despised the divine precepts and followed human doctrines. "This people," he says, "honor me with their lips, but their heart is widely removed from me; but in vain do they worship me, teaching human doctrines and commandments."[66] This also the Lord repeats in the gospel, and says, "You reject the commandment of God, that you may establish your own tradition."[67] Having which things before our eyes, and solicitously and religiously considering them, we ought in the ordinations of priests to choose none but unstained and upright ministers, who, holily and worthily offering sacrifices to God, may be heard in the prayers which they make for the safety of the Lord's people, since it is written, "God does not listen to a sinner; but God listens to anyone who is a worshiper of God and does God's will."[68] On which account it is fitting, that with full diligence and sincere investigation those should be chosen for God's priesthood whom it is manifest God will hear.

3. Nor let the people flatter themselves that they can be free from the contagion of sin, while communicating with a priest who is a sinner, and yielding their consent to the unjust and unlawful episcopacy of their overseer, when the divine reproof by Hosea the prophet threatens, and says, "Their sacrifices shall be as the bread of mourning; all that eat thereof shall be polluted";[69] teaching manifestly and showing that all are absolutely bound to the sin who have been contaminated by the sacrifice of a profane and unrighteous priest. Which, moreover, we find to be manifested also in Numbers, when Korah, and Dathan, and Abiram claimed for themselves the power of sacrificing in opposition to Aaron the priest. There also the Lord commanded by Moses that the people should be separated from them, lest, being associated with the wicked, themselves

---

64. Ex. 28:43 (LXX).
65. Lev. 21:17 (LXX); cf. 21:18ff.!
66. Isa. 29:13 as quoted in Mark 7:6-7 (in a variant reading; contrast Matt. 15:8-9), following the LXX.
67. Mark 7:9.
68. John 9:31, q.v.! Who is the speaker? Who is referred to?
69. Hos. 9:4.

also should be bound closely in the same wickedness. "Separate your-selves," said he, "from the tents of these wicked and hardened ones, and touch not those things which belong to them, lest you perish together in their sins."[70] On which account a people obedient to the Lord's precepts, and fearing God, ought to separate themselves from a sinful prelate, and not to associate themselves with the sacrifices of a sacrilegious priest, especially since they themselves have the power either of choosing worthy priests, or of rejecting unworthy ones.[71]

4. Which very thing, too, we observe to come from divine authority, that the priest should be chosen in the presence of the people under the eyes of all, and should be approved worthy and suitable by public judgment and testimony; as in the book of Numbers the Lord commanded Moses, saying, "Take Aaron your brother, and Eleazar his son, and place them in the mount, in the presence of all the assembly, and strip Aaron of his garments, and put them upon Eleazar his son; and let Aaron die there, and be added to his people."[72] God commands a priest to be appointed in the presence of all the assembly; that is, he instructs and shows that the ordination of priests ought not be solemnized except with the knowledge of the people standing near, that in the presence of the people either the crimes of the wicked may be disclosed, or the merits of the good may be declared, and the ordination, which shall have been examined by the suffrage and judgment of all, may be just and legitimate. And this is subsequently observed, according to divine instruction, in the Acts of the Apostles, when Peter speaks to the people of ordaining an apostle in the place of Judas. "Peter," it says, "stood up in the midst of the disciples, and the multitude were in one place."[73] Neither do we observe that this was regarded by the apostles only in the ordinations of bishops and priests, but also in those of deacons, of which matter itself also it is written in their Acts: "And they twelve called together," it says, "the whole congregation of the disciples, and said to them";[74] which was done so diligently and

---

70. Num. 16:26.

71. The (im)purity of the priest is shared with the laity, although Augustine would later argue that the people cannot be held accountable. Notice that Cyprian's argument is related to the people's ability to depose the priest. What if they cannot, or know not to do it? Tertullian had demanded purity of the entire congregation, but Cyprian, having to respond to events, demanded purity from the clergy. There was an implicit danger here, in that separate theologies of laity and of clergy began to emerge. What pastoral problems does this split in expectations raise? See Gregory the Great, Pastoral Rule part 2, below p. 203; Basil, canon 27, p. 110; and Chrysostom, On the Priesthood 6.4, p. 183.

72. Num. 20:25, 26. On the publicity of choice, see Augustine, Ep. 213, pp. 149ff., and also the circumstances outlined in section 5 of this letter.

73. Acts 1:15.

74. Acts 6:2.

carefully, with the calling together of the whole of the people, surely for this reason, that no unworthy person might creep into the ministry of the altar, or to the office of a priest. For that unworthy persons are sometimes ordained, not according to the will of God, but according to human presumption, and that those things which do not come of a legitimate and righteous ordination are displeasing to God, God manifests by Hosea the prophet, saying, "They have crowned for themselves a ruler, but not by me."[75]

9. Wherefore, although there have been found some among our colleagues who think that the godly discipline may be neglected, and who rashly hold communion with Basilides and Martialis, such a thing as this ought not to trouble our faith, since the Holy Spirit threatens such in the Psalms, saying, "But you hate instruction, and cast my words behind you: when you saw a thief, you consented unto him, and have been partaker with adulterers."[76] He shows that they become sharers and partakers of other people's sins who are associated with the delinquents. And besides, Paul the apostle writes, and says the same thing: "Whisperers, backbiters, haters of God, injurious, proud, boasters of themselves, inventors of evil things, who, although they knew the judgment of God, did not understand that they which commit such things are worthy of death, not only they which commit those things, but they also which consent unto those who do these things."[77] Since they, says he, who do such things are worthy of death, he makes manifest and proves that not only they are worthy of death, and come into punishment who do evil things, but also those who consent unto those who do such things—who, while they are mingled in unlawful communion with the evil and sinners, and the unrepenting, are polluted by the contact of the guilty, and, being joined in the fault, are thus not separated in its penalty. For which reason we not only approve, but applaud, dearly beloved, the religious solicitude of your integrity and faith, and exhort you as much as we can by our letters, not to mingle in sacrilegious communion with profane and polluted priests, but maintain the sound and sincere constancy of your faith with religious fear. I bid you ever heartily farewell.

Letter 68.8

Peter speaks there[78] . . . teaching in the name of Christ, that although a rebellious and arrogant multitude of those who will not obey depart, yet

---

75. Hos. 8:4.
76. Ps. 50:17, 18.
77. Rom. 1:30-32.
78. John 6:68. For more of Cyprian's thoughts on unity, see Treatise 1: *On the Unity of the Church.*

the church does not depart from Christ; and they are the church who are a people united to the priest, and the flock which adheres to its pastor. Whence you ought to know that the bishop is in the church and the church in the bishop; and that if anyone be not with the bishop, he is not in the church, and that those flatter themselves in vain who creep in, not having peace with God's priests, and think that they communicate secretly with some; while the church, which is catholic and one, is not cut nor divided, but is indeed connected and bound together by the cement of the priests who cohere with one another.

4

ALEXANDRIA:
THE MONASTIC PASTOR

Athanasius
Epistle 49.3–6, to Dracontius

Ep. 49 concerns not forsaking the episcopacy. See also Ep. 55 to Rufinianus, the Synodal Letter to Antioch, and, of course, the *Life of Anthony*. NPNF 2.4, from which this epistle is taken, is the largest collection of Athanasius's works; the newest translation of the *Life of Anthony* and the Letter to Marcellinus is in Classics of Western Spirituality. There is, surprisingly, no full-scale treatment of Athanasius, but Robertson's Prolegomena to NPNF 2.4; Meijoring (1968), wherein "synthesis" is the answer; and Frend (1976) can help.

Athanasius, ca. 295–373, lived one of the most dramatic lives of the Fathers. As secretary to patriarch Alexander of Alexandria, he attracted attention at the Council of Nicaea. He became patriarch in 328, but suffered exile five times, totaling seventeen years, for his staunch defense of the Nicene faith, his ability to marshal the orthodox forces (Gregory Nazianzen called him the pillar of the church), and his great popularity among the Alexandrian populace and the monks. During his second exile, he formed important ties with the Western church, and he spent the third exile, 355–361, with the monks in the desert.

His opposition to the Arians was strong and direct, even brutal, but toward the large but largely unorganized group called semi-Arians he was patient and conciliatory, trying to show how their position in fact led them to the Nicene position.

Verba Seniorum

Also called the *Apophthegmata Patrum*, these thirty-eight sayings[1] are selected from O. Chadwick (1958), an extensive collection. Benedicta Ward has several volumes of translations, for example, 1981. There are a number of other shorter selections, for example, T. Merton (1970) and especially the delightful H. Waddell (1936). Parallel material from the Syriac translations was collected by E. Wallis Budge. Chitty (1966) is classic. Lietzmann (1951, vol. 4, ch. 6) has many facts, but beware his (Lutheran-biased) summary. Ramsey (1985) has a nice appreciation of monastic themes. P. Brown (1971) is an important advance in historical understanding.

Among the monks, a genre developed (from the classical *chreia*): a young monk, when finishing a visit with an elder, would ask for a word, a sentence to meditate on and be guided by. Since silence was a great virtue, these occasional breaks were seen as prophetic and holy. Soon people were making collections of the sayings and adding exemplary vignettes. These became hot property (see 8.6 in Chadwick) and translated collections were widely circulated. At their best, they are some of the most attractive literature of the period.

Slowly, popular modern antipathy to monasticism is fading. Giving a single absurd example of monastic extravagance, as if found in a freak show, no longer passes as a critical evaluation. The sayings have a compact sensibility guided by long experience and common sense. They are best summed up in 10.91, or perhaps in 12.2. It is said that there is little theology among them: this is an overstatement. We ought to remember that theology is more appropriate to other genres: Athanasius and Basil were part of the monastic movement *and* great theologians. It is said that the monks were poor and uneducated: many among the myriads in the Egyptian monasteries were, but the frequent presence among the elders of people such as Arsenius and Syncletice shows us the leading presence of upper-class, educated people. Monasticism was a complicated, multifaceted phenomenon.

---

1. Namely, 1.10, 11, 22; 3.14, 16; 4.51; 5.3, 13, 28, 29, 38, 40; 6.5; 7.18; 8.2, 19; 9.10; 10.1, 8, 13, 51, 53, 62, 71c, 85, 91; 11.15, 38; 12.2; 13.7, 11; 14.9; 15.1, 3, 58; 16.10; 17.10, 18.

Syncletice, unfortunately this book's only female author, must
have been a striking woman. In Chadwick, she is cited two dozen
times; perhaps three monks have significantly more attributions in
the index. Her concentration on poverty and her varied uses of the
ship/sea metaphors (a common group of images in patristic literature) reveal an upper-class background. Given the often oppressive strictures of a woman's duties to husband and household,
one can see how the chaste monastic life opened up avenues of
self-fulfillment and even of leadership and scholarship. Consider
the philosopher Hypatia, or the heroines of the very popular
genre, the lives of holy women (Brock and Harvey, 1987). Monasticism was often liberating, as Hickey (1987) discusses, somewhat
pedantically.

John Cassian
Conference 15: The Gifts of God

This is the second conference of Nesteros, from Luibheid (1985). A
good selection and introduction is in O. Chadwick (1958). All of
Cassian's works are found in NPNF 2.11, along with related
works. O. Chadwick (1968²) is foundational, and Rousseau (1978)
describes Cassian within the creation of European monasticism.

John Cassian, ca. 360–435, through his introductory book, *The
Divine Institutes,* and the *Conferences,* became an initial and important guide to the nascent European monasticism in Gaul and a
mediator of the Egyptian monastic achievements. Born in the Latin
region on the west coast of the Black Sea, in modern Romania,
Cassian learned the Latin classics and style well, as his writings
show. He spent time in Bethlehem and Egypt, which he left partly
because of the Origenist/Evagrian controversies. He served Chrysostom, that great bishop-monk, and was part of a delegation to
Rome in 404. By 415 he was ordained and settled in Marseille, to
found two monasteries and to compose his monastic instructions,
published in the late 420s.

You will notice that we introduce Cassian, not Nesteros, and
relate him to the retiring philosopher Evagrius of Pontus and the
activist ascetic Chrysostom. Monasticism was often associated with
the simple and the uneducated, but its ideology was articulated by
a learned, dedicated elite: Athanasius, Basil, Chrysostom, and
Jerome, among others.

ATHANASIUS, LETTER TO DRACONTIUS

49.3–6

3. I beseech you, spare yourself and us. Yourself, lest you run into peril; us, lest we be grieved because of you. Take thought of the church, lest many of the little ones be injured on your account, and the others be given an occasion of withdrawing. Nay, but if you feared the times and acted as you did from timidity, your mind is not mature; for in such a case you ought to manifest zeal for Christ, and rather meet circumstances boldly, and use the language of blessed Paul: "in all these things we are more than conquerors";[2] and the more so in that we ought to serve not the time, but the Lord.[3] But if the organizing of the churches is distasteful to you, and you do not think the ministry of the episcopate has its reward, why, then you have brought yourself to despise the Savior that ordered these things. I beseech you, dismiss such ideas, nor tolerate those who advise you in such a sense, for this is not worthy of Dracontius. For the order the Lord has established by the apostles abides fair and firm; but the cowardice of the community shall cease.[4]

4. For if all were of the same mind as your present advisers, how would you have become a Christian, since there would be no bishops? Or if our successors are to inherit this state of mind, how will the churches be able to hold together? Or do your advisers think that you have received nothing, that they despise it? If so, surely they are wrong. For it is time for them to think that the grace of the font is nothing, if some are found to despise it. But you have received it, beloved Dracontius; do not tolerate your advisers nor deceive yourself. For this will be required of you by the God who gave it. Have you not heard the Apostle say, "Neglect not the gift that is in thee"?[5] or have you not read how he accepts the steward that had doubled his money, while he condemned the one that had hidden it?[6] But may it come to pass that you may quickly return, in order that you too may be one of those who are praised. Or tell me, whom do your advisers wish you

---

2. Rom. 8:37.

3. Rom. 12:11.

4. Given what Athanasius had to face as bishop, including attacks by imperial troops, added to the scruples against unworthily filling holy office, which we noted in Origen (above p. 35), one can understand a certain reticence to take up episcopal authority. There were certain tensions as well between the "official" clergy and the monks in Egypt, as one can see in the *Verba Seniorum* (e.g., 15.13, 25, 27, 29, in Chadwick). Athanasius, although very popular, still had to work to keep his church in order. Here he writes to the monk Dracontius, in 354–55, pointing out the obvious: someone must do it, and if God called him, God would give him the strength. How would Athanasius respond to Chrysostom, ch. 9?

5. 1 Tim. 4:14.

6. Matt. 25:14ff.

to imitate? For we ought to walk by the standard of the saints and our forebears, and imitate them, and to be sure that if we depart from them we put ourselves also out of their fellowship. Whom then do they wish you to imitate? The one who hesitated, and while wishing to follow, delayed it and took counsel because of family,[7] or blessed Paul, who, the moment the stewardship was entrusted to him, "straightway conferred not with flesh and blood"?[8] For although he said, "I am not worthy to be called an apostle,"[9] yet, knowing what he had received, and being not ignorant of the giver, he wrote, "For woe is me if I preach not the gospel."[10] But, as it was "woe to me" if he did not preach, so, in teaching and preaching the gospel, he had his converts as his joy and crown.[11] This explains why the saint was zealous to preach as far as Illyricum, and not to shrink from proceeding to Rome,[12] or even going as far as the Spains,[13] in order that the more he labored, he might receive so much the greater reward for his labor. He boasted then that he had fought the good fight, and was confident that he should receive the great crown.[14] Therefore, beloved Dracontius, whom are you imitating in your present action? Paul, or others unlike him? For my part, I pray that you, and myself, may prove an imitator of all the saints.[15]

5. Or possibly there are some who advise you to hide, because you have given your word upon oath not to accept the office if elected. For I hear that they are buzzing in your ears to this effect, and consider that they are thus acting conscientiously. But if they were truly conscientious, they would above all have feared God, who imposed this ministry upon you. Or if they had read the divine scriptures, they would not have advised you contrary to them. For it is time for them to blame Jeremiah also, and to impeach the great Moses, in that they did not listen to their advice, but

---

7. Luke 9:61.
8. Gal. 1:16.
9. 1 Cor. 15:9.
10. 1 Cor. 9:16.
11. 1 Thess. 2:19.
12. Rom. 1:15.
13. Rom. 15:19, 28.
14. 2 Tim. 4:7, 8.
15. The theme of imitation is classic. It runs throughout Paul, e.g., 1 Thess. 1:6; Phil. 4:8-9; cf. 2:1-4. It is common among the moralists as well: Seneca said, "Why should we not keep by us the portraits of great men for the sake of our inspiration, and celebrate their birthdays?" An excellent example is in Cicero's *Pro Archia* 14, where he says he models his official behavior on the good examples in classical literature. Basil, Ep. 2, writes similarly: "Most important . . . is also the study of the . . . scriptures. For in them are . . . found . . . the lives of saintly men, recorded . . . before us like living images of God's government, for our imitation of their good works" (Loeb 1:14–15). See Gregory, *On the Death of His Father* 16, below p. 124, and Chrysostom, *On the Priesthood* 3.14, p. 170, and Gregory the Great, p. 198.

fearing God fulfilled their ministry, and prophesying were made perfect. For they also, when they had received their mission and the grace of prophecy, refused. But afterward they feared, and did not set at nought God that sent them. Whether then you be of stammering utterance, and slow of tongue, yet fear God that made you, or if you call yourself too young to preach, yet reverence God who knew you before you were made. Or if you have given your word (now their word was to the saints as an oath), yet read Jeremiah, how he too had said, "I will not name the name of the Lord,"[16] yet afterwards he feared the fire kindled within him, and did not do as he had said, nor hid himself as if bound by an oath, but reverenced God that had entrusted to him his office, and fulfilled the prophetic call. Or are you not aware, beloved, that Jonah also fled, but met with the fate that befell him, after which he returned and prophesied?

6. Do not then entertain counsels opposite to this. For the Lord knows our case better than we ourselves, and he knows to whom he is entrusting his churches. For even if a person be not worthy, yet let him not look at his former life, but let him carry out his ministry, lest, in addition to his life he incur also the curse of negligence. I ask you, beloved Dracontius, whether knowing this, and being wise, you are not pricked in your soul? Do you not feel anxious lest any of those entrusted to you should perish? Do you not burn, as with a fire in your conscience? Are you not in fear of the day of judgment, in which none of your present advisers will be there to aid you? For each shall give account of those entrusted to his hands. For how did his excuse benefit the man who hid the money? Or how did it benefit Adam to say, "The woman beguiled me"?[17] Beloved Dracontius, even if you are really weak, yet you ought to take up the charge, lest, the church being unoccupied, the enemies injure it, taking advantage of your flight. You should gird yourself up, so as not to leave us alone in the struggle; you should labor with us, in order to receive the reward also along with all.

VERBA SENIORUM

1. Progress in Perfection

10. Abba Cassian related this story of one Abba John, who ruled over a community because he was great in his way of life. When he was dying, cheerfully, and with his mind set upon the Lord, his brothers stood around him and asked for a sentence which would sum the way to salvation, and which he could bestow on them as a legacy by which they might mount to

---

16. Jer. 20:9.
17. Gen. 3:12. *Give Account:* Heb. 13:17; contrast its use, pp. 177, 182.

the perfection which is in Christ. With a sigh he said, "I never obeyed my own will, and I never taught anyone to do anything which I did not first do myself."

11. A brother asked an old man: "What thing is so good that I may do it and live by it?" And the old man said, "God alone knows what is good. Yet I have heard that one of the fathers asked the great Abba Nesteros, who was a friend of Abba Antony, and said to him, 'What good work shall I do?' And Antony replied, 'Cannot all works please God equally? Scripture says, Abraham was hospitable and God was with him. And Elijah loved quiet and God was with him. And David was humble and God was with him. So whatever you find your soul wills in following God's will, do it, and keep your heart.'"

22. An old man said: "This is the life of a monk: work, obedience, meditation, not to judge others, not to speak evil, not to murmur. For it is written 'You who love God, hate evil.'[18]

"This is the life of the monk: not to go in with the unrighteous, not to see evil, not to be inquisitive, not to be curious, not to hear gossip: not to use the hands for taking, but for giving: not to be proud in heart or wicked in thought: not to fill the belly: in everything to judge wisely.

"That is where you find a monk."

3. Compunction

14. Athanasius of holy memory asked Abba Pambo to come down from the desert to Alexandria. When he arrived, he saw a woman that was an actress, and wept. And the bystanders asked him why he wept. And he said, "Two things grieved me. The first was her damnation; the second, that I take less trouble about pleasing God than she takes about pleasing the dregs of society."[19]

16. Syncletice of holy memory said: "People endure sore travail and conflict when they are first converted to the Lord, but later they have joy unspeakable. They are like those trying to light a fire, the smoke gets into their eyes, their eyes begin to drop tears—but they succeed in what they want. It is written: 'Our God is a consuming fire': and so we must kindle the fire of God with tears and trouble."

4. Self-Control

51. Abba Hyperichius said: "It is better to eat flesh and drink wine than to eat the flesh of the brothers by disparaging them."

---

18. Ps. 97:10.
19. A parallel to Pelagia of Antioch's story, noted above p. 54, n. 33.

5. Lust

3. Abba Cassian said: "Abba Moses told us: 'It is good not to hide the thoughts but to disclose them to discreet and devout elders; but not to those who are old merely in years, for many have found final despair instead of comfort by confessing to those whom they saw to be aged, but who in fact were inexperienced.' "

13. Another brother was goaded by lust. He rose up in the night and went to tell his temptations to an old man, and the old man consoled him. So he returned, comforted, to his cell. But again the spirit of lust tempted him. And a second time he went to the old man. This happened several times. The old man did not reproach him, but spoke words to his profit: "Yield not to the devil, and guard your soul. Whenever the demon troubles you, come to me, and rebuke him, and so he will go away. Nothing troubles the demon of lust more than disclosure of his pricks. Nothing pleases him more than the concealment of the temptation."

Eleven times the brother went to the old man, and blamed himself for his imaginings. And then the brother said to the old man, "Of thy charity, Abba, speak to me a word." The old man said to him, "Believe me, my son, if God allowed the imaginings which goad me to be passed to you, you would not bear them but would be utterly destroyed." And so by his words and deep humility, that brother found rest from the goad of lust.

28. Once a brother came to an old man and said, "My brother keeps leaving me, and goes traveling everywhere, and I am suffering for it." And the old man besought him: "Bear it calmly, brother. And God will see your earnestness and endurance, and will bring him back to you. It is not possible for a person to be recalled from his purpose by harshness and severity—demon cannot drive out demon: you will bring him back to you better by kindness. That is how God acts for our good, and draws us to himself."

29. A brother, being tempted by a demon, went to an old man and said, "Those two monks over there who live together, live wickedly." But the old man knew that a demon was playing with him, and he sent and called them to him. And at evening he put a mat for them, and covered them with a single blanket and said, "They are children of God, and holy persons." But he said to his disciple, "Shut this slandering brother up in a cell by himself: he is suffering from the passions of which he accuses them."

38. A brother was assailed by lust. By chance he came to a village in Egypt, and saw the daughter of the heathen priest there, and greatly loved her. And he said to her father, "Give her to be my wife." He answered, "I cannot give her to you until I have besought my god." And he went to the

demon whom he served and said, "Here is a monk wanting to marry my daughter. Do I give her to him?" The demon answered, "Ask him if he denies his God, and his baptism, and his monastic vow." And the priest came and said to the monk, "If you deny your God, and your baptism, and your monastic vow, I will give you my daughter." The monk agreed. And at once he saw something like a dove fly out of his mouth and up into the sky. Then the priest went to the demon and said, "He has promised to do the three things you said." Then the devil answered, "Do not give your daughter to be his wife, for his God has not left him, but will yet help him." And the priest went back and said to the monk, "I cannot give her to you, because your God is still helping you, and has not left you."

When the monk heard this, he said to himself, "If God has shown me such kindness, though like a wretch I have denied him, and my baptism and my monastic vow, if God is so good that he still helps me though I am wicked, why am I running away from him?" And he was restored to his right and sober mind, and came into the desert to a great old man, and told him what had happened. And the old man replied, "Stay with me in this cave and fast for three weeks, and I will pray God for you." And the old man travailed on behalf of the brother, and prayed God thus: "I beseech thee, O Lord, grant me this soul, and accept its penitence."

And God heard his prayer. At the end of the first week, the old man came to the brother and asked, "Have you seen anything?" And the brother replied, "Yes, I saw a dove above in the sky over my head." And the old man answered, "Look to your heart, and pray God earnestly." After the second week the old man came again to the brother, and asked him, "Have you seen anything?" And he replied, "I have seen a dove coming down by my head," and the old man charged him: "Pray, and pray seriously." And at the end of the third week, the old man came again and asked him, "Have you seen anything else?" And he answered, "I saw a dove and it came and sat on my head, and I stretched out my hand to catch it, and it entered my mouth."

And the older man thanked God, and said to the brother, "Look, God has accepted your penitence. In future be careful, and on your guard." And the brother answered, "See, I will stay with you now, until I die."

40. They said this of a father, that he had been a man who lived in the world, and had turned to God, but was still goaded by desire for his wife; and he told this to the fathers. When they saw him to be a true laborer, one who did more than his duty, they laid on him a course of discipline which so weakened his body that he could not stand up. By God's providence a father came to visit Scete. And when he came to this man's cell, he saw it open, and he passed on, surprised that no one came to meet him. But then

he thought that perhaps the brother inside was ill, and returned, and knocked on the door. And after knocking, he went in, and found the monk gravely ill. And he said, "What's the matter, father?" And he told him, "I was living in the world, and the enemy still troubles me because of my wife. And I told the fathers, and they laid upon me various burdens to discipline my life. And in trying to carry them out obediently, I have fallen ill—and yet the goad is worse." When the old man heard this, he was vexed, and said, "The fathers are powerful men, and did well in laying these burdens upon you. But if you will listen to me who am but a child in these matters, stop all this discipline, take a little food at the proper times, recover your strength, join in the worship of God for a little, and turn your mind to the Lord—for this is a thing you cannot conquer by your own efforts. The human body is like a coat. If you treat it carefully, it will last a long time. If you neglect it, it will fall into tatters."

The sick man did as he was told, and in a few days the incitement to lust vanished.

6. To Possess Nothing

5. Abba Evagrius said that there was a brother who had no possessions but a Gospel, and sold it to feed the poor. And he said a word which is worth remembering: "I have even sold the word which commands me to sell all and give to the poor."[20]

7. Patience, or Fortitude

18. Saint Syncletice said: "People in the world who commit crime are thrown into prison against their will. For our sins, let us put ourselves under guard, and by willingly accepting it now we shall avoid punishment in the future. If you fast, you should avoid saying that by weakening your frame you have fallen ill, for people who do not fast, fall ill in the same way. If you have begun some good work, you should not be turned from it by the enemy's attempts to hinder you; indeed, your endurance will conquer the enemy. Seamen beginning a voyage set the sails and look for a favorable wind—and later they meet a contrary wind. Just because the wind has turned, they do not throw the cargo overboard or abandon ship: they wait a little and battle against the storm until they can again set a direct course. And when we run into headwinds, let us put up the cross for our sail, and we shall voyage through the world in safety."

8. To Do Nothing for Show

2. The monks praised a brother to Abba Antony. But Antony went to him and tested whether he could endure abuse. And when he perceived that

---

20. Cf. Matt. 19:21.

he could not bear it, he said: "You are like a house with a highly decorated facade, where burglars have stolen all the furniture out of the back door."

19. Saint Syncletice said: "An open treasury is quickly spent. And any virtue will be annihilated if it is published abroad and becomes famous. If you put wax in front of a fire it melts; and if you pour vain praises on the soul, it goes soft and weak in seeking goodness."

9. Not to Judge

10. An old man said: "Judge not the adulterer if you are chaste—or you will break the law of God likewise. For he who said 'Do not commit adultery' also said 'Judge not.' "21

10. Discretion

1. Abba Antony said: "Some wear down their bodies by fasting. But because they have no discretion, it puts them further from God."

8. Abba Peter, the disciple of Abba Lot, told this story. "I was once in the cell of Abba Agatho, when a brother came to him and said, 'I want to live with the monks; tell me how to live with them.' The old man said, 'From the first day you join them, remember you are a pilgrim all the days of your life, and do not be too confident.' Abba Macarius said to him, 'What does confidence do?' The old man said, 'It is like a fierce drought. When it is so dry, everyone flees the land because it destroys even the fruit on the trees.' Abba Macarius said, 'Is bad confidence like that?' Abba Agatho said, 'No passion is worse than confidence—it is the mother of all passion. It is best for the monk's progress that he should not be confident, even when he is alone in his cell.' "

13. Abba Agatho said: "If an angry person raises the dead, God is still displeased with the anger."

51. Abba Poemen said: "He who knows himself is mature."

He also said: "One person seems silent of speech, but is condemning other people within his heart—he is really talking incessantly. Another person seems to talk all day, yet keeps silence: for he always speaks in a way that is useful to his hearers."

53. He also said: "Wickedness cannot drive out wickedness. If anyone hurts you, do him good, and so by your good work you will destroy his wickedness."

62. Abba Abraham, who was a disciple of Abba Agatho, once asked Abba Poemen: "Why do the demons attack me?" And Abba Poemen said

---

21. An interesting chord of biblical echoes: it sums up the point of the Pericope Adulterae, John 8:1-8, and of Rom. 1:26—2:4; similar logic is found in James 2:8-13; the nonjudgment clause comes from the Sermon on the Mount, Matt. 7:1-5 // Luke 6:37-38; the Sixth Commandment is from Ex. 20:13, (LXX) = Deut. 5:17.

to him, "Do the demons attack you? The demons do not attack us when we follow our self-wills, because then our wills become demons and themselves trouble us to obey them. If you want to know the kind of people with whom the demons fight, it is Moses and those like him."

71c. Saint Syncletice said: "It is dangerous for a person to try teaching before being trained in the good life. One whose house is about to fall down may invite travelers inside to refresh them, but instead they are hurt in the collapse of the house. It is the same with teachers who have not carefully trained themselves in the good life: they ruin their hearers as well as themselves. Their mouth invites to salvation; their way of life leads to ruin."

85. An old man said that a man once committed a grave sin. Stricken with penitence, he went to confess to an old man. He did not tell him what he had done, but put it in the form of a question: "If such a thought rose in a person's mind, would he be saved?" The old man, who had no discretion, answered, "You have lost your soul."

When the brother heard this, he said, "Well, if I perish, I will go to the world." But on his way he considered the matter and decided to tell his temptations to Abba Silvanus, who possessed great discretion in these matters. The brother went to him and did not tell him what he had done, but again put it in the form of the question: "If such a thought arose in a person's mind, would he be saved?" Silvanus began to speak to him with texts from scripture and said, "That judgement does not fall on people *tempted* to sin." The brother perceived the force of the saying, and took hope, and told him what he had done. When Abba Silvanus learned what he had done, he acted like a skilled physician and put on his soul a poultice made of texts from scripture, showing him that repentance is available for them who in truth and in charity turn to God. After some years Abba Silvanus met the old man who had driven the brother to despair and told him what had happened, and said, "That brother, who despaired because of your words, and had gone back to the world, is now a bright star among the brothers." He told him this so that we may know how perilous it is when someone confesses his thoughts or sins to people without discretion.

91. An old man was asked by a brother: "How do I find God? With fasts, or labor, or watchings, or works of mercy?" The old man replied, "In all that you have said, and in discretion. I tell you that many have afflicted their body, but have gained no profit because they did it without discretion. Even if our mouths stink with fasting, and we have learnt all the scriptures, and memorized the whole Psalter, we still lack what God wants—humility and charity."

11. To Live Soberly

15. There was an old man in Scete, with a reasonable rule of bodily life, but not at all careful in remembering what he heard. So he went to Abba John the Short to ask him about forgetfulness. He listened to Abba John, went back to his cell, and forgot what he had been told. He came a second time and asked him, listened, went back, and forgot what he had heard the moment he had reached his cell. Many times he went backward and forward, but could never remember.

He happened to meet the old man and said, "Do you know, father, that I again forgot what you told me? I did not wish to trouble you, so I did not come again." Abba John said to him, "Go, light a lamp." And he lit it. And he said, "Bring more lamps and light them from the first." And he did so. And Abba John said to the old man, "Was the first lamp harmed, because you used it to light others?" And he said, "No." "So John is not harmed: even if all the monks of Scete should come to me, it does not keep me from God's love. So come to me whenever you want, and do not hesitate."

And so, by patience on both sides, God cured the forgetfulness of the old man. This was the work of the men of Scete, to strengthen those who were attacked by passion; their own experience in the moral struggle enabled them to help others along the road.

38. An old man visited another old man. In their conversation one said, "I am dead to the world." And the other said, "Do not be self-confident until you die. You may say about yourself that you are dead: but Satan is not dead."

12. To Pray Unceasingly

2. The brothers asked Abba Agatho: "Father, which virtue in our way of life needs most effort to acquire?" And he said to them, "Forgive me, I think nothing needs so much effort as prayer to God. If one is wanting to pray, the demons infest him in the attempt to interrupt the prayer, for they know that prayer is the only thing that hinders them. All the other efforts of a religious life, whether they are made vehemently or gently, have room for a measure of rest. But we need to pray till we breathe out our dying breath. That is the great struggle."

13. Hospitality and Cheerful Mercy

7. A brother came to a hermit, and as he was taking his leave, he said: "Forgive me, Abba, for hampering you in keeping your rule." The hermit answered, "My rule is to welcome you with hospitality, and to send you on your way in peace."

11. An old man in Egypt lived in a desert place. And far away lived a Manichaean who was a priest, at least was one of those whom Man-

ichaeans call priests. While the Manichaean was on a journey to visit another of that erroneous sect, he was caught by nightfall in the place where lived this orthodox and holy man. He wanted to knock and go in and ask for shelter, but was afraid to do so, for he knew that he would be recognized as a Manichaean and believed that he would be refused hospitality. But, driven by his plight, he put the thought aside, and knocked.

The old man opened the door and recognized him, and he welcomed him joyfully, made him pray with him, gave him supper and a bed. The Manichaean lay thinking in the night, and marvelling: "Why was he not hostile to me? He is a true servant of God." And at break of day he rose, and fell at his feet, saying, "Henceforth I am orthodox, and shall not leave you." And so he stayed with him.

14. Obedience

9. Saint Syncletice said: "I reckon that for coenobites[22] obedience is a higher virtue than continence, however perfect. Continence carries pride with it, obedience has the promise of due humility."

15. Humility

1. Abba Antony was baffled as he meditated upon the depths of God's judgements, and prayed thus: "Lord, how is it that some die young and others grow old and infirm? Why are there some poor and some wealthy? And why are the rich unrighteous and grind the faces of the righteous poor?"

And a voice came to him: "Antony, look to yourself: these are the judgements of God, and it is not good for you to know them."

3. Abba Antony also said: "I saw all the devil's traps set upon the earth, and I groaned and said, 'Who do you think can pass through them?' And I heard a voice saying, 'Humility.' "

58. An old man, asked why we are troubled by demons, answered: "Because we throw away our armor—humility, poverty, patience and others' scorn."

16. Patience

10. A brother who was hurt by another brother went to the Theban Abba Sisois and said: "I want to avenge myself on a brother who has hurt me." The old man begged him, "Don't, my son; leave vengeance in the hands of

---

22. Coenobites = koino + bios (common life), i.e., those monastics who lived in community rather than in isolation.

God." But he said, "I cannot rest until I avenge myself." The old man said, "My brother, let us pray." The old man stood up and said, "O God, we have no further need to think of you, for we take vengeance of ourselves." The brother heard it and fell at the old man's feet, saying, "No longer will I quarrel with my brother; I beg you to forgive me."

17. Charity

10. Abba Poemen said: "There is nothing greater in love than that one should lay down his life for his neighbor. When someone hears a complaining word and struggles against himself, and does not himself begin to complain; when one bears an injury with patience, and does not look for revenge; that is when one lays down his life for his neighbor."[23]

18. A brother asked an old man: "There are two monks: one stays quietly in his cell, fasting for six days at a time, and laying many austerities upon himself; and the other ministers to the sick. Which of them is more acceptable to God?" The old man answered, "If the brother who fasts six days even hung himself up by his nostrils, he could never be the equal of him who ministers to the sick."

JOHN CASSIAN, CONFERENCE 15.1–2, 6, 8

Nesteros on the Gifts of God

1. After the evening meal we sat on the mats, as monks do, and we waited for the discussion which had been promised us. Out of deference to the old man we remained silent for a while. Then he interrupted our respectful silence with the following words.

"The direction taken by our earlier discussion has brought us now to the need to state the nature of spiritual gifts, and the tradition of our elders, as we know, tells us that this takes a threefold form.

"The first cause of the gift of healing is the merit earned by holiness. The grace of working miracles is to be found among specially chosen and just persons. It is quite evident that the apostles and many saints worked miracles and wonders. This was in accordance with what the Lord himself had commanded when he said, 'Heal the sick, raise the dead, cleanse the lepers, expel the demons. You have freely received. Give freely.'[24]

"Second, for the edification of the church or of those who bring forward their own patients or of those who have to be healed, the virtue of healing

---

23. Monasticism as inheriting the role of martyrs was an important theme; Malone (1950) and van Loveren (1982). Cf. John 15:13.
24. Matt. 10:8.

comes even from sinners and from the unworthy. Of such people the Savior had this to say in the gospel: 'They will say to me on that day: Lord, Lord, did we not prophesy in your name, and did we not drive out devils in your name, and did we not do many wonders in your name? And I will say out loud to them, I do not know you. Leave me, you workers of iniquity.'[25] But by contrast, if faith is lacking in those who bring forward the sick, then it will not be permitted, even to those with the gift of healing, to work a cure. The evangelist Luke had this to say: 'And Jesus could not work miracles among them because of their unbelief.'[26] It was at this time that the Lord said: 'There were many lepers in Israel in the days of Elisaeus the prophet and no one of them was cured except Naaman the Syrian.'[27]

"The third kind of healing is a trick and deception worked by demons. One caught up in obvious wrongdoing is an object of admiration because of the wonders worked by him. He acquires the reputation of being a holy man and a servant of God and he becomes, for evil spirits, the means of enticing others to imitate him even to the extent of doing wrong like him. The way is now open for scandal and even the sanctity of religion is maligned. And it is quite certainly the case that this man who credits himself with the gift of healing is brought crashing down all the harder because of the pride in his heart.

"The demons have also the following trick. They cry out the names of those whom they know to have none of the merits of holiness and to possess none of the fruits of the spirit. They pretend to be burnt up by the merits of such people and to take flight from the bodies of the possessed. Deuteronomy has this to say about such persons: 'If a prophet should arise among you or one claiming visionary dreams, and if he foretells a sign and a portent, and if what he says should actually happen, and if he should say to you, "Let us go and follow strange gods who are unknown to you and let us serve them," do not listen to the words of that prophet or dreamer. For the Lord your God is putting you to the test, bringing out into the open whether or not you love God with all your heart and with all your soul.'[28] And in the gospel he says this: 'Fake Christs and fake prophets will rise up and they will perform great signs and wonders so that if possible even the chosen will be led into error.'[29]

---

25. Matt. 7:22-23.

26. Mark 6:5-6; cf. Matt. 13:58; this is *not* in Luke 4:16-30.

27. Luke 4:27.

28. Deut. 13:1-3; cf. Didache 11.

29. Matt. 24:24. The role of miracles was always seen as somewhat ambiguous in early Christian literature. See, e.g., *Verba Seniorum* 15.65, etc.; in the N.T., the role of signs in John, and Peter's and Paul's activities and opponents in Acts, in light of Garrett (1989). Augustine's case is instructive; see P. Brown (1967), 413ff., and contrast *City of God* 22.8 and Sermon 317 with *On True Religion* 25.47, *Retractationes* 1.13.7, and Letter 52.

2. "Therefore we must never be admirers of those who pretend to do such things out of virtuousness. We must note, instead, whether they have become perfect as a result of driving out their sins and because of the improvement of their way of life. This is something that is certainly not achieved through the act of faith of someone else or for reasons that are obscure to us. It happens because of one's own zeal and the divine gift of grace.

"Such, then, is the practical knowledge which is otherwise called 'charity' by the apostle and which, on his apostolic authority, is to be preferred to all human or angelic speech, to the full faith which can even move mountains, to all knowledge and prophetic power, to the utter abandonment of the things of the world, and, finally, even to glorious martyrdom. He listed all the types of charismatic gifts and had this to say: 'To one the Spirit grants wisdom in preaching, to another knowledgeable discourse, to another faith, to another the gift of healing, to another the working of cures,'[30] and all the rest. But he will go on to speak of love, and notice how he put this before all the charisms: 'I will show you a way that is better than any of them.'[31]

"In this way it is clearly shown that the high point of perfection and blessedness does not lie in the working of those miracles but rather in the purity of love. And not without good reason. The former have to vanish and to be done away with. But love will endure forever. Hence we never see the Fathers caught up in these wonderworkings. By the grace of the Holy Spirit they were possessors of such capacities, but they never wanted to use them unless they were coerced by utter, unavoidable necessity.

6. "These people did not make selfish use of the power to work such miracles. They proclaimed that these had been done not through any merit of their own but by the Lord's mercy. Faced with the awe evoked by these wonders, they resorted to the words of the apostles in order to ward off glory among humans. 'Friends, why are you amazed at this? Or why do you keep looking at us, as if it were our power and our piety which caused this man to walk?'[32] They believed that no one should draw praise upon himself because of the gifts and the miracles of God. Instead, praise should be given for the fruits of one's virtue since these came into being from the zeal of a mind and the excellence of achievements.

"But as was already said, it often happens that those of corrupt disposition and spurious faith can drive out demons in God's name and work the very greatest miracles. The apostle once complained about the like:

---

30. 1 Cor. 12:8-10.
31. 1 Cor. 12:31.
32. Acts 3:12.

'Master, we saw a man driving out demons in your name. We told him not to do so, because he does not go around with us.'[33] Christ was immediately able to say to them, 'Do not stop him. Anyone who is not against us is on our side.'[34] However, there are those who at the end of time will say, 'Lord, Lord, did we not prophesy in your name, did we not work great wonders in your name?'[35] And he says that this is what he will say in reply: 'I never knew you. Go away from me, you workers of evil.'[36] In this way he gives a warning to those to whom, as a reward for holiness, he had given this glory of working signs and miracles: 'Do not be exultant because demons have submitted to you. Rather be delighted because your names are written in heaven.'[37]

8. "Actually, the greater miracle is to root out the tinder of luxury from one's flesh rather than to drive unclean spirits from the bodies of others. A more resplendent wonder is the restraint exercised over the wild stirrings of anger by the virtue of patience, rather than the capacity to hold sway over the creatures of the air. Much more important is the exclusion of ravening gloom from one's heart than the ability to drive out the sicknesses and the bodily fevers of someone else. Lastly, it is in many ways more remarkable and more sublime virtue to be able to heal the weaknesses of one's own soul rather than the failings of another's body. The more exalted the soul is by comparison with the body, the more its salvation is to be preferred; the more valuable and excellent its substance, the graver and more deadly its ruin."

---

33. Luke 9:49.
34. Luke 9:50.
35. Matt. 7:22.
36. Matt. 7:23.
37. Luke 10:20.

5

SYRIA: IN THE CHAMBERS
OF THE EAST

Syria comprised the area from modern Lebanon to Iran, the eastern sector of the Roman Empire and the western of the Sassanid. Throughout most of it, Syriac, an Aramaic dialect, became the primary language. There is no good short history on early Syriac Christianity. The best places to start are the fine introductory essays in Brock and Harvey (1987) and R. Murray (1975). McCullough (1982) is not totally unhelpful. Many texts are in ANF 8 and NPNF 2.13, but they must be used with care.

There is a special reason for our including this chapter. American Christians by and large know only a Christianity strongly shaped by Western European culture: this causes tension and conflict with people of other cultures. In order to help ease this tension, we can develop our sense of the rich variety among Christian cultural traditions, for example, through the study of Syriac Christianity and its strong spiritual tradition. Hymnody, for instance, was deeply influenced by Syrians like Ephrem (fourth century) and Romanus (early sixth century). We should recall as well that the science and philosophy given to the medieval world by the Arabs was given to the Arabs by Syriac Christianity.

Pseudo-Clement
First Letter on Virginity, 10, 11

This section is from ANF 8. See Quasten 1.58f., and, placing it in a cultural background, Lane Fox (1987), ch. 7.

This work, later broken in two and preserved in Syriac, was written in Greek in the earlier third century in western Syria or Palestine. The whole work is relevant.

Pseudo-Clement
Homily 3.63–72

Also from ANF 8. Clement, for some reason, became a popular name to place on pseudepigraphical works, as in the epistle above, and especially in the *Homilies* and the closely related Latin *Recognitions,* versions of a Christian romantic novel. The *Homilies* and *Recognitions* have been at the center of a long scholarly battle; see F. Jones (1982) and, cautiously, Hennecke and Schneemelcher, vol. 2, ch. 12, 14. We, luckily, can ignore these fights, and take the *Homilies*'s final form from mid-fourth-century western Syria. One might also read the two introductory *Letters* from Peter and Clement to James.

Apostolic Constitutions
Book 8.16–20, 23–24

The Apostolic Constitutions, found in ANF 7, is a large grab bag of earlier documents and traditions, compiled in Syria in the late fourth century. See ODCC and Quasten 2.184 for this, and the many confusingly similar compilations. Book 8.3–27 is based on the Antiochene liturgy. The various sections are distributed among the twelve apostles, which was a common literary conceit. 8.16 then is attributed to John the Evangelist.

The Teaching of the Apostles
Introduction and Canons 1, 5, 8, 10–17, 20, 22–26

This document, which we have taken from ANF 8, is also called the *Teaching* or *Doctrine of Addai.* It is one of a number of texts very popular in Syria, whose histories are intertwined and extremely convoluted, and not yet adequately sorted out. Compiler after compiler worked older documents into new collections. The original date of these canons is unknown, but the earliest manuscripts of them date from the fifth or sixth centuries (see Baumstark, *Geschichte der syr. Lit.,* 1922, sec. 12g [p. 83] n.1, and Vööbus, CSCO 317, ch. 7.1: C, H, L). The document turns up again in an important later collection called the *Synodicon,* which has been published and translated by Vööbus, CSCO 367–68, 1975, whose introduction, in particular pp. 3 and 20, should be consulted. Our text is section 39 of the *Synodicon,* translated on pp. 187–97.

Aphrahat
Demonstration 10: On Pastors, 1–6

Our only author who did not live under Roman rule, Aphrahat lived in Eastern Syria, perhaps in Adiabene, under the persecuting King Shapur II. All we know dependably of Aphrahat comes from his twenty-three *Demonstrations*, published between 337 and 345. Number 10 dates from 337, and is taken from NPNF 2.13.

PSEUDO-CLEMENT, FIRST LETTER ON VIRGINITY

10–11

10. Now, we are persuaded of you, my brethren, that your thoughts are occupied about those things which are requisite for your salvation. But we speak thus in consequence of the evil rumors and reports concerning shameless men, who, under pretext of the fear of God, have their dwelling with maidens, and so expose themselves to danger, and walk with them along the road and in solitary places alone—a course which is full of dangers, and full of stumbling blocks and snares and pitfalls; nor is it in any respect right for Christians and those who fear God so to conduct themselves.[1] Others, too, eat and drink with them at entertainments indulging themselves in loose behavior and much uncleanness—such behavior ought not to be among believers, and especially among those who have chosen for themselves a life of holiness. Others, again, meet together for vain and trifling conversation and merriment, and that they may speak evil of one another; and they hunt up tales against one another, and are idle: persons with whom we do not allow you even to eat bread. Then, others gad about among the houses of virgin brethren or sisters, on pretense of visiting them, or reading the scriptures to them, or exorcising them. Forasmuch as they are idle and do no work, they pry into those things which ought not to be inquired into, and by means of plausible words make merchandise of the name of Christ. These are they from whom the divine apostle kept aloof, because of the multitude of their evil

---

1. Concerning *subintroductae*, virgin women who would share quarters chastely, in theory, with men, see ODCC and E. Clark (1977). It has always been difficult to live out a practice of perfection like this when the practice invites misinterpretation by outsiders. Does it matter what "they" think? Consider Titus 2:7-8; 1 Peter 2:11-12; and Cyprian, *On the Dress of Virgins* 5, above p. 55. Notice that the people addressed are those who would claim to be leaders or models, or otherwise advanced. Similar charges were lodged against Paul of Samosata about this time (Eusebius, HE 7.30.6–16); Jerome, somewhat later, strikes sharply against these practices, in Rome and elsewhere, in, e.g., Ep. 22 and 125 (in Loeb); the *Verba Seniorum* show similar opportunities to stumble in Egypt. We usually remember the asceticism of the time, but there seems to have been a counterbalancing luxury that could be indulged in to a great degree. Sexual activity, even among the monks, appears to have been more prevalent than generally thought. It is very difficult to judge the relationship between articulated ideology, de facto moral codes, and actual practice, even today.

deeds; as it is written: "Thorns sprout in the hands of the idle";[2] and, "The ways of the idle are full of thorns."[3]

11. Such are the ways of all those who do not work, but go hunting for tales, and think to themselves that this is profitable and right. For such persons are like those idle and prating widows "who go wandering about among houses"[4] with their prating, and hunt for idle tales, and carry them from house to house with much exaggeration, without fear of God. And besides all this, barefaced as they are, under pretense of teaching, they set forth a variety of doctrines. And would that they taught the doctrines of truth! But it is this which is so disquieting, that they understand not what they mean, and assert that which is not true: because they wish to be teachers, and to display themselves as skillful in speaking; because they traffic in iniquity in the name of Christ—which it is not right for the servants of God to do. And they hearken not to that which the scripture has said: "Let not many be teachers among you, and be not all of you prophets."[5] For "one who does not transgress in word is perfect, able to keep down and subjugate his whole body."[6] And, "If anyone speak, let him speak in the words of God."[7] And, "If there is in you understanding, give an answer to your friend; but if not, put your hand on your mouth."[8] For, "at one time it is proper to keep silence, and at another time to speak."[9] And again it says: "When one speaks in season, it is honorable."[10] And again it says: "Let your speech be seasoned with grace. For it is required to know how to give an answer to everyone in season."[11] For "one who utters whatsoever comes to his mouth produces strife; and one that utters a superfluity of words increases vexation; and one that is hasty with his lips falls into evil. For because of the unruliness of the tongue comes anger; but the perfect keeps watch over his tongue, and loves his soul's life."[12] For these are they "who by good words and fair speeches lead astray the hearts of the simple, and, while offering them blessings, lead them astray."[13]

---

2. Prov. 26:9.
3. Prov. 15:19 (LXX). Gossip was part of the social fabric, frequently attacked by some. Cf. Jerome, Ep. 52, p. 153 and often; Verba Seniorum 1.22, p. 72.
4. 1 Tim. 5:13.
5. James 3:1; 1 Cor. 12:29. Consult Didache 11.
6. James 3:2.
7. 1 Pet. 4:11.
8. Ben Sira 5:12.
9. Eccles. 3:7.
10. Prov. 15:23.
11. Col. 4:6.
12. This recalls Prov. 18:6; 13:3; 21:23; Ben Sira 1:22 and similar passages.
13. Rom. 16:17-19.

Let us, therefore, fear the judgment which awaits teachers. For a severe judgment will those teachers receive "who teach, but do not,"[14] and those who take upon them the name of Christ falsely, and say: We teach the truth, and yet go wandering about idly, and exalt themselves, and make their boast "in the mind of the flesh."[15] These, moreover, are like "the blind who lead the blind and they both fall into the ditch."[16] And they will receive judgment, because in their talkativeness and their frivolous teaching they teach natural wisdom, and the "frivolous error of the plausible words of human wisdom,"[17] "according to the will of the prince of the dominion of the air, and of the spirit which works in those who will not obey, according to the training of this world, and not according to the doctrine of Christ."[18] But if you have received "the word of knowledge, or the word of instruction, or of prophecy,"[19] blessed be God, "who helps everyone without grudging—that God who gives to everyone and does not upbraid him."[20] With the gift, therefore, which you have received from our Lord, serve your spiritual family, the prophets who know that the words which you speak are those of our Lord; and declare the gift which you have received in the church for the edification of the Christian community (for good and excellent are those things which help the children of God), if so be that they are truly with you.

PSEUDO-CLEMENT, HOMILY 3

3.63–72

63. [Peter said:] "But of those who are present, whom shall I choose but Zacchaeus, to whom also the Lord went in and rested, judging him worthy to be saved?" And having said this, he laid his hand upon Zacchaeus, who stood by, and forced him to sit down in his own chair. But Zacchaeus, falling at his feet, begged that he would permit him to decline the rulership; promising, at the same time, and saying, "Whatever it behooves the ruler to do, I will do; only grant me not to have this name; for I am afraid of assuming the name of the rulership, for it teems with bitter envy and danger."[21]

---

14. Matt. 23:3.
15. Col. 2:18.
16. Matt. 15:14.
17. Col. 2:8.
18. Eph. 2:2; Col. 2:8.
19. 1 Cor. 12:8-10.
20. James 1:5.
21. On the theme of the hazards of office, see Origen, above p. 35.

64. Then Peter said: "If you are afraid of this, do not be called ruler, but the appointed one, the Lord having permitted you to be so called, when he said, 'Blessed is the one whom the Lord shall appoint to the ministry of his fellow servants.'[22] But if you wish it to be altogether unknown that you have authority of administration, you seem to me to be ignorant that the acknowledged authority of the president has great influence as regards the respect of the multitude. For everyone obeys those who have received authority, having conscience as a great constraint. And are you not well aware that you are not to rule as the rulers of the nations,[23] but as a servant ministering to them, as a father to the oppressed, visiting them as a physician, guarding them as a shepherd—in short, taking all care for their salvation? And do you think that I am not aware what labors I compel you to undertake, desiring you to be judged by multitudes whom it is impossible for anyone to please? But it is most possible for one who does well to please God. Wherefore I entreat you to undertake it heartily, by God, by Christ, for the salvation of the faithful, for their ordering, and your own profit.

65. "And consider this other thing, that in proportion as there is labor and danger in ruling the church of Christ, so much greater is the reward. And yet again the greater is also the punishment to him who can, and refuses. I wish, therefore, knowing that you are the best instructed of my attendants, to turn to account those noble powers of judging with which you have been entrusted by the Lord, in order that you may be saluted with the 'Well done, good and faithful servant,'[24] and not be found fault with, and declared liable to punishment, like he who hid the one talent.[25] But if you will not be appointed a good guardian of the church, point out another in your stead, more learned and more faithful than yourself. But you cannot do this; for you associated with the Lord, and witnessed his marvelous doings, and learned the administration of the church.

66. "And your work is to order what things are proper; and that of the faithful is to submit, and not to disobey. Therefore submitting they shall be saved, but disobeying they shall be punished by the Lord, because the president is entrusted with the place of Christ. Wherefore, indeed, honor

---

22. Matthew 24:45//Luke 12:42, and Matthew 25:21. "Ruler," from the Greek *archōn,* was a normal term for a governor or other high civil official. This is perhaps a warning against those who would turn the episcopate into a governmental department. See Hom. 3.72; *Teaching of the Apostles,* canon 5; and Gregory, *On . . . His Father* 22, p. 126.

23. Mark 10:42-45//Matt. 20:25-28.

24. Matt. 25:21, 23.

25. Matt. 25:14ff.

or contempt shown to the president is handed on to Christ, and from Christ to God. And this I have said, that the faithful may not be ignorant of the danger they incur by disobedience to you, because whosoever disobeys your orders, disobeys Christ; and he who disobeys Christ offends God.[26]

67. "It is necessary, therefore, that the church, as a city built upon a hill, have an order approved of God, and good government. In particular, let the bishop, as chief, be heard in the things which he speaks; and let the elders give heed that the things ordered be done. Let the deacons, going about, look after the bodies and the souls of the faithful, and report to the bishop. Let all the rest of the brethren bear wrong patiently; but if they wish judgment to be given concerning wrongs done to them, let them be reconciled in presence of the elders; and let the elders report the reconciliation to the bishop.

68. "And let them inculcate marriage not only upon the young, but also upon those advanced in years, lest burning lust bring a plague upon the church by reason of whoredom or adultery. For, above every other sin, the wickedness of adultery is hated by God, because it not only destroys the person who sins, but those also who eat and associate with him. For it is like the madness of a dog, because it has the nature of communicating its own madness. For the sake of chastity, therefore, let not only the elders, but even all, hasten to accomplish marriage. For the sin of one who commits adultery necessarily comes upon all. Therefore, to urge the faithful to be chaste, this is the first charity. For it is the healing of the soul. For the nourishment of the body is rest.

69. "But if you love the faithful, take nothing from them, but share with them such things as you have. Feed the hungry; give drink to the thirsty; clothe the naked; visit the sick; so far as you can, help those in prison; receive strangers gladly into your own abodes; hate no one.[27] And how you must be pious, your own mind will teach you, judging rightly. But before all else, if indeed I need say it to you, come together frequently, if it were every hour, especially on the appointed days of meeting. For if you do this, you are within a wall of safety. For disorderliness is the beginning of perdition. Let no one therefore forsake the assembly on the ground of envy towards another. For if any one of you forsake the assembly, he shall be regarded as of those who scatter the church of Christ, and shall be cast out with adulterers.

70. "However, hear your bishop, and do not weary of giving all honor to him; knowing that, by showing it to him, it is borne to Christ, and from Christ it is borne to God; and to him who offers it, is requited manifold.

---

26. Cf. Ignatius, p. 22f.
27. Matt. 25:35-45.

Honor, therefore, the throne of Christ. For you are commanded even to honor the chair of Moses, and that although they who occupy it are accounted sinners.[28] And now I have said enough to you; and I deem it superfluous to say to him how he is to live unblamably, since he is an approved disciple of him who taught me also.

71. "But there are some things that you must not wait to hear, but must consider of yourselves what is reasonable. Zacchaeus alone having given himself up wholly to labor for you, and needing sustenance, and not being able to attend to his own affairs, how can he procure necessary support? Is it not reasonable that you are to take forethought for his living? not waiting for his asking you, for this is the part of a beggar. But he will rather die of hunger than submit to do this. And shall not you incur punishment, not considering that the laborer is worthy of his hire?[29] And let no one say, 'Is, then, the word sold which was freely given?' Far be it. For if anyone has the means of living, and takes anything, he sells the word; but if he who has not takes support in order to live—as the Lord also took at supper and among his friends, having nothing, though he alone is the owner of all things—he sins not. Therefore suitably honor elders, catechists, useful deacons, widows who have lived well, orphans as children of the church. But wherever there is need of any provision for an emergency, contribute all together. Be kind one to another, not shrinking from the endurance of anything whatever for your own salvation."

72. And having thus spoken, he placed his hand upon Zacchaeus, saying, "O Ruler and Lord of all, Father and God, guard the shepherd with the flock. You are the cause, you the power. We are that which is helped; you the helper, the physician, the savior, the wall, the life, the hope, the refuge, the joy, the expectation, the rest. In a word, you are all things to us. In order to the eternal attainment of salvation, cooperate, preserve, protect. You can do all things. For you are the Ruler of rulers, the Lord of lords, the Governor of kings. Give power to the president to loose what ought to be loosed, to bind what ought to be bound. Make him wise. Protect the church of thy Christ as a fair bride. For thine is eternal glory. Praise to the Father and the Son and the Holy Ghost to all ages. Amen."

APOSTOLIC CONSTITUTIONS

Book 8.16–20, 23–24

16. Concerning the ordination of presbyters, I who am loved by the Lord make this constitution for you the bishops: When you ordain a presbyter,

---

28. Matt. 23:2-3.
29. Matt. 10:10; Luke 10:7; 1 Tim. 5:18.

O bishop, lay your hand upon his head, in the presence of the presbyters and deacons, and pray, saying: O Lord Almighty, our God, who has created all things by Christ, and does in like manner take care of the whole world by him; for he who had power to make different creatures, has also power to take care of them, according to their different natures; on which account, O God, you take care of immortal beings by bare preservation, but of those that are mortal by succession—of the soul by the provision of laws, of the body by the supply of its wants. Therefore now also look down upon your holy church, and increase the same, and multiply those that preside in it, and grant them power, that they may labor both in word and work for the edification of your people. Do you now also look down upon this your servant, who is put into the presbytery by the vote and determination of the whole clergy; and replenish him with the Spirit of grace and counsel, to assist and govern your people with a pure heart, in the same manner as you did look down upon your chosen people, and did command Moses to choose elders, whom you did fill with your Spirit.[30] Do you also now, O Lord, grant this, and preserve in us the Spirit of your grace, that this person, being filled with the gifts of healing and the word of teaching, may in meekness instruct your people, and sincerely serve you with a pure mind and a willing soul, and may fully discharge the holy ministrations for your people, through your Christ, with whom glory, honor, and worship be to you, and to the Holy Ghost, forever. Amen.

17. Concerning the ordination of deacons, I, Philip, make this constitution: You shall ordain a deacon, O bishop, by laying your hands upon him in the presence of the whole presbytery, and of the deacons, and shall pray, and say:

18. O God Almighty, the true and faithful God, who are rich to all that call upon you in truth, who are fearful in counsels, and wise in understanding, who are powerful and great, hear our prayer, O Lord, and let your ears receive our supplication, and cause the light of your countenance to shine upon this your servant, who is to be ordained for you to the office of a deacon; and replenish him with your Holy Spirit, and with power, as you did replenish Stephen, who was your martyr, and follower of the sufferings of your Christ. Render him worthy to discharge acceptably the ministration of a deacon, steadily, unblamably, and without reproof, that thereby he may attain a higher degree, through the mediation of your only begotten Son, with whom glory, honor, and worship be to you and the Holy Spirit forever. Amen.

19. Concerning a deaconess, I, Bartholomew, make this constitution: O bishop, you shall lay your hands upon her in the presence of the presbytery, and of the deacons and deaconesses, and shall say:

---

30. Num. 11:16-30.

20. O Eternal God, the Father of our Lord Jesus Christ, the Creator of man and of woman, who did replenish with the Spirit Miriam, and Deborah, and Anna, and Huldah; who did not disdain that your only begotten Son should be born of a woman; who also in the tabernacle of the testimony, and in the temple, did ordain women to be keepers of your holy gates, do you now also look down upon this your servant, who is to be ordained to the office of a deaconess, and grant her your Holy Spirit, and "cleanse her from all filthiness of flesh and spirit,"[31] that she may worthily discharge the work which is committed to her to your glory, and the praise of your Christ, with whom glory and adoration be to you and the Holy Spirit forever. Amen.

23. And I, James, the son of Alphaeus, make a constitution in regard to confessors: A confessor is not ordained; but is so by choice and patience, and is worthy of great honor, as having confessed the name of God, and of his Christ, before nations and kings. But if there be occasion, he is to be ordained either a bishop, priest, or deacon. But if anyone of the confessors who is not ordained snatches any such dignity upon account of his confession, let the same person be deprived and rejected; for he is not in such an office, since he has denied the constitution of Christ, and is "worse than an infidel."[32]

24. I, the same, make a constitution in regard to virgins: A virgin is not ordained, for we have no such command from the Lord;[33] for this is a state of voluntary trial, not for the reproach of marriage, but on account of leisure for piety.

THE TEACHING OF THE APOSTLES

Introduction, 1, 5, 8, 10–17, 20, 22–26

And, when the disciples were cast into this perplexity, how they should preach his gospel to those of foreign tongues which were unknown to them, and were speaking thus to one another: Although we are confident that Christ will perform by our hands mighty works and miracles in the presence of strange peoples whose tongues we know not, and who themselves also are unversed in our tongue, yet who shall teach them and make them understand that it is by the name of Christ who was crucified that these mighty works and miracles are done?—while, I say, the disciples were occupied with these thoughts, Simon Cephas rose up, and said to them, "My brethren, this matter, how we shall preach his gospel, pertains not to us, but to our Lord; for he knows how it is possible for us to preach

---

31. 2 Cor. 7:1.
32. 1 Tim. 5:8. See ch. 3 concerning confessors.
33. 1 Cor. 7:25.

his gospel in the world; and we rely on his care for us, which he promised us, saying: "When I am ascended to my Father I will send you the Spirit, the Paraclete, that he may teach you everything which it is meet for you to know, and to make known."[34]

And, while Simon Cephas was saying these things to his fellow apostles, and putting them in remembrance, a mysterious voice was heard by them, and a sweet odor, which was strange to the world, breathed upon them;[35] and tongues of fire, between the voice and the odor, came down from heaven toward them, and alighted and sat on every one of them; and, according to the tongue which every one of them had severally received, so did he prepare himself to go to the country in which that tongue was spoken and heard.

And, by the same gift of the Spirit which was given to them on that day, they appointed ordinances and laws—such as were in accordance with the gospel of their preaching, and with the true and faithful doctrine of their teaching:

1. The apostles therefore appointed: Pray ye towards the east: because, "as the lightning which lighten from the east and is seen even to the west, so shall the coming of the Son of man be":[36] that by this we might know and understand that he will appear from the east suddenly.

5. The apostles further appointed: Let there be elders and deacons, like the Levites; and subdeacons, like those who carried the vessels of the court of the sanctuary of the Lord; and an overseer, who shall likewise be the guide of all the people, like Aaron, the head and chief of all the priests and Levites of the whole camp.[37]

8. The apostles further appointed: At the conclusion of all the scriptures let the Gospel be read, as being the seal of all the scriptures; and let the

---

34. Cf. John 14:16-26; 16:5-15.

35. *Voice* and *odor:* this is a development of Acts 2:2-3 in Syriac, where one noisy wind could be interpreted as both a voice and a strong vapor. The impression left is of a liturgy with incense and candles.

36. Matt. 24:27.

37. This canon has some echoes in Torah, but none very strong, e.g., Num. 1:47-51; 3:5-10. *Elder:* see Joshua 6:21; 7:6; etc. but it is not the Syriac word usually used of the Seventy elders. It is the normal Syriac word for "presbyter/elder" or "priest." *Subdeacon:* The Syriac word used is a Greek loanword and equals the normal Greek term. The subdiaconate here is slightly subordinated to the other orders; see Basil. Ep. 54, p. 118, and *Apostolic Constitutions* 8.46.13 *Overseer:* an overly cautious translation, although supported by Vööbus. It is a general word, but it can mean "bishop" as, given the context, it clearly means here. *Guide:* it can also mean "judge," "governor," "bishop," or "abbot" (see Ps.-Clement *Hom.* 3.64, p. 89; contrast Matt. 23:10). *Camp:* or *army;* in Lev. 4:12; 6:11; Num. 2:17; etc., it refers to the whole of the Israelites. This canon's terminology is archaicizing and recalls Israelite priestly, rather than civil, hierarchy, that is, Aaron and the Levites rather than Joshua and the Seventy elders.

people listen to it standing upon their feet: because it is the gospel of the redemption of all.

10. The apostles appointed: That, beside the Old Testament, and the Prophets, and the Gospel, and the Acts (of their exploits), nothing should be read on the pulpit in the church.

11. The apostles further appointed: Whosoever is unacquainted with the faith of the church and the ordinances and laws which are appointed in it, let him not be a guide and ruler; and whosoever is acquainted with them and departs from them, let him not minister again: because, not being true in his ministry, he has lied.

12. The apostles further appointed: Whosoever swears, or lies, or bears false witness, or has recourse to magicians and soothsayers and Chaldeans,[38] and puts confidence in fates and birthdays, which they hold fast who know not God—let him also, as one who knows not God, be dismissed from the ministry, and not minister again.

13. The apostles further appointed: If there be any one that is divided in mind touching the ministry, and who follows it not with a steadfast will, let not this one minister again: since the Lord of the ministry is not served by him with a steadfast will; and he deceives people . . . not God, "before whom crafty devices avail not."[39]

14. The apostles further appointed: Whosoever lends and receives usury, and is occupied in merchandise and covetousness, let not this one minister again, nor continue in the ministry.

15. The apostles further appointed: That whosoever loves the Jews, like Iscariot, who was their friend, or the pagans, who worship creatures instead of the Creator, should not enter in among them and minister; and moreover, that if he be already among them, they should not suffer him to remain, but that he should be separated from among them, and not minister with them again.

16. The apostles further appointed: That, if anyone from the Jews or from the pagans come and join himself with them, and if after he has joined himself with them he turn and go back again to the side on which he stood before, and if he again return and come to them a second time, he should not be received again; but that, according to the side on which he was before, so those who know him should look upon him.[40]

---

38. Chaldeans were thought to possess esoteric Eastern wisdom and power.

39. 1 Sam. 2:3 (Syriac version).

40. Jews and pagans, in Christian ideology, represented the two theological extremes of error; politically, especially under or near Sassanid and Vandal rule, they were often allied against Byzantine power. See Meeks and Wilken (1978). The various interrelations, though often bad, were not like medieval and later European anti-Semitism.

17. The apostles further appointed: That it should not be permitted to the guide to transact the matters which pertain to the church apart from those who minister with him; but that he should issue commands with the counsel of them all, and that that only should be done which all of them should concur in and not disapprove.

20. The apostles further appointed: If any divest themselves of mammon and run not after the gain of money, let these be chosen and admitted to the ministry of the altar.

22. The apostles further appointed: If it be seen that those who are accustomed to hear causes show partiality, and pronounce the innocent guilty and the guilty innocent, let them never again hear another cause: thus receiving the rebuke of their partiality, as it is fit.

23. The apostles further ordained: Let not those that are high-minded and lifted up with the arrogance of boasting be admitted to the ministry: because of this text: "That which is exalted among humanity is abominable before God";[41] and because concerning them it is said: "I will return a recompense upon those that vaunt themselves."[42]

24. The apostles further appointed: Let there be a ruler[43] over the elders who are in the villages, and let him be recognized as head of them all, at whose hand all of them shall be required: for Samuel[44] also thus made visits from place to place and ruled.

25. The apostles further appointed: That those kings who shall hereafter believe in Christ should be permitted to go up and stand before the altar along with the guides of the church: because David[45] also, and those who were like him, went up and stood before the altar.

26. The apostles further appointed: Let no one dare to do anything by the authority of the priesthood which is not in accordance with justice and equity, but in accordance with justice, and free from the blame of partiality, let all things be done.

All these things did the apostles appoint, not for themselves, but for those who should come after them—for they were apprehensive that in time to come wolves would put on sheep's clothing: since for themselves the Spirit, the Paraclete, which was in them, was sufficient: that, even as he had appointed these laws by their hands, so he would guide them lawfully.

---

41. Luke 16:15.
42. Cf. Isa. 2:12.
43. Vööbus translates *ruler* as "superintendent," and in a note glosses it as "director, a procurator"; it is used of civil and ecclesiastical offices.
44. 1 Sam. 3ff.
45. 2 Sam. 6:17f. *Kings:* a sign of post-Constantinian date: Constantine, not yet baptized, preached at the Council of Nicaea, and after him emperors had quasi-clerical status.

For they, who had received from our Lord power and authority, had no need that laws should be appointed for them by others.[46]

APHRAHAT, DEMONSTRATION 10: ON PASTORS

1–6

1. Pastors are set over the flock, and give the sheep the food of life. Whosoever is watchful and toils in behalf of the sheep, is careful for the flock, and is the disciple of our Good Shepherd, who gave himself in behalf of his sheep.[47] And whosoever brings not back the flock carefully, is likened to the hireling who has no care for the sheep. Be like, O pastors, those righteous pastors of old. Jacob fed the sheep of Laban, and guarded them and toiled and was watchful, and so received the reward. For Jacob said to Laban, "Lo! twenty years am I with you. Your sheep and your flocks I have not robbed and the males of your sheep I have not eaten. That which was broken I did not bring to you, but you required it at my hands! In the daytime the heat devoured me and the cold by night.[48] My sleep departed from my eyes." Observe, you pastors, that pastor, how he cared for his flock. He used to watch in the nighttime to guard it and was vigilant; and he used to toil in the daytime to feed it. As Jacob was a pastor, so Joseph was a pastor and his brethren were pastors. Moses was a pastor, and David also was a pastor. So Amos was a pastor. These all were pastors who fed the sheep and led them well.

2. Now, why, my beloved, did these pastors first feed the sheep, and were then chosen to be pastors of people? Clearly that they might learn how a pastor cares for the sheep, and is watchful and toils in behalf of the sheep. And when they had learned the manners of pastors, they were chosen for the pastoral office. Jacob fed the sheep of Laban and toiled and was vigilant and led them well; and then he tended and guided well his sons, and taught them the pattern of pastoral work. And Joseph used to tend the sheep along with his brethren; and in Egypt he became guide to a numerous people, and led them back, as a good pastor does his flock. Moses fed the sheep of Jethro, his father-in-law, and he was chosen from (tending) the sheep to tend his people, and as a good pastor he guided them.

3. But those pastors who did not care for the sheep, those were hirelings who used to feed themselves alone. On this account the prophet[49] ad-

---

46. Conclusion: Notice how the past is made relevant and its authority is co-opted.
47. John 10:11ff.
48. Gen. 31:38, 40.
49. Ezek. 34:2-4, 9, 10-12, 18, 19.

dresses them, saying to them, "O you pastors who destroy and scatter the sheep of my pasture, hear the word of the Lord. Thus says the Lord: Lo! I will visit my sheep as the pastor visits the flock in the day of the whirlwind, and I will require my sheep at your hands. O foolish pastors, with the wool of the sheep do you clothe yourselves and the flesh of the fatlings do you eat, and the sheep you do not feed. That which was sick you did not heal, and that which was broken you did not bind up. The weak you did not strengthen, and the lost and the scattered you did not gather together. The strong ones and the fatlings you did not guard, but with harshness you subdued them. The good pastures you yourselves graze upon, and what remains you trample with your feet. The pleasant waters do you drink, and whatever remains you defile with your feet. And my sheep have eaten the trampled (herbage) which your feet have trampled, and they have drunk the waters which your feet have defiled." These are the greedy and base pastors and hirelings, who did not feed the sheep, or guide them well, or deliver them from the wolves. But when the Great Pastor, the chief of pastors, shall come, he will call and visit his sheep and will take knowledge of his flock. And he will bring forward those pastors, and will exact an account from them, and will condemn them for their deeds. And those who fed the sheep well, them the Chief of Pastors will cause to rejoice and to inherit life and rest: "O stupid and foolish pastor, to whose right hand and to whose right eye I committed my sheep. Because you did say concerning the sheep, let that which die, die, and let that which perish, perish, and whatever is left, let them devour the flesh of one another; therefore, behold I will make blind your right eye and I will wither up your right arm. Your eye which regarded a bribe shall be blinded, and your hand which did not rule in righteousness shall waste away."[50] And as for you, my sheep, the sheep of my pasture, you are mortal; but I am the Lord your God.[51] Behold henceforth I will feed you in a good and rich pasture.[52]

4. "The good shepherd gives himself for the sake of the sheep."[53] And again he said: "I have other sheep and I must bring them also hither. And the whole flock shall be one, and one shepherd, and my Father because of this loves me; that I give myself for the sake of the sheep."[54] And again he said: "I am the door of the sheep. Every one that enters by me shall live and shall go in and go out and find pasture."[55] O pastors, be made like unto

---

50. Zech. 11:7–17.
51. Ezek. 34:31.
52. Ezek. 34:14.
53. John 10:11.
54. John 10:16, 17.
55. John 10:9.

that diligent pastor, the chief of the whole flock, who cared so greatly for his flock. He brought nigh those that were afar off. He brought back the wanderers. He visited the sick. He strengthened the weak. He bound up the broken. He guarded the fatlings. He gave himself up for the sake of the sheep. He chose and instructed excellent leaders, and committed the sheep into their hands, and gave them authority over all his flock. For he said to Simon Cephas: "Feed my sheep and my lambs and my ewes."[56] So Simon fed his sheep; and he fulfilled his time and handed over the flock to you, and departed. Do you also feed and guide them well. For the pastor who cares for the sheep engages in no other pursuit along with that. He does not make a vineyard, nor plant gardens, nor does he fall into the troubles of this world.[57] Never have we seen a pastor who left the sheep in the wilderness and became a merchant, or one who left the flock to wander and became a farmer. But if he deserts his flock and does these things he thereby hands over the flock to the wolves.

5. And remember, my beloved, that I wrote to you concerning our ancestors that they first learned the ways of tending sheep and in that received trial of carefulness, and then were chosen for the office of guides, that they might learn and observe how much the pastor cares for the flock, and as they used to guide the sheep carefully, so also might be perfected in this office of guidance. Thus Joseph was chosen from the sheep, to guide the Egyptians in the time of affliction. And Moses was chosen from the sheep, to guide his people and tend them. And David was taken from following the sheep, to become king over Israel. And the Lord took Amos from following the sheep, and made him a prophet over his people. Elisha likewise was taken from behind the yoke, to become a prophet in Israel. Moses did not return to his sheep, nor did he leave his flock that was committed to him. David did not return to his father's sheep, but guided his people in the integrity of his heart.[58] Amos did not turn back to feed his sheep, or to gather (the fruit of) trees, but he guided them and performed his office of prophecy. Elisha did not turn back to his yoke, but served Elijah and filled his place. And [Gehazi] who was for him as a shepherd, because he loved fields and merchandise and vineyards and oliveyards and tillage, did not wish to become his disciple; and (therefore) he did not commit the flock into his hand.

6. I beseech you, pastors, that you set not over the flock leaders who are foolish and stupid, covetous also and lovers of possessions. Everyone who

---

56. John 21:15-17.
57. The pastor does not make a vineyard: see Elvira canon 19, p. 102.
58. Ps. 78:72.

feeds the flock shall eat of their milk.[59] And everyone who guides the yoke shall be ministered to from his labor. The priests have a right to partake of the altar, and the Levites shall receive their tithes. Whoever eats of the milk, let his heart be upon the flock; and let each one who is ministered to from the labor of his yoke, take heed to his tillage. And let the priests who partake of the altar serve the altar with honor. And as for the Levites who receive the tithes, they have no portion in Israel. O pastors, disciples of our great Pastor, don't be like hirelings; because the hireling cares not for the sheep. Be like our sweet Pastor, whose life was not dearer to him than his sheep. Rear up the youths and bring up the maidens; and love the lambs and let them be reared in your bosoms; that when you shall come to the Chief Pastor, you may offer to him all your sheep in completeness, and so he may give you what he has promised: "Where I am, you also shall be."[60] These things, brief as they are, will be sufficient for the good pastors and leaders.

---

59. 1 Cor. 9:7ff.
60. John 12:26.

6

SELECT CANONS:
THE DOS AND THE DON'TS

The largest convenient collection of conciliar canons and canonical epistles in English is Percival's NPNF 2.14 (from which most of these selections are taken), who also prints some of the standard commentaries and much interesting material. Basil's Epistles, with text, are in the Loeb series;.*The Detailed Rules'* Question 7 is from Ayer. Canons in Greek and Latin are fairly well covered; much less is known of those in other languages. Some material from Syria is found in ch. 5. A large and mixed collection of canons in Syriac is in A. Vööbus, CSCO volumes 307, 317, 367–68, 375–76. Much from J. Chabot (1902) is summarized in McCullough (1982, ch. 9–10). For secondary sources, besides Percival and ODCC (s.v. Canon, Canon Law), there is J. Gaudemet (1985).

Councils and major church leaders found it necessary, from time to time, to publish lists of rules for Christian living, or more usually for avoidance, and these rules are called canons. The early collections have been extensively studied, but mostly by canon lawyers, whose interests tend towards the medieval collections and to systematic and legal, not social or historical, concerns. As sources for the social, quotidian history of late antiquity, they are marvelous but underutilized. Our collection is only a small sample of these most practical of sources. In them you will find a familiar and modern-sounding groping for solutions to familiar problems; you will find as well unfamiliar characterizations of personal self-reform and the Christian life. We can learn from both.

THE COUNCIL OF ELVIRA, CANONS 18–20, 56

Southern Spain, ca. 300 (Shippee's translation)

18. Should bishops, presbyters, or deacons, once installed in office, be discovered to be adulterers, it is resolved, both because of the offense and

because of the impious crime, that they not be allowed into communion even at death.

19. Bishops, presbyters, and deacons should not leave their locations in order to do business, nor, going about the provinces, should they search out lucrative markets. Instead, for the pursuit of a livelihood, let them send either a son or freedman or agent or friend or whomever. Should they wish to do business, let them do business within the province.[1]

20. Should one of the clergy be found receiving interest, it is resolved that he be defrocked and excommunicated. If, however, a layperson is judged to have accepted interest and, upon correction, promises that the debt be canceled nor anything else be exacted, it is resolved to grant him a pardon. If, however, he persists in this iniquity, he must be ejected from the church.[2]

56. It is resolved that a magistrate, while in office, be restrained so that he keep himself away from church.

THE COUNCIL OF ANCYRA, CANONS 1–2

Central Asia Minor, 314

1. With regard to those presbyters who have offered sacrifices and afterwards returned to the conflict, not with hypocrisy, but in sincerity, it has seemed good that they may retain the honor of their chair; provided they had not used management, arrangement, or persuasion, so as to appear to be subjected to the torture, when it was applied only in seeming and pretense. Nevertheless, it is not lawful for them to make the oblation, nor to preach, nor in short to perform any act of sacerdotal function.

2. It is likewise decreed that deacons who have sacrificed and afterwards resumed the conflict, shall enjoy their other honors, but shall abstain from every sacred ministry, neither bringing forth the bread and the cup, nor making proclamations. Nevertheless, if any of the bishops shall

---

1. On a pastor and personal finances, see the canons Elvira 19, 20; Laodicea 4; Basil 14; Chalcedon 3; and ch. 5, Ps.-Clem. Hom. 3.69, 71 and Aphrahat, 10.4; and also Cyprian, *On the Lapsed* 6. Questions and problems existed from the beginning: 1 Thess. 2; Luke 10; Acts 5; 1 Tim. 3, 5; Didache 11–13; etc.

2. *Interest:* In Latin *usura* means any interest; the modern capitalist differentiation between fair interest and usury is a late Renaissance development, notably supported by Calvin. Under this canon, the lender-at-interest loses all his capital (perhaps excepting what has been paid) as well. Banking made up a very small part of the economy and was not a road to large wealth. One did not generally borrow to invest or develop, but to meet some emergency, such as paying taxes or rent. The medieval situation was quite different, See ODCC, s.v. Usury, and, with caution, the excursus in NPNF 2.14, pp. 36–38, and also Leo the Great, Ep. 4. 4–6, below p. 188f.

observe in them distress of mind and meek humiliation, it shall be lawful to the bishops to grant more indulgence, or to take away [what has been granted].

THE COUNCIL OF NICAEA, CANONS 4–5, 15

Northwest Asia Minor, 325

4. It is by all means proper that a bishop should be appointed by all the bishops in the province; but should this be difficult, either on account of urgent necessity or because of distance, three at least should meet together, and the suffrages of the absent [bishops] also being given and communicated in writing, then the ordination should take place. But in every province the ratification of what is done should be left to the metropolitan.

5. Concerning those, whether of the clergy or of the laity, who have been excommunicated in the several provinces, let the provision of the canon be observed by the bishops which provides that persons cast out by some be not readmitted by others. Nevertheless, inquiry should be made whether they have been excommunicated through captiousness, or contentiousness, or any such like ungracious disposition in the bishop. And, that this matter may have due investigation, it is decreed that in every province synods shall be held twice a year, in order that when all the bishops of the province are assembled together, such questions may by them be thoroughly examined, so that those who have confessedly offended against their bishop may be seen by all to be for just cause excommunicated, until it shall seem fit to a general meeting of the bishops to pronounce a milder sentence upon them. And let these synods be held, the one before Lent (that the pure gift may be offered to God after all bitterness has been put away), and let the second be held about autumn.

15. On account of the great disturbance and discords that occur, it is decreed that the custom prevailing in certain places contrary to the canon must wholly be done away; so that neither bishop, presbyter, nor deacon shall pass from city to city. And if anyone, after this decree of the holy and great synod, shall attempt any such thing, or continue in any such course, his proceedings shall be utterly void, and he shall be restored to the church for which he was ordained bishop or presbyter.

THE COUNCIL OF ANTIOCH, CANONS 5, 11–12

Syria, 341

5. If any presbyter or deacon, despising his own bishop, has separated himself from the church, and gathered a private assembly, and set up an

altar; and if, when summoned by his bishop, he shall refuse to be persuaded and will not obey, even though he summon him a first and a second time, let such a one be wholly deposed and have no further remedy, neither be capable of regaining his rank. And if he persist in troubling and disturbing the church, let him be corrected, as a seditious person, by the civil power.[3]

11. If any bishop, or presbyter, or anyone whatever of the canon shall presume to betake himself to the emperor without the consent and letters of the bishop of the province, and particularly of the bishop of the metropolis, such a one shall be publicly deposed and cast out, not only from communion, but also from the rank which he happens to have; inasmuch as he dares to trouble the ears of our emperor beloved of God, contrary to the law of the church. But, if necessary business shall require anyone to go to the emperor, let him do it with the advice and consent of the metropolitan and other bishops in the province, and let him undertake his journey with letters from them.

12. If any presbyter or deacon deposed by his own bishop, or any bishop deposed by a synod, shall dare to trouble the ears of the emperor, when it is his duty to submit his case to a greater synod of bishops, and to refer to more bishops the things which he thinks right, and to abide by the examination and decision made by them; if, despising these, he shall trouble the emperor, he shall be entitled to no pardon, neither shall he have an opportunity of defense, nor any hope of future restoration.

THE COUNCIL OF GANGRA, EPILOGUE

North of Ancyra, Mid-Fourth Century

These things we write, not to cut off those who wish to lead in the church of God an ascetic life, according to the scriptures; but those who carry the pretense of asceticism to superciliousness; both exalting themselves above those who live more simply, and introducing novelties contrary to the scriptures and the ecclesiastical canons. We do, assuredly, admire virginity accompanied by humility; and we have regard for continence, accompanied by godliness and gravity; and we praise the leaving of worldly occupations, [when it is made] with lowliness of mind; [but at the same time] we honor the holy companionship of marriage, and we do not condemn wealth enjoyed with uprightness and beneficence; and we commend plainness and frugality in apparel [which is worn] only from

---

3. Schism is considered extremely dangerous. Cf. Ancyra 1, 2, and notice the provision to hand a schismatic cleric over to the civil authorities.

attention, [and that] not overfastidious, to the body; but dissolute and effeminate excess in dress we eschew; and we reverence the houses of God and embrace the assemblies held therein as holy and helpful, not confining religion within the houses, but reverencing every place built in the name of God; and we approve of gathering together in the church itself for the common profit; and we bless the exceeding charities done by the community to the poor, according to the traditions of the church; and, to sum up in a word, we wish that all things which have been delivered by the holy scriptures and the apostolical traditions may be observed in the church.

THE COUNCIL OF LAODICEA, CANONS 3–5, 12–13, 35–36

Southwest Asia Minor, Mid-late Fourth Century

3. One who has been recently baptized ought not to be promoted to the sacerdotal order.[4]

4. They who are of the sacerdotal order ought not to lend and receive usury, nor what is called hemioliae.[5]

5. Ordinations are not to be held in the presence of hearers.[6]

12. Bishops are to be appointed to the ecclesiastical government by the judgment of the metropolitans and neighboring bishops, after having been long proved both in the foundation of their faith and in the conversation of an honest life.

13. The election of those who are to be appointed to the priesthood is not to be committed to the multitude.

35. Christians must not forsake the church of God, and go away and invoke angels and gather assemblies, which things are forbidden. If, therefore, anyone shall be found engaged in this covert idolatry, let him be anathema; for he has forsaken our Lord Jesus Christ, the Son of God, and has gone over to idolatry.

36. They who are of the priesthood, or of the clergy, shall not be magicians, enchanters, mathematicians, or astrologers; nor shall they make what are called amulets, which are chains for their own souls. And those who wear such, we command to be cast out of the church.[7]

---

4. Ambrose is one of many notable exceptions.

5. *Hemioliae:* one and a half, i.e., principal plus 50 percent. See p. 102, nn 1–2.

6. *Hearers:* those excluded from full communion, either because of disciplinary sentence or non-baptism. See Basil, canon 22.

7. *Mathematicians,* i.e., numerologers. Amulets were very popular, often made with psalm texts. Ps. 91 was a favorite.

BASIL, CANONS

From Three Canonical Letters[8]
Letter 188

"To a fool, if he ask questions," it is said, "shall wisdom be accounted."[9]
But questions asked by the wise, as it seems, make even a fool wise—the
thing which, by the grace of God, happens in our case as often as we
receive the letters of your industrious spirit. For we become a more
prudent administrator than before and wiser by this very questioning,
learning many things that we do not know; and our solicitude about
making answer becomes, as it were, our teacher. Doubtless on this present
occasion also, though we have never before taken up for study the
questions you raise, we have been obliged to examine into them accurately, both to recall whatever we have heard from our elders, and independently to draw conclusions akin to what we have been taught.

3. If a deacon commit fornication after receiving the diaconate, he shall
be removed from the diaconate, but after he has been reduced to the
station of a layperson he shall not be barred from communion. Wherefore
there is an old canon[10] that those who have fallen from their grade shall be
subjected to this form of punishment only, the ancients following, as I
think, the law, "You shall not exact the penalty twice for the same offense";[11] and also for another reason—those in the ranks of the laity, after
being expelled from the place of the faithful, are again taken back into the
place from which they fell, but the deacon once and for all incurs the
lasting penalty of deposition. On the ground, therefore, that the diaconate
is not restored to him, they have taken their stand on this punishment
alone. These, then, are the conclusions from their decrees. But in general a
truer remedy is withdrawal from sin. Thus one who for pleasure of the
flesh has rejected grace, but by chastisement of the flesh and by complete
subjection of it through continency has abandoned the pleasures whereby
he was mastered, will furnish us a complete proof of his cure. We should,
therefore, know both what is according to strict rule and what is according
to custom, and in matters which do not admit of the strictest interpretation
we should follow the decision handed down.

6. The. fornications of canonical persons must not be accounted as
marriage, but their union must by all means be dissolved. For this is both
advantageous for the safety of the church and will not give heretics an

---

8. Probable dates are 188: 374–375; 199: 375–376; 217: 376–377.
9. Prov. 17:28 (LXX).
10. Which is not known; contrast Elvira 18.
11. Nahum 1:9 (LXX).

opportunity to attack us on the ground that we have won others to ourselves by granting them license to sin.[12]

10. Those who swear that they do not receive ordination and decline it under oath should not be forced to commit perjury. For even if there seems to be a canon[13] that condones such behavior, yet by experience we have learned that those who have committed perjury do not prosper. Consideration, however, must be given to the form of the oath, and its words, and the disposition under which it was taken, and the subtle additions in the words; since if no excuse exists at all such persons must be altogether dismissed. The case of Severus, however, that is, the case of the presbyter ordained by him, seems to me to have some such excuse—if it likewise seems so to you. Order that region which is subject to Mestia and to which the man has been assigned to come under Vasoda, for thus he will not commit perjury since he will not be withdrawing from the place, and Longinus, since he will have Cyriacus with him, will not desert the church, and will not damn his own soul through idleness. And we shall seem to be doing nothing contrary to the canons by making concessions to Cyriacus, who swore that he would remain at Mindana but accepted the transfer. For his return will be a safeguarding of his oath. And his yielding to the arrangement will not be accounted against him as perjury, because it was not added in the oath that he would not depart from Mindana for a little while but that he would remain there for the future. But to Severus who pleads forgetfulness we shall grant forgiveness, saying that God who knows secret things[14] will not allow his church to be ravaged by such a man, who first of all acts uncanonically, and then binds by oath contrary to the gospels, and teaches others to commit perjury by the means employed in the transfer, and now lies in that he pretends forgetfulness. But since we are not judges of the human heart, but judge from what we hear, let us leave vengeance to the Lord, and ourselves receive him without discrimination, granting pardon to his forgetfulness as a human failing.

12. Digamists the canon[15] has completely excluded from the ministry.

---

12. Whether canonical means all orders or just professed virgins is not clear (cf. Loeb, ad loc., and Antioch, canon 11, p. 104). If the latter, then the vow of virginity is to be enforced over marriage.

13. I.e., by forced ordination; which canon is unknown. The situation is complicated (see Loeb , ad loc., for details) and Basil must balance the competing interests of canon law, vows, etc. Of interest to us is the variety of criteria Basil used to solve the problem: canon law; experience; expediency; etc. Note especially the treatment of Severus (and the reference to Susanna's accusers, Sus. 42ff.!): it is clear he is lying, but his excuse must be accepted, and his due left to God.

14. Sus. 42, aptly cited.

15. Cf. 1 Tim. 3:2-13; Titus 1:5-9.

14. One who takes usury, if he consents to spend his unjust gain upon the poor, and thereafter to be freed of the disease of avarice, shall be received into holy orders.

Letter 199

18. Concerning fallen virgins who, after professing to the Lord the life in holiness, then, by succumbing to the lusts of the flesh, have made their vows void, our predecessors, in simple terms and gently showing indulgence to the weaknesses of the fallen, decreed that they should be received after a year, ranking them on the principle of a likeness to digamists. But it seems to me, since by God's grace the church as it advances is becoming stronger, and the order of virgins is now increasing, that we should give strict attention both to the act as it appears to us on reflection, and to the meaning of scripture as it is possible to discover it through inference. For widowhood is inferior to virginity: consequently the sin also of widows is much less than that of virgins. Let us see accordingly what is written to Timothy by Paul;[16] "But the younger widows avoid. For when they have grown wanton in Christ, they will marry: having damnation, because they have made void their first faith." If, then, a widow lies under a very heavy charge, on the ground that she has made void her faith in Christ, what must we think of the virgin who is a spouse of Christ and a sacred vessel dedicated to the Lord! A great sin indeed it is that even a handmaid giving herself over to secret marriage should fill the house with corruption, and through her evil life do an affront to her master; but it is far worse, of course, that the bride should become an adulteress and, dishonoring her union with the bridegroom, give herself over to licentious pleasures. Therefore while the widow, as a corrupted handmaid, is condemned, the virgin lies under the charge of adultery.[17] Just as, therefore, we call him an adulterer who associates with the wife of another, not receiving him into communion until he cease from the sin, so clearly shall we also decree in the case of him who keeps the virgin. But we must now agree beforehand on this—that she is named a virgin who willingly has consecrated herself to the Lord, and has renounced marriage, and has preferred the life of holiness. And we sanction their professions from that time at which their age possesses the fullness of reason. For it is not proper to consider children's words entirely final in such matters, but she who is above sixteen or seventeen years, and is mistress of her faculties, who has been examined carefully and has remained constant and has persisted in her petitions for admittance, should then be enrolled

---

16. 1 Tim. 5:11, 12.
17. For which Basil's canon 58 sets 15 years' punishment.

among the virgins, and we should ratify the profession of said virgin, and inexorably punish her violation of it. For parents, and brothers, and other relatives bring forward many girls before the proper age, not because these girls have an inner urge toward celibacy, but in order that their relatives may provide some worldly advantage for themselves.[18] Such should not be received readily, until we shall have clearly examined into their own personal inclination.[19]

19. But we do not recognize the professions of men except such as have enrolled themselves in the order of monks; these seem to have taken up celibacy in silence. Yet even as regards them I think that the following course of action should precede; they should be questioned and a clear profession received from them, so that whenever they return to the life of the flesh and pleasure they may undergo the punishment of fornicators.

20. As to such women as have professed virginity while in heresy and then afterwards have preferred marriage, I do not think that these ought to be condemned. For "What things soever the law speaks, it speaks to them that are in the law."[20] And those who have not yet come under the yoke of Christ do not recognize the laws of the Lord. Therefore, they should be received by the church, sharing with all the remission that is accorded in these things because of their faith in Christ. And in general such things as are committed in the catechumenical state are not called into account. But these persons, of course, the church does not receive without baptism. Therefore it is most necessary in these cases to observe the rights of birth.

22. Regarding men who hold women by abduction, if they have carried off women who had been betrothed to others, they must not be received before they have separated from them and have placed them in the power of those to whom they were originally betrothed, whether the latter wish to receive them or to give them up. But if anyone takes a girl who is not betrothed, it is necessary to take her away and restore her to her relatives, and commit her to their discretion, whether they are parents or brothers, or whoever have authority over the maiden; and if they choose to surrender her to him, the union shall be valid, but if they refuse, violence is not to be employed. However, he who holds a wife by secret or somewhat violent seduction must acknowledge the punishment for fornication. And punishment for four years has been prescribed for fornicators. In the first year they must be excluded from the prayers, and weep for themselves at the door of the church; in the second year they are to be admitted to the

---

18. I.e., dowry.

19. Notice the specific discussion of hermeneutics. What rules of interpretation are used? How absolute are these rules?

20. Rom. 3:19.

place of the "hearers"; in the third to penance; in the fourth to "standing" with the laity, abstaining from the oblation; then the communion with the Good is to be permitted them.

27. In the case of the presbyter who through ignorance has been implicated in an unlawful marriage, I have laid down what must be done—he should retain his seat, but abstain from the rest of his offices. For it is enough to pardon such a one. But for him who should heal his own wounds to bless another is unfitting. For benediction is the communication of sanctification. But how will he, who does not possess this because of his transgression through ignorance, impart it to another! Therefore let him bless neither publicly nor privately, nor let him distribute the body of Christ to others, nor perform any other function, but being satisfied with his seat of dignity let him with tears call upon the Lord to pardon him the sin which he committed through ignorance.[21]

32. Those clerics who commit the sin unto death[22] are deposed from their rank, but are not shut out from the communion of the laity, "For you shall not punish twice for the selfsame."[23]

44. The deaconess who committed fornication with the Greek is to be admitted to repentance, and she shall be admitted to the oblation in the seventh year, that is, if she live in chastity. But the Greek who, after accepting the faith, again enters upon the sacrilege, returns to his vomit.[24] But the body of the deaconess, on the ground that it has been consecrated, we no longer permit to remain in carnal usage.

45. If anyone, after receiving the name of Christian, revile Christ, there shall be no profit from the title.

Letter 217

51. Regarding clerics, the canons have not expounded definitely about them, having commanded that one punishment be laid down for the fallen, namely, deposition from the ministry, whether they happen to be in orders or whether they adhere to a ministry without ordination.[25]

55. Those who march out to meet robbers, if they be laics, are debarred from the communion of the Good; but if they be clerics, they are deposed

---

21. Just what is the case is not clear. Notice how it was just this sort of question of priestly purity that so exercised the Western church. It was never seen as so dangerous or divisive in the East.

22. 1 John 5:16, 17. Which sin is not clear.

23. Nah. 1:9 (LXX).

24. Cf. Prov. 26:11. *Greek* here means "non-Christian."

25. *Cleric* is here construed broadly, beyond those ordained by laying on of hands, to the various minor orders, such as lay readers.

from orders. "For all," he says, "that take the sword, shall perish with the sword."[26]

60. She who has professed virginity and has failed in her promise shall fulfill the time for the sin of adultery in the rule of a life by herself.[27] The same also applies to those who have professed the monastic life and have fallen.

69. A reader, if he should have intercourse with his betrothed before marriage, after being inactive for a year, shall be admitted to reading, although remaining without promotion. But one who had illicit intercourse without betrothal shall cease from the ministry. The same also in the case of a minister.[28]

70. A deacon whose lips have become defiled[29] and has confessed that he has sinned to that extent, shall be removed from the ministry; but he shall be deemed worthy of partaking of the sacraments, together with the deacons. Likewise the presbyter also. But if one be discovered to have sinned further than this, in whatever order he may be, he shall be deposed.

71. One who has knowledge of each of the foregoing sins, and has not confessed, but has been exposed, shall undergo punishment for as long a period as the perpetrator of the evil is punished.[30]

73. One who has denied Christ and violated the mystery of salvation should mourn and is obligated to do penance for the whole period of his life; at the time of his departure from life being deemed worthy of the sacraments by reason of his faith in the mercy of God.[31]

74. If, however, each of those who have been guilty of the aforesaid sins be earnest in performing penance, he who has been entrusted by the mercy of God with loosing and binding, if he should become more merciful in diminishing the time of punishment on seeing the magnitude of the sinner's penance, shall not be worthy of condemnation; since the story in the scriptures makes known to us that those who do penance with greater labor quickly obtain the mercy of God.

84. All these things do we write that the fruits of penance may be tested. For we do not judge such things entirely by time, but we attend to the manner of the repentance. But if it is difficult to tear them away from their

---

26. Matt. 26:52.

27. I.e., in continence; see Loeb, ad loc.

28. Probably a subdeacon; see Loeb, ad loc.

29. Probably the expression of intent, but not the deed; see Loeb, ad loc. The meaning is not entirely clear.

30. Perhaps of the accomplice, and not of mere knowledge; see Loeb, ad loc.

31. This is the only life-long penance ordered in Basil's canons; see also 81, in Loeb.

own habits, and they wish to serve the pleasures of the flesh rather than the Lord, and do not accept the life according to the gospel, there is no common ground between them and us. For in a disobedient and contradicting people we have been taught to hear: "Saving, save your life."[32] Therefore, let us not allow ourselves to perish with such; but fearing the serious judgment and having before our eyes the dread day of the retribution of the Lord, let us not be willing to perish through the sins of others. For if the terrible things of the Lord have not instructed us, and such scourges have not brought us to a realization that the Lord has deserted us because of our iniquities and has delivered us into the hands of barbarians, and that the people has been led captive to the enemy and given over to dispersion because those who bore the name of Christ dared these things; if they did not know or understand that because of these things the anger of God has come upon us, what common ground is there between them and us? Nay, we ought to protest to them night and day and publicly and privately; but let us not permit ourselves to be snatched away together with their iniquities, praying if possible to profit them and to draw them away from the snare of the wicked one; but if we are unable to do this, let us strive zealously to save at least our own souls from eternal damnation.

BASIL, THE DETAILED RULES FOR MONKS

From Question 7.1, 3, 4

Question 7. Since your words have given us full assurance that the life [that is, the coenobitic life] is dangerous with those who despise the commandments of the Lord, we wish accordingly to learn whether it is necessary that one who withdraws should remain alone or live with others of like mind who have placed before themselves the same goal of piety.[33]

Response 1. I think that the life of several in the same place is much more profitable. First, because for bodily wants no one of us is sufficient for himself, but we need each other in providing what is necessary. For just as the foot has one ability, but is wanting another, and without the help of the other members it would find neither its own power strong nor sufficient of itself to continue, nor any supply for what it lacks, so it is in the case of the solitary life: what is of use to us and what is wanting we cannot provide for ourselves, for God who created the world has so ordered all things that

---

32. Gen. 19:17 (LXX), spoken to Lot.

33. *The Detailed Rules* were compiled from stenographic notes of conversations; see Quasten 3.212–14. Solitary vs. community life was a very important monastic issue, and some form or combination of both continued. Basil's rules form the basis of Eastern monastic orders, and influenced the Western orders.

we are dependent upon each other, as it is written that we may join ourselves to one another.[34] But in addition to this, reverence to the love of Christ does not permit each one to have regard only to his own affairs, for love, he says, seeks not its own.[35] The solitary life has only one goal, the service of its own interests. That clearly is opposed to the law of love, which the Apostle fulfilled, when he did not in his eyes seek his own advantage but the advantage of many, that they might be saved.[36]

Further, no one in solitude recognizes his own defects, since he has no one to correct him and in gentleness and mercy direct him on his way. For even if correction is from an enemy, it may often in the case of those who are well disposed rouse the desire for healing; but the healing of sin by him who sincerely loves is wisely accomplished. . . . Also the commands may be better fulfilled by a larger community, but not by one alone; for while this thing is being done another will be neglected; for example, by attendance upon the sick the reception of strangers is neglected; and in the bestowal and distribution of the necessities of life (especially when in these services much time is consumed) the care of the work is neglected, so that by this the greatest commandment and the one most helpful to salvation is neglected; neither the hungry are fed nor the naked clothed.[37] Who would therefore value higher the idle, useless life than the fruitful which fulfills the commandments of God?

3. . . . Also in the preservation of the gifts bestowed by God the coenobitic life[38] is preferable. . . . For one who falls into sin, the recovery of the right path is so much easier, for he is ashamed at the blame expressed by so many in common, so that it happens to him as it is written: It is enough that the same therefore be punished by many.[39] . . . There are still other dangers which we say accompany the solitary life, the first and greatest is that of self-satisfaction. For he who has no one to test his work easily believes that he has completely fulfilled the Commandments . . .

4. For how shall he manifest his humility, when he has no one to whom he can show himself the inferior? How shall he manifest compassion, cut off from the society of many? How will he exercise himself in patience, if no one opposes his wishes?

---

34. 1 Cor. 12:12-27.
35. 1 Cor. 13:5.
36. Cf. 1 Cor. 10:33; Phil. 1:19-26.
37. Matt. 25:31ff.
38. Coenobitic = *koino* + *bios*, common life.
39. 2 Cor. 2:6.

THE COUNCIL OF CHALCEDON, CANONS 3–4

Northwest Asia Minor, 451[40]

3. It has come to [the knowledge of] the holy synod that certain of those who are enrolled among the clergy have, through lust of gain, become hirers of other people's possessions, and make contracts pertaining to secular affairs, lightly esteeming the service of God, and slip into the houses of secular persons, whose property they undertake through covetousness to manage. Wherefore the great and holy synod decrees that henceforth no bishop, clergy, nor monk shall hire possessions, or engage in business, or occupy himself in worldly engagements, unless called by the law to the guardianship of minors, from which there is no escape; or unless the bishop of the city shall commit to him the care of ecclesiastical business, or of unprovided orphans or widows and of persons who stand especially in need of the church's help, through the fear of God. And if anyone shall hereafter transgress these decrees, he shall be subjected to ecclesiastical penalties.[41]

4. Let those who truly and sincerely lead the monastic life be counted worthy of a becoming honor; but, forasmuch as certain persons using the pretext of monasticism bring confusion both upon the churches and into political affairs by going about promiscuously in the cities, and at the same time seeking to establish monasteries for themselves; it is decreed that no one anywhere build or found a monastery or oratory contrary to the will of the bishop of the city; and that the monks in every city and district shall be subject to the bishop, and embrace a quiet course of life, and give themselves only to fasting and prayer, remaining permanently in the places in which they were set apart; and they shall meddle neither in ecclesiastical nor in secular affairs, nor leave their own monasteries to take part in such; unless, indeed, they should at any time through urgent necessity be appointed thereto by the bishop of the city. And no slave shall be received into any monastery to become a monk against the will of his master. And if anyone shall transgress this our judgment, we have decreed that he shall be excommunicated, that the name of God be not blasphemed. But the bishop of the city must make the needful provision for the monasteries.[42]

---

40. In 451, a Roman and German army stopped Attila the Hun at Châlons.

41. Cf. Elvira 19, 20. Plus ça change.

42. Monasticism produced its share of less than heroic figures, who could create serious problems within the church. In fact, mobs of monks played considerable roles at Chalcedon and other councils. Outsiders could also be hostile: see Libanius, Oration 30; Eunapius, *Lives of the Sophists* 6.11; and Rousseau (1978, ch. 1).

7

THE CAPPADOCIANS

Basil the Great
Selected Letters

Gregory Nazianzen
On the Death of His Father

These selected letters of Basil's (53, 54, 93, 270, 333, 334, 366) are from Deferrari (1926–34), vol. 4 of which contains his *To Adolescents on . . . Pagan Literature*. More useful than NPNF 2.8 are W. Clarke (1925) and Wagner (1950). The books by Fedwick cover many important aspects, and he has promised a full biography. See also Gregg (1975) and Constantelos (1981).

Gregory's *On the Death of His Father* (Oration 18.1, 2, 6, 15–16, 18, 20–28, 32, 36, 38) is taken from NPNF 2.7, the only extensive collection. Also profitable are Orations 1, 2 (the chief source for Chrysostom's and Gregory the Great's works on the priesthood; see ch. 9 and 10 below), 12, 37, 39, 40, and so on, and many of his letters, for example, 76, 182, 197, and those to Basil. Consult Gregg (1975) and Ruether (1969).

With regret, we can only make reference to Gregory Nyssen, for example, the introduction to his Catechetical Oration, the five homilies on the Lord's Prayer, the *Life of Moses*, and the *Life of Macrina*.

"Cappadocians" refers in particular to three great pastors and theologians from central Asia Minor: Basil the Great, Metropolitan of Caesarea (ca. 330–379); his childhood friend and co-worker Gregory Nazianzen (that is, of Nazianzus; ca. 330–ca. 390); and Basil's brother Gregory Nyssen (mid-330s to mid-390s). They represent, however, two families which greatly enriched Christian life and theology and which numbered many saints. Among

Nazianzen's family, besides his siblings, Caesarius and Gorgonia, we must recall his parents, Gregory, bishop of Nazianzus, and Nonna, and his cousin Amphilochius of Iconium. Basil and Gregory's brother Peter was a bishop; their sister, Macrina, was influential in molding their theology and dedication to a Christian life, and she was the third saint in the female line. Her grandmother, Macrina, was also a formidable woman.

Gregory and Basil were childhood friends and later they cemented their friendship during their education in Athens (still then the Oxford of antiquity), two Christian boys in a largely pagan atmosphere. They were trained in rhetoric and philosophy, toward careers in law or rhetoric. Basil began his Christian vocation first, through Macrina's influence, and visited some of the great monastic centers of Palestine and Egypt, and then invited Gregory to share his retirement.

Gregory, however, was the more truly retiring personality. He was constantly being called to action from withdrawal. He fled after his father coerced him into ordination (on his return he delivered his Oration 2, analyzing pastoral duties). Basil made him bishop of Sasima, to oppose political moves by Arian bishops, but he never resided there. He helped his father in Nazianzus and continued his duties after his death, but refused to follow his father as bishop. He was called from a monastery to aid the small Nicene party in Constantinople in 379, and his brilliant preaching began the Orthodox resurgence. Upon the Emperor Theodosius's arrival in 380, he was made bishop and presided over the great Council of Constantinople in 381. The politicking of the council was too much, however, and during it he resigned his office to return to Nazianzus. The most public of his qualities was his preaching, brilliant in form and solid and clear in content. His description of the conflict between his duties and his desires is the product of a deeply self-reflective soul. He was also a poet. His last will survives, leaving all to the "Catholic community of Nazianzus, for the benefit of the poor."

Basil was by instinct a man of action and filled the last twenty years of his life with any number of accomplishments in a variety of fields. He sponsored many public works, especially hospitals and orphanages. He reordered the church's administration and reformed its liturgy (the two great Byzantine liturgies are named after Basil and Chrysostom). All Orthodox monastic rules are based on

Basil's reforms. Besides being the architect of such changes, he was their master builder as well, for he was a powerful preacher and a champion of moral simplicity and rigor. He and Athanasius were the two great defenders of Nicene Orthodoxy when Arians controlled the imperial court and many major bishoprics. Through his letters, treatises, and tireless activity, he helped formulate the theological response and rallied his allies to withstand the great political pressures.

A millennium and a half have passed, but Basil has remained a popular hero in the Orthodox church, the defender of his faith and of his flock. It is quite proper that he is known as Basil the Great.

BASIL, SELECTED LETTERS

Letter 53, To the Chorepiscopi[1]

The enormity of the matter about which I write (which is why it is generally suspected and discussed) has filled my soul with grief; yet hitherto the thing has seemed to me incredible. So let what I write on the matter be received by anyone who has qualms of conscience as a medicine, by anyone who has no qualms as a precaution, and by anyone who is indifferent (I pray that none such may be found among you) as a solemn protest.

But what is it that I have in mind? The report is that some of you take money from candidates for ordination, and cover it up under the name of piety.[2] But that only makes the matter worse. For if anyone does an evil thing under the guise of good, he deserves a twofold punishment, because he not only does what is in itself not good, but also makes use of the good as a co-worker, so to speak, for the accomplishment of sin. If this be true, let it not happen in future, but be corrected; for we must say to anyone who accepts this money what the apostles said to the man who wanted to pay for participation in the Holy Spirit: "May your money perish with you."[3] For one who through ignorance wants to buy is less guilty than one who sells the gift of God. For the transaction has become a matter of business; and if you sell what you have received as a free gift, you will be

---

1. Common dates given for these letters are: 53, 54: 370; 93: 372; 270: 377; the others are unknown. Fedwick (1981) cautiously dates the first four in the period 370–378.

A chorepiscopus was bishop of a smaller, rural see, with limited authority and dependent on the metropolitan; see ODCC.

2. *Piety:* i.e., the money "proving" the candidate's piety. The sale of civil office was regular practice.

3. Acts 8:20.

deprived of all its grace, as if you yourself were sold to Satan. For you are
bringing the huckster's traffic into spiritual affairs, and into the church,
where we are entrusted with the body and blood of Christ. These things
must not be done in this way. I will tell you what the artifice is. They think
that they commit no sin, because they receive the money after and not
before the ordination. But to take is to take, whenever it happens.

Therefore, I beg you, abandon this way to revenue, or rather, this road to
hell. Do not pollute your hands with such earnings, and so make yourselves unworthy to perform the holy mysteries. But forgive me. I began as
not believing; but now I threaten as though convinced. If, after this letter of
mine, anyone do any such thing, he will withdraw from the altars of this
diocese and will seek a place where he may buy and sell the gift of God.
"For we and the churches of God have no such custom."[4]

One·word I will add, and then cease. These actions arise from covetousness; and covetousness is both the root of all evils and is called
idolatry.[5] Therefore do not honor idols above Christ for petty gain, nor yet,
on the other hand, imitate Judas, betraying for gain a second time Christ
who was once crucified for our sakes. For both the lands and the hands of
those who accept the fruits of such things shall be called Haceldama.[6]

Letter 54, To the Chorepiscopi

It gives me great pain that the canons of the Fathers have lately fallen
into neglect, and that all discipline has been banished from the churches. I
fear that, as this indifference proceeds, the affairs of the church will
gradually come to complete ruin. The practice that has long been followed
in God's churches was to accept subdeacons for the service of the church
only after a very careful investigation. Their conduct was inquired into in
every detail, to learn if they were not railers, or drunkards, or quick to
quarrel,[7] and whether they so controlled their youthful spirits as to be able
to achieve that "holiness without which no one shall see God."[8] Now
while this examination was conducted by priests and deacons living with
the candidates, these would then refer the matter to the chorepiscopi,
who, after receiving the votes of those who were in the strict sense of the

---

4. 1 Cor. 11:16.
5. 1 Tim. 6:10; Col. 3:5.
6. Acts 1:18-19.
7. Cf. 1 Cor. 5:11. It is not clear whether any specifically legislated canons, as opposed to a clear custom, were meant. Canons 9–10 of the Council of Antioch, and 20–25 of Laodicea are relevant. *Subdeacon:* the duties and rank of this order varied, especially between East and West; Basil here is apparently closer to a Latin under-standing. See *Teaching of the Apostles,* canon 5, p. 94. On testing, see Chrysostom, *On the Priesthood* 3.10, p. 168, and Cyprian, Ep. 67.2, p. 62.
8. Heb. 12:14.

word witnesses, and giving notice to their bishop, then enrolled the subdeacon as a member of the sacred orders.

But now you, in the first place, thrusting me aside, and not even consenting to refer such matters to me, have arrogated to yourselves the entire authority. In the second place, becoming careless in the matter, you have allowed priests and deacons, selecting whomsoever they pleased, without examining into their lives, through motives of partiality based either upon kinship or upon some other friendly relationship, to introduce into the church the unworthy. Consequently, though there are many numbered as subdeacons in every village, yet there is not one worthy to conduct the service at the altar, as you yourselves testify, since you have difficulty in finding candidates at the elections.

Therefore, since I perceive that the situation is already approaching the incurable, especially now that vast numbers are forcing themselves into the subdiaconate through fear of the conscription,[9] I have been compelled to resort to the renewal of the canons of the Fathers; and I bid you by this letter to send me the list of the subdeacons in each village, stating by whom each has been introduced, and what is his mode of life. Do you also keep the list in your own possession, so that your records may be compared with those deposited with me, and that no one may be able illegally to enter his own name at will. With this proviso, however, that if any of the names on the list have been introduced by priests after the first year of the indiction,[10] these persons are to be cast back among the laity. Let them all be examined by you anew; and if they are worthy, let them be accepted by your vote. Purge the church by excluding those who are unworthy, and henceforth examine and accept only worthy candidates; but do not enroll these others before you have referred them to us. Otherwise rest assured that anyone who has been received into the subdiaconate without my approval will be still a layperson.

Letter 93, To the Patrician, Caesaria, on Communion

And also to take communion every day, that is to say, to partake of the holy body and blood of Christ, is good and beneficial, since he himself clearly says: "He that eats my flesh, and drinks my blood, has everlasting life."[11] For who can doubt that sharing continually in the life is nothing else than living in many ways? We for our part, however, take communion four

---

9. *Conscription:* into the army, freedom from which was an early "privilege" granted to the clergy. Similar privileges were a common political tool, often abused.

10. *Indiction:* fifteen-year dating cycles; the previous first year would have begun in September, 372, or perhaps 357.

11. John 6:54. On home communion, see also Justin Martyr, *Apology* 1.85; Tertullian, *On Prayer* 19 and *To His Wife* 2.5; Cyprian, *On the Lapsed* 132; Jerome, Ep. 125.

times each week—on Sunday, on Wednesday, on Friday, and on Satur-
day—and on the other days only when there is a commemoration of a
saint.

On the question of a person being compelled, in times of persecution
when no priest or ministrant is present, to take communion with his own
hand, it is superfluous to point out that this is in no wise sinful, since long
custom has sanctioned this practice from the very force of circumstances.
For all who live the monastic life in the solitudes, where there is no priest,
keep the communion at home and partake of it from their own hands. At
Alexandria also and in Egypt, each person, even those belonging to the
laity, as a rule keeps the communion in his own home, and partakes of it
with his own hands when he so wishes. For when the priest has once
consummated the offering and has given it, one who has received it ought
confidently to believe that he is partaking of it, even as he has received it,
all at once, even when he partakes of it daily. So it is when the rite is
performed in the church also—the priest hands over the portion, and the
recipient in receiving it has complete right of possession, and by such right
raises it to his mouth with his own hand. It is, therefore, in respect of
authority, one and the same thing, whether a communicant receives a
single portion from the priest or many portions at once.

Letter 270, Without Address, concerning Rape[12]

I am greatly grieved that I do not find you either indignant over deeds
which are forbidden or able to understand that this rape which is going on
is an unlawful outrage and a tyranny against life itself and human existence, and an insult to free people. For I know that if you all had such an
opinion, nothing would have prevented this wicked custom from being
driven long ago out of our country. Therefore assume in the present
instance the zeal of a Christian, and be moved in a manner worthy of the
injustice. And as for the girl, wherever you find her, take her by all force
and restore her to her parents; and as for the man, debar him from the
prayers, and declare him excommunicated; and as for those who accompanied the man, according to the canon already published by us, debar
them with their whole household from the prayers for a period of three
years. And as for the village that received her who was raped, and kept her,
or even fought to keep her, put it also with all its people outside the
prayers; that all may learn, considering the ravager as a common foe like a
snake or any other wild beast, to pursue him accordingly and to champion
those who are wronged.

---

12. Kidnapping a woman to force marriage by bedding her was legal, if not generally smiled upon. Our society's ambiguous response to acquaintance rape is a
similar case. The canon is probably the thirtieth of Ep. 199. See canon 22, p. 109.

Letter 333,[13] To a Scribe

Words are by nature winged. On this account they require symbols—that when they are in flight the writer may attain their speed. Do you, then, my child, make your strokes perfect, and punctuate your passages to match them. For by a slight error a great saying has failed of its purpose, but by care on the part of the writer that which is said succeeds.

Letter 334, To a Calligraphist

Write straight and keep straightly to your lines; and let the hand neither mount upwards nor slide downhill. Do not force the pen to travel slant-wise, like the crab in Aesop; but proceed straight ahead, as if traveling along a carpenter's rule, which everywhere preserves the even course and eliminates all irregularity. For that which is slantwise is unbecoming, but that which is straight is a joy to those who see it, not permitting the eyes of those who read to bob up and down like well-sweeps. Something of the sort has happened to me when reading your writing. For since your lines rest ladderwise, when I had to pass from one to another I was obliged to lift my eyes to reach the beginning of the next line. And then when no sequence was evident at that point, I had to run back again and seek the order, retracing my steps and "following the furrow," just as they say Theseus did the thread of Ariadne. Therefore write straight and do not confuse our mind by your oblique and slanting writing.

Letter 366, Ps.-Basil to Urbicius, a Monk, on Continence[14]

You do well in making strict rules for us, that we may see not only continence but also its fruit. Now its fruit is communion with God. For to

---

13. This and the next short letter cover aspects of necessary secretarial care. Secretarial office, a path of advancement through the civil service, was an important career. The former letter may cover tachygraphy (ancient stenography) and its correct transcription. The latter addressee let his handwriting curve down as it crossed the page, so that the reader could lose his place. Well-sweeps are the long levering poles with buckets, still used in wells in many places.

14. Ep. 366 is spurious and of uncertain date.

Continence, *enkrateia* in Greek, concerns self-control, or the withstanding of passion. The word *passions* in early Christian writings has a specific meaning very often misunderstood by the modern reader. It has nothing to do with intensity of feeling. *Passionless* does not imply flaccid or uninterested. Rather, passions were seen as coercive feelings that could lead one to do something clearly wrong against one's will. An addiction would be a passion, as would a quick temper poorly controlled. It is in this sense that freedom from passion was considered a great virtue, and an attribute of God. God's impassibility means that God cannot be coerced. Chrysostom, *On the Priesthood* 5.8, below p. 181, states this clearly. (Cf. Clement, *Who Is the Rich Person?* 34, p. 31.) The "denial of the body," then, was not dualistic, but presumed a person's freedom of choice, between choosing to prize things bound to rot, and choosing to prize God, who can preserve one from corruption.

Denial of body and confession to God: the two actions are opposites, as illustrated in John 1:20. Cyprian, *On the Dress of Virgins*, above, pp. 52ff., makes similar points.

be free from corruption is to partake of God, just as the state of corruption is communion with the world. For continence is denial of body and confession to God. It departs from everything mortal, having as it were a body in the Spirit of God; and it causes us to mingle with God, having neither rivalry nor envy. For anyone who loves a body envies another, but one who has not brought the disease of corruption into his heart is strengthened thereafter for every labor, although dying in body, yet living in incorruption. And to me, as I strive to learn the matter thoroughly, God seems to be continence, because he desires nothing, but has everything in himself; and he strives after nothing, nor has he passion in his eyes, neither in his ears, but being without need, he is in every way satisfied. Desire is a disease of the soul, whereas its health is continence.

But we should not look upon continence as of only one kind, in regard to sexual things, for example, but also in relation to all the other things which the soul wrongly desires, not being satisfied with the bare necessities for it: thus envy arises on account of gold, and countless wrongful deeds on account of other desires. Both refraining from drunkenness is continence, and avoidance of bursting through overeating. Both the control of the body is continence, and exercising mastery over evil thoughts. How often has the mind, neither good nor true, disturbed the soul and distracted the heart to consider many things vainly? Certainly continence sets the soul free, at one and the same time healing its ailments and being a source of power to it; for it does not teach sobriety, but furnishes it.

Continence is a grace of God. Jesus was continence made manifest, becoming light and without weight on both land and sea. For neither did the earth feel his weight, nor the sea, but just as he walked upon the sea, so did he not weigh down the earth. For if from a state of corruption comes death, and from being free from corruption comes freedom from death, then Jesus wrought divinity, not mortality. He ate and drank in a peculiar way, not excreting his food; so great a power within him was his continence that his nourishment was not corrupted in him, since he himself had no corruption.

If continence exist in us in but a slight degree, we are superior to all things. For we have heard that even angels, being incontinent, have been cast down from heaven, because of lust. For they were convicted, they did not descend of themselves; for what business had this disease of incontinence in heaven unless there was some competent eye to detect it? It is on this account that I said: "If we possess continence in but a slight degree, and do not love the world but the life above, we shall be found there, whither we direct our mind's eye." For it seems that this is the eye which can see invisible things. And indeed we have the saying: "The mind sees and the mind hears." These things, though they seem to you little, I have written out at length, because each expression is a thought, and I know that when you have read them you will perceive this.[15]

GREGORY NAZIANZEN, ON THE DEATH OF HIS FATHER

Or. 18

1. O man of God,[16] and faithful servant,[17] and steward of the mysteries of God,[18] and man of desires[19] of the Spirit: for thus scripture speaks of persons advanced and lofty, superior to visible things.

2. . . . . Are you come to inspect us, or to seek for the pastor, or to take the oversight of the flock? You find us no longer in existence, but for the most part having passed away with him, unable to bear with the place of our affliction, especially now that we have lost our skillful steersman, our light of life, to whom we looked to direct our course as the blazing beacon of salvation above us: he has departed with all his excellence, and all the power of pastoral organization, which he had gathered in a long time, full of days and wisdom, and crowned, to use the words of Solomon, with the hoary head of glory.[20]

6. Even before he was of our fold, he was ours. His character made him one of us. For, as many of our own are not with us, whose life alienates them from the common body, so, many of those without are on our side, whose character anticipates their faith, and need only the name of that which indeed they possess. My father was one of these, an alien shoot, but inclined by his life towards us. He was so far advanced in self-control, that he became at once most beloved and most modest, two qualities difficult to combine. What greater and more splendid testimony can there be to his justice than his exercise of a position second to none in the state, without enriching himself by a single farthing. . . . It was as a reward for such conduct, I think, that he attained to the faith.[21]

---

15. This letter quotes silently from Clement's *Stromateis* 3.1, 7, about the types of continence, the angels' fall, and Jesus' no-waste digestion. The last, in fact, Clement explicitly quoted with approval from Valentinus, the Christian Gnostic "heretic"— an interesting history of traditions.

16. Josh. 14:6. Addressed to Basil.

17. Num. 12:7.

18. 1 Cor. 4:1.

19. Dan. 9:23 (LXX).

20. Prov. 16:31. This description, florid to modern tastes but normal to its time, shows how social organization was deemed crucial to civilization, and that the role of patron (here, the bishop) was the linchpin of that organization.

21. Jerome spoke of "our Seneca." The quest for virtue was prized by some, but not by many, and Christianity had no monopoly on it: the pagan rhetor Libanius complained that the Christian emperor's court suffered from spending too much

15. .... For he was most consistent with himself and his early days, and kept in harmony his life before the priesthood with its excellence, and his life after it with what had gone before.[22]

16. He received a woodland and rustic church, the pastoral care and oversight of which had not been bestowed from a distance, but it had been cared for by one of his predecessors of admirable and angelic disposition, and a more simple man than our present rulers of the people; but, after he had been speedily taken to God, it had, in consequence of the loss of its leader, for the most part grown careless and run wild; accordingly, he at first strove without harshness to soften the habits of the people, both by words of pastoral knowledge, and by setting himself before them as an example, like a spiritual statue, polished into the beauty of all excellent conduct.[23] He next, by constant meditation on the divine words, though a late student of such matters, gathered together so much wisdom within a short time that he was in no wise excelled by those who had spent the greatest toil upon them, and received this special grace from God, that he became the father and teacher of orthodoxy—not, like our modern intellectuals, yielding to the spirit of the age, nor defending our faith by indefinite and sophistical language, as if they had no fixity of faith, or were adulterating the truth; but, he was more pious than those who possessed rhetorical power, more skilled in rhetoric than those who were upright in mind; or rather, while he took the second place as an orator, he surpassed all in piety.[24]

---

money on coiffures. A number of goals motivated people to become Christian: some to do good, others to become famous; some to fight evil, some to flee evil, and some to be protected from evil. Is the church to judge among motivations? How might one be led from "a good first step" to "a more perfect way"? (Augustine discussed this question in his pamphlet *On Catechizing the Uninstructed*, found in NPNF 1.3 or ACW 2.) How might the church react when attractions that once brought people to the church now draw them somewhere else?

The testimony to Gregory is impressive, since the main purpose of high imperial office was to gain fame (Greek, *doxa*) and wealth. Various degrees of "influence peddling" were standard: one aspect of the theory of friendship was the regulation of patronage and favors. See the classical discussion in Plutarch's Moralia, *Praecepta gerendae reipublicae*, in vol. 10 of the Loeb.

22. I.e., his progress in virtue did not cease when he was baptized, nor when ordained: he did not rest on his oars.

23. Pastor as exemplar: see above, p. 70, on Athanasius.

24. Rhetorical power was greatly prized, so that the line between the skill's serving the congregation and the skill as an end in itself could easily be lost. This danger attends any skill for or model of ministry: oratory or managerial; intellect or social work. See Chrysostom, *On the Priesthood* 5.1, 8, pp. 177, 180.

Rhetoric was the ancient equivalent to the Madison Avenue advertising game, and the sophistic goal was primarily to convince. From the church's beginning, however, it was realized that the Christian faith should not be presented as dependent on a human skill like rhetoric. Beginning with Paul's Corinthian correspon-

18. To give a proof of what I say [that he was "like the great Noah"]. When a tumult of the overzealous part of the church was raised against us,[25] and we had been decoyed by a document and artful terms into association with evil, he alone was believed to have an unwounded mind, and a soul unstained by ink, even when he had been imposed upon in his simplicity, and failed from his guilelessness of soul to be on his guard against guile. He it was alone, or rather first of all, who by his zeal for piety reconciled to himself and the rest of the church the faction opposed to us, which was the last to leave us, the first to return, owing to both their reverence for the man and the purity of his doctrine, so that the serious storm in the churches was allayed, and the hurricane reduced to a breeze under the influence of his prayers and admonitions; while, if I may make a boastful remark, I was his partner in piety and activity, aiding him in every effort on behalf of what is good, accompanying and running beside him, and being permitted on this occasion to contribute a very great share of the toil. Here my account of these matters, which is a little premature, must come to an end. . . .

20. Who was more anxious than he for the common weal? Who more wise in domestic affairs, since God, who orders all things in due variation, assigned to him a house and suitable fortune? Who was more sympathetic in mind, more bounteous in hand, towards the poor, that most dishonored portion of the nature to which equal honor is due? For he actually treated his own property as if it were another's, of which he was but the steward, relieving poverty as far as he could, and expending not only his super-fluities but his necessities—a manifest proof of love for the poor, giving a

---

dence (1 Cor. 2:1-7; 2 Cor. 4:7, "But we have this treasure in earthen vessels, to show that the transcendent power belongs to God, and not to us"), quite specific claims were made about the language of scripture, which is often so rough and artless. The Bible is so poor in style on purpose, because a rhetorical brilliance would prove only a source of distraction and pride. Many patristic writers commented on this, including Origen, *On First Principles* 4.1.7–4.2.3; Augustine, *On Catechizing the Uninstructed* 9 (13) and *Confessions* 3.5; and Chrysostom, *On the Priesthood* 4.7. (Jerome's dream, Ep. 22.30, is instructive.) The point remains valid today, for there are many who are ready to tell the church how to increase its membership through more effective advertisement and media involvement, but the church's job is to preach the truth. It is not, however, a simple opposition: these writers who critiqued the role of rhetoric were all fine stylists. The question is one of clarity of focus and simplicity of heart.
25. Factionalism was rife, and the frequent attempts to find compromise solutions often led to compromising situations, especially since the theological vocabulary was still fluid and liable both to honest misapprehension and to duplicity. The particular incident here was the Council of Rimini (359, of dubious reputation), which published a creed calling the Word *homoiousios*, and not *homoousios*. While it is clear, on reflection, that the former is a useless term, it is equally clear how some might have seen it as a possible compromise.

portion, not only to seven, according to the injunction of Solomon,[26] but if an eighth came forward, not even in his case being niggardly, but more pleased to dispose of his wealth than we know others are to acquire it; taking away the yoke and election (which means, as I think, all meanness in testing as to whether the recipient is worthy or not) and word of murmuring[27] in benevolence. This is what most people do: they give indeed, but without that readiness, which is a greater and more perfect thing than the mere offering. For he thought it much better to be generous even to the undeserving for the sake of the deserving, than from fear of the undeserving to deprive those who were deserving. And this seems to be the duty of casting our bread upon the waters,[28] since it will not be swept away or perish in the eyes of the just Investigator, but will arrive yonder where all that is ours is laid up, and will meet with us in due time, even though we think it not.

21. But what is best and greatest of all, his magnanimity was accompanied by freedom from ambition. Its extent and character I will proceed to show. In considering their wealth to be common to all, and in liberality in bestowing it, he and his consort rivaled each other in their struggles after excellence; but he intrusted the greater part of this bounty to her hand, as being a most excellent and trusty steward of such matters. What a woman she is! Not even the Atlantic Ocean, or if there be a greater one, could meet her drafts upon it. So great and so boundless is her love of liberality.

22. . . . Who was more under the divine guidance in admitting candidates to the sanctuary, or in resenting dishonor done to it, or in cleansing the holy table with awe from the unholy? Who with such unbiased judgment, and with the scales of justice, either decided a suit,[29] or hated vice, or honored virtue, or promoted the most excellent? Who was so compassionate for the sinner, or sympathetic towards those who were running well? Who better knew the right time for using the rod and the staff,[30] yet relied most upon the staff? Whose eyes were more upon the faithful in the land,[31] especially upon those who, in the monastic and unwedded life, have despised the earth and the things of earth?

23. Who did more to rebuke pride and foster lowliness? And that in no assumed or external way, as most of those who now make profession of

---

26. Eccles. 11:2.
27. Isa. 58:9 (LXX).
28. Eccles. 11:1.
29. *Decided a suit:* Constantine empowered bishops to hear civil suits, a decision by which the church gained standing and he gained a new, loyal civil service. What might the church have lost? See Chrysostom, *On the Priesthood* 3.17, below p. 175, and Ps.-Clement, Hom. 3.64, above p. 89.
30. Ps. 23:4.
31. Ps. 101:6.

virtue ... For his lowliness was no matter of dress, but of spiritual disposition, nor was it expressed by a bent neck, or lowered voice, or downcast
look, or length of beard, or close-shaven head, or measured gait, which
can be adopted for a while, but are very quickly exposed, for nothing
which is affected can be permanent. No! he was ever most lofty in life,
most lowly in mind; inaccessible in virtue, most accessible in intercourse.
His dress had in it nothing remarkable, avoiding equally magnificence and
sordidness, while his internal brilliancy was supereminent. . . .[32]

He held that doing and saying everything by which fame among externs
might be won, is the characteristic of the politician, whose chief happiness
is found in the present life: but that the spiritual and Christian person
should look to one object alone, salvation, and think much of what may
contribute to this, but detest as of no value what does not; and accordingly
despise what is visible, but be occupied with interior perfection alone, and
estimate most highly whatever promotes his own improvement, and at-
tracts others through himself to that which is supremely good.

24. But what was most excellent and most characteristic, though least
generally recognized, was his simplicity, and freedom from guile and
resentment. For among those of ancient and modern days, each is supposed to have had some special success, as each chanced to have received
from God some particular virtue: Job unconquered patience in misfortune,[33] Moses[34] and David[35] meekness, Samuel prophecy, seeing into the
future,[36] Phineas zeal,[37] for which he has a name, Peter and Paul eagerness in preaching,[38] the sons of Zebedee magniloquence, whence also
they were entitled sons of thunder.[39] But why should I enumerate them all,
speaking as I do among those who know this? Now the specially dis-
tinguishing mark of Stephen and of my father was the absence of malice.

---

32. *Avoiding equally:* Many have said that it was not ostentatious "poverty," but
moderation that was true freedom from ostentatious wealth, and Aristippus's reply
to Diogenes the Cynic (D. Laertius 2.68) was proverbial. What Gregory described
was the stereotype of the philosopher's mein. There was also Aesop's fable about the
apes dressed as men, who mimicked polite behavior correctly, until someone threw
them food. The satirist Lucian often parodied those whose obvious disdain of
wealth was but tinplate. Some sayings among the *Verba Seniorum* weigh the conflicting claims of fasting, and hospitality and humility: hospitality and humility win.

33. Job 1:21. *Some particular virtue:* This important hermeneutical principle, that
biblical characters each personified some great virtue, entered Christian exegesis
chiefly through Origen from Philo of Alexandria; see, e.g., Gregory Nyssen's *Life of
Moses*, and Gregory the Great, *Pastoral Rule* 1.11, below p. 199.

34. Num. 12:3.

35. Ps. 132:1 (LXX).

36. 1 Sam. 9:9.

37. Num. 25:7.

38. Gal. 2:7.

39. Mark 3:17.

For not even when in peril did Stephen hate his assailants, but was stoned while praying for those who were stoning him[40] as a disciple of Christ, on whose behalf he was allowed to suffer, and so, in his longsuffering, bearing for God a nobler fruit than his death: my father, in allowing no interval between assault and forgiveness, so that he was almost robbed of pain itself by the speed of pardon.

25. ... My father kept no grudge against those who provoked him, indeed he was absolutely uninfluenced by anger, ... except when he had been prepared and armed and set in hostile array against that which was advancing to injure him. So that this sweet disposition of his would not, as the saying goes, have been stirred by tens of thousands. For the wrath which he had was not like that of the serpent,[41] smoldering within, ready to defend itself, eager to burst forth, and longing to strike back at once on being disturbed; but like the sting of the bee, which does not bring death with its stroke; while his kindness was superhuman. The wheel and scourge were often threatened, and those who could apply them stood near; and the danger ended in being pinched on the ear, patted on the face, or buffeted on the temple: thus he mitigated the threat.[42]

... How could anyone be more conclusively proved to be good, and worthy to offer the gifts to God? For often, instead of being himself roused, he made excuses for anyone who assailed him, blushing for another's faults as if they had been his own.

26. The result of this was most unusual, not that he was the only one to give rebuke, but the only one to be both loved and admired by those whom he reproved, from the victory which his goodness gained over warmth of feeling. ... Indeed, a forgiving spirit often has great saving power, checking the wrongdoer by the sense of shame, and bringing him back from fear to love, a far more secure state of mind.

27. Such and so remarkable being his gentleness, did he yield the palm to others in industry and practical virtue? By no means. Gentle as he was, he possessed, if anyone did, an energy corresponding to his gentleness. For although, for the most part, the two virtues of benevolence and severity are at variance and opposed to each other, the one being gentle but without practical qualities, the other practical but unsympathetic, in his case there was a wonderful combination of the two, his action being as energetic as that of a severe person, but combined with gentleness; while his readiness to yield seemed unpractical but was accompanied with

---

40. Acts 7:59.
41. Ps. 58:4 (LXX).
42. Corporal punishment was fierce and ubiquitous, and not normally an idle threat.

energy, in his patronage, his freedom of speech, and every kind of official duty.... Such being his birth, such his exercise of the priestly office, such the reputation which he won at the hands of all, what wonder if he was thought worthy of the miracles by which God establishes true religion?

28. One of the wonders which concern him was that he suffered from sickness and bodily pain. But what wonder is it for even the holy to be distressed, either for the cleansing of their clay, slight though it may be, or a touchstone of virtue and test of philosophy, or for the education of the weaker, who learn from their example to be patient instead of giving way under their misfortunes?

32. But I imagine that some of those who have had an accurate knowledge of his life must have been for a long while wondering why we ... postponed the mention of the difficulties of his times, against which he conspicuously arrayed himself. The first ... evil of our day, was the emperor who apostatized from God and from reason, and thought it a small matter to conquer the Persians, but a great one to subject to himself the Christians;[43] and so, together with the demons who led and prevailed upon him, he failed in no form of impiety, but by means of persuasions, threats, and sophistries, strove to draw others to him, and even added to his various artifices the use of force....

Who can be found who more utterly despised or defeated him? One sign, among many others, of his contempt, is the mission to our sacred buildings of the police and their commissary, with the intention of taking ... possession of them: he had attacked many others, and came hither with like intent, demanding the surrender of the temple according to the imperial decree, but was so far from succeeding in any of his wishes that, had he not speedily given way before my father, ... he would have had to retire with his feet mangled, with such wrath and zeal did the priest boil against him in defense of the shrine. And who had a manifestly greater share in bringing about his end, both in public, by the prayers and united supplications which he directed against the accursed one, without regard to the [dangers of] the time; and in private, arraying against him his nightly armory, of sleeping on the ground, by which he wore away his aged and tender frame, and of tears, with whose fountains he watered the ground for almost a whole year, directing these practices to the Searcher of hearts alone, while he tried to escape our notice, in his retiring piety of which I have spoken. And he would have been utterly unobserved, had I not once suddenly rushed into his room, and noticing the tokens of his lying upon

---

43. The Emperor Julian, 361–363, who was killed in battle against the Persians outside Ctesiphon.

the ground, inquired of his attendants what they meant, and so learned the mystery of the night.

36. The things of the Spirit were exactly known to the man of the Spirit, and he felt that he must take up no submissive position, nor side with factions and prejudices which depend upon favor rather than upon God, but must make the advantage of the church and the common salvation his sole object. Accordingly he wrote, gave advice, strove to unite the people and the clergy, whether ministering in the sanctuary or not, gave his testimony, his decision and his vote, even in his absence, and assumed, in virtue of his gray hairs, the exercise of authority among strangers no less than among his own flock. At last, since it was necessary that the consecration should be canonical,[44] and there was lacking one of the proper number of bishops for the proclamation, he tore himself from his couch, exhausted as he was by age and disease, and bravely went to the city, or rather was borne, with his body dead though just breathing, persuaded that, if anything were to happen to him, this devotion would be a noble winding-sheet. Hereupon once more there was a prodigy, not unworthy of credit. He received strength from his toil, new life from his zeal, presided at the function, took his place in the conflict, enthroned the bishop, and was conducted home, no longer borne upon a bier, but in a divine ark. His longsuffering, over whose praises I have already lingered, was in this case further exhibited. For his colleagues were annoyed at the shame of being overcome, and at the public influence of the old man, and allowed their annoyance to show itself in abuse of him; but such was the strength of his endurance that he was superior even to this, finding in modesty a most powerful ally, and refusing to bandy abuse with them. For he felt that it would be a terrible thing, after really gaining the victory, to be vanquished by the tongue. In consequence, he so won upon them by his long-suffering, that, when time had lent its aid to his judgment, they exchanged their annoyance for admiration, and knelt before him to ask his pardon, in shame for their previous conduct, and flinging away their hatred, submitted to him as their patriarch, lawgiver, and judge.

38. In general, he was a man of great endurance, and superior to his robe of flesh: but during the pain of his last sickness, a serious addition to the risks and burdens of old age, his weakness was common to him and all others; but this fitting sequel to the other marvels, so far from being common, was peculiarly his own. He was at no time free from the anguish

---

44. It was the consecration of Basil to succeed Eusebius as bishop of Caesarea (not the church historian, who was Eusebius of Caesarea Maritima in Palestine). Basil, having assisted Eusebius for several years, was the obvious choice, but, because of political pressures and favoritisms, he needed allies.

of pain, but often in the day, sometimes in the hour, his only relief was the liturgy, to which the pain yielded, as if to an edict of banishment. At last, after a life of almost a hundred years, exceeding David's limit of our age,[45] forty-five of these, the average life of a person, having been spent in the priesthood, he brought it to a close in a good old age. And in what manner? With the words and forms of prayer, leaving behind no trace of vice, and many recollections of virtue.

---

45. Ps. 90:10.

8

THE LATIN
TRIUMVIRATE

Ambrose
On the Duties of the Clergy

Our selections from *On the Duties of the Clergy* are taken from
NPNF 2.10, which contains *On Repentance* and Ep. 63, both quite
relevant. Ambrose's work *On Tobit* (Zucker, 1933) attacked usury
and avarice, as did *On Naboth* (Vasey, 1982; see 1 Kings 21). Several
other letters are helpful (Beyenka, 1968[2], FoC 26, is complete).
Two important contemporary views of Ambrose are the biography
by his secretary, Paulinus, written at Augustine's request (Lacy,
1952); and Augustine's own recollections in the *Confessions*, books
5–8. P. Brown (1967, ch. 8) traces Ambrose's powerful influence;
F. Homes-Dudden (1935) gives a full, if old-fashioned, account;
whereas Monachino (1973) focuses on pastoral aspects.

Ambrose, Augustine, and Jerome, along with Gregory the
Great, are reckoned the four Latin Doctors of the Church, and the
very basic influence of Ambrose on Augustine, the dialogue of
Augustine and Jerome, and their combined influences on Gregory
made them a four-square foundation to the medieval church's life
and thought.

Ambrose was born in Trier about 339, and his father, who died
young, was the prefect of Gaul. Ambrose's prestigious rhetorical
and legal education in Rome set him along a similar career, and in
about 370 he became the civil governor of Aemilia-Liguria. Its
capital was Milan, which was also an imperial residence. When
Auxentius, the imperially appointed Arian bishop of twenty years,
died in 374, riots over his successor began between the Catholic
local majority and the Arian imperial court and Arian Gothic army.
Ambrose moved to quell the riots, but found himself a candidate,

put forward by the Catholics and acceptable to the court. Finally he was prevailed upon to take up the office. He was, however, still a catechumen, as was usual for Christians in government, so he had to be baptized and ordained quickly before his installation. He gave all his cash and even his land to the church, took up an ascetic discipline, and began intensive biblical and theological instruction with Simplicianus, an influential Catholic intellectual.

Ambrose took these episcopal aspects—the administrative, financial, moral, and scholastic—very seriously. Besides his local and regional duties, he was active in imperial affairs, working to forge an ideology of the state aiding the church to oppose pagan, Arian, and Jewish foes. In part through his own persuasiveness and commanding personality, he several times enforced his episcopal authority even over the emperor's authority. He curbed exploitation of the populace, furthered charitable works, and wrote passionately on personal and official morality. Through his diligent work with Simplicianus, he gained and put to work a command of the Bible, especially the Old Testament, informed by Greek theological and philosophical currents drawn largely from Origen and Plotinus. It was his learned and eloquent preaching that led Augustine, after leaving the Manichees, to reconsider Christianity as an intellectually viable way of life. Returning to Milan from an episcopal election, Ambrose fell sick, and two months later he died in Milan in 397.

Some initial remarks about our selection are in order. Ambrose modeled the content and form of his *On the Duties of the Clergy* directly on Cicero's thoroughly Stoic *On Offices* (de Officiis), modifying and blending them with much Christian and biblical material. Both are divided into three books on, respectively, what is virtuous, what is advantageous, and how to act when these two conflict. Each author began from the four cardinal virtues of Plato: prudence, justice, fortitude, and temperance. Ambrose drew so heavily on Cicero that he has been called a plagiarist, as our notes witness. Ambrose, however, pushed beyond Stoic ethics in important places, adding an eschatological motivation and emphasizing stricter ascetic and charitable disciplines. It is an instructive study to see how Ambrose copied or developed his sources. Cicero (and Seneca as well) is widely available, and *On Offices* and *On Friendship* are in the Loeb Cicero vols. 20–21. Hagendahl (1958, 3.2) sets out in detail the case for Ambrose as plagiarist (not only a modern view: Jerome called him a crow decked in peacock feathers for swiping from Origen's commentary on Luke). Two other interesting comparisons are those with the monastic moral material (e.g., the *Verba Seniorum*) and especially with Clement of Alexandria's *Stromateis*. What specific duties are enjoined? What reasons and motives are adduced?

That Ambrose's Christian ethics are stricter than Cicero's Stoic ethics raises a historical dilemma for the church. A.H.M. Jones (1964, p. 979) noted that during the period when great numbers of people were flocking to join the church and when the church had so many great moral preachers, such as Chrysostom, Basil, Ambrose, and Augustine, "the general standards of conduct . . . have remained in general static, and in some respects have sunk." If so much of Christian ideology dwelt on urging, demanding the choice of a moral life, why can we not see its effects? Jones suggests that an unreachably high, self-defeating standard was set, which is likely to be part of the reason. In part, too, the conflict may reflect competing understandings of what Christianity provided: for some, a moral call to virtue; for others, a patron's protection against evil. Greer (1989) studies a similar conflict between freedom and power. It is a fascinating and disturbing conundrum.

Yet another, more modern point emerges. One might call Stoic charity haughty: it was understood as the superior's largess. Our authors (see pp. 19 and 31 for examples, but contrast p. 89) tried to inculcate a humbler, gospel-inspired understanding: since wealth is God's largesse, the rich are required to deliver God's gifts to the poor. They owe the poor, and their charity redounds to no one's glory but God's. Since the Enlightenment, however, the educated have grown up reading more in Cicero and Seneca than in patristic writers, which is evident in Western theories of the duties of welfare. The common assumption is that those with the funds, public or private, are the superiors, and so their duties include the prerogatives to decide the management and goals of charity. An example highlights the difference: one who passes a beggar on the street might debate whether one should give the person money, lest it be misused or perhaps could be put to better use; that is, one must judge the beggar. According to Christian ideology, this is not an allowable question. One must both give to the specific beggar, judging not, as well as treat systemic problems. This position is uncomfortable and problematic, but it is the gospel's word, a word followed by the church's moral leaders during its first centuries.

Augustine
Letter 213

Letter 213, dated September 26, 426, is taken from NPNF 1.1. Augustine is extensively translated in many volumes in the major series and in many individual volumes. The standard and classic biography is P. Brown (1967). Kevane (1964) is relevant. There are many good short appreciations of Augustine: Marrou (1957) has also a number of photographs and a nice selection of short passages, and Pellegrino (1986) is a fine collection.

To begin to do justice to Augustine's place as pastor to the Latin church would have required the major portion of this volume. On the other hand, many others have done him some manner of justice, and his *Confessions* must rank as by far the most frequently read patristic work. We have, therefore, chosen to give a short, unusual glimpse into Augustine's life and to point the reader to some of his many important relevant works. These are readily available, often in several translations: the *Confessions*, of course; the *Enchiridion on Faith, Hope, and Love*, a charming handbook; his pamphlet on catechetical method, *On Catechizing the Uninstructed; On True Religion; On Faith and Works; On the Christian Struggle; On Christian Doctrine* (book 4 covers Bible study); NPNF 1.3, which has works on various moral topics; *On the Gift of Perseverance;* and *On the Sermon on the Mount.* Many of his sermons and letters are interesting. Among the sermons, for example, are 53, on Matt. 5:3, 8; 69–70, on Matt. 11:28; and 137–138, on John 10 and "I am the Good Shepherd"; and all of Pellegrino (1986). Among the letters, see 21, reflections on his first experience of the difficulties of the ministry; 78 and 122, to his congregation at Hippo; 130, on prayer; 211, to his sister's convent; and 245, on ornaments and amulets.

Augustine was born at Thagaste in 354 and died in 430 in Hippo Regius, some fifty miles distant. Still, he managed to internalize the crucial elements of North African, Latin, and Greek Christianity and to synthesize them, but according to his own distinctive frame of mind. His fertile mind and practical skills were fully exercised by a broad range of opportunities and oppositions:

studying Bible with his colleague Jerome; gaining command of platonizing Christian philosophical theology from Ambrose and Simplicianus; opposing the dualistic fatalism of Manichaeism, the faith of his youth; opposing the vigorous schismatic Donatist church and the quick spread of Pelagian anthropology; and formulating a theory of history to answer pagan critiques that Christianity was causing the empire's collapse. Out of the variety of his duties and works, he formed a coherent worldview that has guided the religious life and thought of Europe ever since.

There is, however, a simple synthesis of his pastoral theology, a touchstone to which he constantly returned: "You shall love the Lord your God with all your heart, and with all your soul, and with all your mind. This is the great and first commandment. And a second is like it: You shall love your neighbor as yourself."

Jerome
Letter 52.1–9, 11–12, 14–17

The portions of Letter 52 (from 394, to Nepotian on the disciplined life) are from NPNF 2.6. The most relevant works are among Jerome's letters; several genres pertain. Others on the ascetic life include the famous Letter 22, the similar 130, from an older and wiser man, and 125. 77 is the eulogy for Fabiola and 13 began a reconciliation with his aunt. Letters of consolation include 118 and 60, to Heliodorus on the death of our Nepotian—sadly, only two years after Jerome wrote Ep. 52 to him. Sections of his homilies are helpful, for example, sermon 95, on obedience (Ewald, 1966). The standard biography is Kelly (1975). See Adams (1971), Hagendahl's works, and Rousseau (1978) on their respective topics. E. Clark (1982[2]) has very little on Jerome, and much more could be written on this complex of issues.

Jerome was born in 331 to a Christian, if not fervent, family in Stridon, near Aquileia. He took to his studies well, gaining extensive learning and a great lucid Latin style. Little is known about him before his pilgrimage to the East in 372, but his movement toward his scholarly ascetic vocation was gradual: a student's varied life in Rome; a time at the court in Trier; and a period of studied retirement with a small Christian circle in Aquileia. Jerome spent about a decade in Antioch and with the hermits in the surrounding desert; here the major traits of his life took shape. He perfected his

Greek and learned Hebrew, for biblical studies; he developed his ascetical ideas; and he practiced his polemical skills with deadly (and alienating) effect. He returned to Rome, 382–385, where his scholarship was encouraged by Pope Damasus and where the circle of learned, ascetic, aristocratic women (among them Marcella, Eustochium, and especially Paula) formed, to whom Jerome was, as it were, a chaplain/tutor. He was a bitter foe of heresy and especially of proud, uncharitable laxity, but his acerbity gained him enemies. After Damasus's death Jerome had to leave Rome. He settled in Bethlehem, not too distant from the great library at Caesarea, where he led a monastery sponsored by Paula, who led her own women's monastery nearby. His exegetical work was built on technical and philological skill and learning rivaled only by Origen's. Much of his exegesis and Bible translation came from this period, along with voluminous correspondence and a series of charming lives of desert saints. He died in 420.

Jerome was a priest and had a clear vocation, but it was never especially to parish work. His scholarly work and ascetic bent paralleled the career of Origen. His attraction to the coenobitic life shows one option of a choice intensely debated in the church, whether one took a road into active service, usually to the priesthood and episcopate, or whether one fled the world's distractions and sought to live simply in obedience. A spectrum of responses can be seen among committed Christians. Ambrose was born to service; Chrysostom and Augustine desired quiet and supported communities, but their senses of duty were too clear; Basil and Gregory's friendship illustrates the tensions well; and the problems attending both options were often discussed among the *Verba Seniorum*. Jerome argued the merits of the retired community in Letter 14, to his friend Heliodorus, who had returned to clerical and later episcopal tasks. These tensions have never been resolved, but they seem to be fertile tensions, each way aiding the other, somewhat like a garden and its mulch pile. They have led, however, to problems in developing theories of ordination and vocation. The Orthodox tradition has long tended to keep the parish and its worship at the center of its priestly thought. Catholic and Protestant thought on who should be ordained to do what is better called flexible than coherent. There remain problems for the church and the individual when the vocation is plain but the office is not.

AMBROSE, ON THE DUTIES OF THE CLERGY

Book 1

1.1. I think I shall not seem to be taking too much on myself, if, in the midst of my children, I yield to my desire to teach, seeing that the master of humility himself has said: "Come, children, hearken unto me: I will teach you the fear of the Lord."[1] Wherein one may observe both the humility and the grace of his reverence for God. For in saying "the fear of the Lord," which seems to be common to all, he has described the chief mark of reverence for God. As, however, fear itself is the beginning of wisdom and the source of blessedness—for they that fear the Lord are blessed[2]—he has plainly marked himself out as the teacher for instruction in wisdom, and the guide to the attainment of blessedness.

2. We therefore, being anxious to imitate his reverence for God, and not without justification in dispensing grace, deliver to you as to children those things which the Spirit of Wisdom has imparted to him, and which have been made clear to us through him, and learned by sight and by example. For we can no longer now escape from the duty of teaching which the needs of the priesthood have laid upon us, though we tried to avoid it: "For God gave some, apostles; and some, prophets; and some, evangelists; and some, pastors and teachers."[3]

3. I do not therefore claim for myself the glory of the apostles (for who can do this save those whom the Son of God himself has chosen?); nor the grace of the prophets, nor the virtue of the evangelists, nor the cautious care of the pastors. I only desire to attain to that care and diligence in the sacred writings, which the Apostle has placed last among the duties of the saints;[4] and this very thing I desire, so that, in the endeavor to teach, I may be able to learn. For one is the true Master, who alone has not learned what he taught all; but people learn before they teach, and receive from Christ what they may hand on to others.

4. But not even this was the case with me. For I was carried off from the judgment seat, and the uniform of office, to enter on the priesthood, and began to teach you, what I myself had not yet learned. So it happened that I began to teach before I began to learn. Therefore I must learn and teach at the same time, since I had no leisure to learn before.

2.5. Now what ought we to learn before everything else, but to be silent, that we may be able to speak? lest my voice should condemn me, before

---

1. Ps. 34:11.
2. Ps. 112:1.
3. Eph. 4:11.
4. Cf. 1 Cor. 12:10.

that of another acquit me; for it is written: "By your words you shall be condemned."[5] What need is there, then, that you should hasten to undergo the danger of condemnation by speaking, when you can be more safe by keeping silent? How many have I seen to fall into sin by speaking, but scarcely one by keeping silent; and so it is more difficult to know how to keep silent than how to speak. I know that most persons speak because they do not know how to keep silent. It is seldom that anyone is silent even when speaking profits nothing. One is wise, then, who knows how to keep silent. Lastly, the Wisdom of God said: "The Lord has given to me the tongue of learning, that I should know when it is good to speak."[6] Justly, then, is one wise who has received of the Lord to know when one ought to speak. Wherefore the scripture says well: "A wise person will keep silence until there is opportunity."[7]

3.13. Let there be a door to your mouth, that it may be shut when need arises, and let it be carefully barred, that none may rouse your voice to anger, and you pay back abuse with abuse. You have heard it read today: "Be angry and sin not."[8] Therefore although we are angry (this arising from the motions of our nature, not of our will), let us not utter with our mouth one evil word, lest we fall into sin; but let there be a yoke and a balance to your words, that is, humility and moderation, that your tongue may be subject to your mind. Let it be held in check with a tight rein; let it have its own means of restraint, whereby it can be recalled to moderation; let it utter words tried by the scales of justice, that there may be seriousness in our meaning, weight in our speech, and due measure in our words.

5.17. But we must also guard against one who can be seen, and who provokes us, and spurs us on, and exasperates us, and supplies what will excite us to licentiousness or lust. If, then, anyone reviles us, irritates, stirs us up to violence, tries to make us quarrel, let us keep silence, let us not be ashamed to become dumb. For anyone who irritates us and does us an injury is committing sin, and wishes us to become like himself.

18. Certainly if you are silent, and hide your feelings, someone is wont to say: "Why are you silent? Speak if you dare; but you dare not, you are dumb, I have made you speechless." If you are silent, he is the more excited. He thinks himself beaten, laughed at, little thought of, and ridiculed. If you answer, he thinks he has become the victor, because he

5. Matt. 12:37. On the virtue of silence, see James 3 and numerously among the *Verba Seniorum*, etc. Chrysostom's catechetical homily Montfaucon 1.30–35 makes similar points with illustrations from the Psalms, Ben Sira 20 and 28, and Matt. 12:37. The Pythagoreans required a five-year novitiate of silence. See also p. 23.
6. Isa. 50:4 (LXX).
7. Ben Sira 20:7.
8. Ps. 4:4; Eph. 4:26.

has found one like himself. For if you are silent, people will say: "That person has been abusive, but this one held him in contempt." If you return the abuse, they will say: "Both have been abusive." Both will be condemned, neither will be acquitted. Therefore it is his object to irritate, so that I may speak and act as he does. But it is the duty of a just person to hide his feelings and say nothing, to preserve the fruit of a good conscience, to trust himself rather to the judgment of good people than to the insolence of a calumniator, and to be satisfied with the stability of his own character. For that is: "To keep silence even from good words";[9] since one who has a good conscience ought not to be troubled by false words, nor make more of another's abuse than of the witness of one's own heart.

11.36. Every duty is either "ordinary" or "perfect,"[10] a fact which we can also confirm by the authority of the scriptures. For we read in the Gospel that the Lord said: "If you will enter into life, keep the commandments." He said, "Which?" Jesus said to him, "You shall do no murder, you shall not commit adultery, you shall not steal, you shall not bear false witness, honor your father and your mother, you shall love your neighbor as yourself."[11] These are ordinary duties, to which something is wanting.

37. Upon this the young man says to him: "All these things have I kept from my youth up, what lack I yet?" Jesus said to him, "If you will be perfect, go and sell all your goods and give to the poor, and you shall have treasure in heaven; and come and follow me."[12] And earlier the same is written, where the Lord says that we must love our enemies, and pray for those that falsely accuse and persecute us, and bless those that curse us.[13] This we are bound to do, if we would be perfect as our Father who is in heaven; who bids the sun to shed its rays over the evil and the good, and makes the lands of the whole universe fertile with rain and dew without any distinction.[14] This, then, is a perfect duty (the Greeks call it *katorthōma*), whereby all things are put right which could have any failings in them.

38. Mercy, also, is a good thing, for it makes people perfect, in that it imitates the perfect Father. Nothing graces the Christian soul so much as

---

9. Ps. 39:2 (LXX), q.v.

10. Cicero, *On Offices* 1.3. Ordinary and perfect were the two types of duties in Stoic ethics. Perfect virtues have no imperfection, i.e., one can never err performing them, but ordinary virtues need to be examined case by case to see if they are honest and helpful. Ambrose found the distinction in Jesus' second response to the young man, "If you would be perfect. . . ." The ordinary virtues receive most of Cicero's and Ambrose's attention.

11. Matt. 19:17-19.

12. Matt. 19:20-21.

13. Matt. 5:44.

14. Matt. 5:45.

mercy; mercy as shown chiefly towards the poor, that you may treat them as sharers in common with you in the produce of nature, which brings forth the fruits of the earth for use to all. Thus you may freely give to a poor person what you have, and in this way help him who is your neighbor and companion. You bestow silver; he receives life. You give money; he considers it his fortune. Your coin makes up all his property.

12.40. But many are kept back from the duty of showing active mercy, because they suppose that God does not care about human actions, or that he does not know what we do in secret, and what our conscience has in view. Some again think that God's judgment in no wise seems to be just; for they see that sinners have abundance of riches, that they enjoy honors, health, and children; while, on the other hand, the just live in poverty and unhonored, they are without children, sickly in body, and often in grief.

41. That is no small point. For those three royal friends of Job declared him to be a sinner, because they saw that he, after being rich, became poor; that after having many children, he had lost them all, and that he was now covered with sores and was full of weals, and was a mass of wounds from head to foot. But holy Job made this declaration to them: "If I suffer thus because of my sins, why do the wicked live? They grow old also in riches, their seed is according to their pleasure, their children are before their eyes, their houses are prosperous; but they have no fear; there is no scourge from the Lord on them."[15]

44. . . . The innocent person dies in the strength of his own simplicity, in the full possession of his own will; having a soul filled as it were with marrow.[16] But the sinner, though he has abundance in life, and lives in the midst of luxury, and is redolent with sweet scents, ends his life in the bitterness of his soul, and brings his last day to a close, taking with him none of those good things which he once enjoyed, carrying away nothing with him but the price of his own wickedness.

---

15. Job 21:7-9. From the psalmists and Job through Ambrose and to our own day, perhaps the most common and pressing question of theology has been how God can be both good and powerful, yet allow the world's manifest injustices. One or the other must give: namely, either God lacks in some virtue (the Manichaean solution, and an inherent trap in process theology), or our perception of the world is incomplete. The Christian tradition chose, obviously, the latter. Ambrose's specific solution, that one sees the rewards of good and evil executed not on the body, but on the soul in this life, was largely Stoic in character, as Cicero described it, e.g., in *On Offices* 3.3. Basic to all Christian answers is the distinction between the first and second deaths, the latter to be part of the true and clear last judgment. But although the theory must guide the pastoral practice, obviously the practice cannot simply be a rehearsal of the theory, like that of Job's friends. The pastoral practice resists summary, but might be guided by Christ's example: Phil. 2:1-13 or John 3:16-17; 10:11-18.

16. Job 21:24; compare the whole chapter.

46. You see the enjoyments of the sinner; but question his conscience. Will he not be more foul than any sepulcher? . . . Thus the wicked is a punishment to himself, but the upright is a grace to himself. And to either, whether good or bad, the reward of his deeds is paid in his own person.

18.67. Lovely, then, is the virtue of modesty, and sweet is its grace! It is seen not only in actions, but even in our words,[17] so that we may not go beyond due measure in speech, and that our words may not have an unbecoming sound. The mirror of our mind often enough reflects its image in our words. Sobriety weighs out the sound even of our voice, for fear that too loud a voice should offend the ear of anyone. Nay, in singing itself the first rule is modesty, and the same is true in every kind of speech, too, so that one may gradually learn to praise God, or to sing songs, or even to speak, in that the principles of modesty grace one's advance.

69. Let no one suppose that this praise belongs to chastity alone. For modesty is the companion of purity, in company with which chastity itself is safer. Shame, again, is good as a companion and guide of chastity, inasmuch as it does not suffer purity to be defiled in approaching even the outskirts of danger. This it is that, at the very outset of her recognition, commends the Mother of the Lord to those who read the scriptures, and, as a credible witness, declares her worthy to be chosen to such an office. For when in her chamber, alone, she is saluted by the angel, she is silent, and is disturbed at his entrance,[18] and the Virgin's face is troubled at the strange appearance of a man's form. And so, though she was humble, yet it was not because of this, but on account of her modesty, that she did not return his salutation, nor give him any answer, except to ask, when she had learnt that she should conceive the Lord, how this should be. She certainly did not speak merely for the sake of making a reply.

70. In our very prayers, too, modesty is most pleasing, and gains us much grace from our God. Was it not this that exalted the publican, and commended him, when he dared not raise even his eyes to heaven?[19] So he was justified by the judgment of the Lord rather than the Pharisee, whom overweening pride made so hideous. "Therefore let us pray in the incorruptibility of a meek and quiet spirit, which is in the sight of God of great price,"[20] as St. Peter says. A noble thing, then, is modesty, which, though giving up its rights, seizing on nothing for itself, laying claim to nothing, and in some ways somewhat retiring within the sphere of its own powers, yet is rich in the sight of God, in whose sight no one is rich. Rich is

17. Cicero, *On Offices* 1.37.
18. Luke 1:29ff.
19. Luke 18:13, 14.
20. 1 Pet. 3:4.

modesty, for it is the portion of God. Paul also bids that prayer be offered up with modesty and sobriety.[21] He desires that this should be first, and, as it were, lead the way of prayers to come, so that the sinner's prayer may not be boastful, but veiled, as it were, with the blush of shame, may merit a far greater degree of grace, in giving way to modesty at the remembrance of its fault.

71. Modesty must further be guarded in our very movements and gestures and gait.[22] For the condition of the mind is often seen in the attitude of the body. For this reason the hidden person of our heart (our inner self) is considered to be either frivolous, boastful, or boisterous, or, on the other hand, steady, firm, pure, and dependable. Thus the movement of the body is a sort of voice of the soul.

72. You remember, my children, that a friend of ours who seemed to recommend himself by his assiduity in his duties, yet was not admitted by me into the number of the clergy, because his gestures were too unseemly. Also that I bade one, whom I found already among the clergy, never to go in front of me, because he actually pained me by the seeming arrogance of his gait. That is what I said when he returned to his duty after an offense committed. This alone I would not allow, nor did my mind deceive me. For both have left the church. What their gait betrayed them to be, such were they proved to be by the faithlessness of their hearts. The one forsook his faith at the time of the Arian troubles; the other, through love of money, denied that he belonged to us, so that he might not have to undergo sentence at the hands of the church. In their gait was discernible the semblance of fickleness, the appearance, as it were, of wandering buffoons.

73. Some there are who in walking perceptibly copy the gestures of actors,[23] and act as though they were bearers in the processions, and had the motions of nodding statues, to such an extent that they seem to keep a sort of time, as often as they change their step.

74. Nor do I think it becoming to walk hurriedly, except when a case of some danger demands it, or a real necessity. For we often see those who hurry come up panting, and with features distorted. But if there is no

---

21. 1 Tim. 2:8.
22. Cicero, *On Offices* 1.35, 41. The need to conform the outward to inward virtues was a commonplace among Latins, e.g., Cicero, Seneca, and Tertullian, as we have seen, and Jerome, Ep. 52.7, below. A tree is known by its fruit, it is said, but a book cannot be judged by its cover. Outward acts can guide a soul's growth, or reveal its disease. This truth, however, is hidden when we move from being pastoral, even when very frank, to being judgmental. Thus Puritan ideals were coarsened by society into caste distinctions. Ambrose sought self-amendment, not judgment; see 1.18.75; 3.22.134.
23. Cicero, *On Offices* 1.36.

reason for the need of such hurry, it gives cause for just offense. I am not, however, talking of those who have to hurry now and then for some particular reason, but of those to whom, by the yoke of constant habit, it has become a second nature. In the case of the former I cannot approve of their slow solemn movements, which remind one of the forms of phantoms. Nor do I care for the others with their headlong speed, for they put one in mind of the ruin of outcasts.

75. A suitable gait is that wherein there is an appearance of authority and weight and dignity, and which has a calm collected bearing. But it must be of such a character that all effort and conceit may be wanting, and that it be simple and plain. Nothing counterfeit is pleasing. Let nature train our movements. If indeed there is any fault in our nature, let us mend it with diligence. And, that artifice may be wanting, let not amendment be wanting.[24]

76. But if we pay so much attention to things like these, how much more careful ought we to be to let nothing shameful proceed out of our mouth, for that defiles a person terribly. It is not food that defiles, but unjust disparagement of others and foul words.[25] These things are openly shameful. In our office indeed must no word be let fall at all unseemly, nor one that may give offense to modesty. But not only ought we to say nothing unbecoming to ourselves, but we ought not even to lend our ears to words of this sort. Thus Joseph fled and left his garment, that he might hear nothing inconsistent with his modesty.[26] For one who delights to listen, urges the other on to speak.

77. To have full knowledge of what is foul is in the highest degree shameful. To see anything of this sort, if by chance it should happen, how dreadful that is! What, therefore, is displeasing to us in others, can that be pleasing in ourselves? Is not nature itself our teacher, who has formed to perfection every part of our body, so as to provide for what is necessary and to beautify and grace its form? However, it has left plain and open to the sight those parts which are beautiful to look upon; among which, the head, set as it were above all, and the pleasant lines of the figure, and the appearance of the face are prominent, while their usefulness for work is ready to hand. But those parts in which there is compliance with the necessities of nature, it has partly put away and hidden in the body itself,

---

24. "Nothing counterfeit is pleasing" paralleled the Stoic maxim, "Nothing dishonest is profitable," and the Stoic "sovereign good" was "to live in conformity with the dictates of nature" (Cicero, *On Offices* 3.3, 8). But how does one discover these dictates? How did Ambrose?

25. Matt. 15:11ff.

26. Gen. 39:12.

lest they should present a disgusting appearance, and partly, too, it has taught and persuaded us to cover them.[27]

20.85. Modesty has indeed its rocks—not any that it brings with it, but those, I mean, which it often runs against, as when we associate with profligate persons, who, under the form of pleasantry, administer poison to the Good. And the latter, if they are very constant in their attendance at banquets and games, and often join in jests, enervate that befitting gravity of theirs. Let us then take heed that, in wishing to relax our minds, we do not destroy all harmony, the blending as it were of all good works. For habit quickly bends nature in another direction.

86. For this reason I think that what you wisely do is befitting to the duties of clerics, and especially to those of the priesthood—namely, that you avoid the banquets of strangers, but so that you are still hospitable to travelers, and give no occasion for reproach by reason of your great care in the matter.[28] Banquets with strangers engross one's attention, and soon produce a love for feasting. Tales, also, of the world and its pleasures often creep in. One cannot shut one's ears; and to forbid them is looked on as a sign of haughtiness. One's glass, too, even against one's will, is filled time after time. It is better surely to excuse oneself once for all at one's own home, than often at another's. When one rises sober, at any rate one's presence need not be condemned by the insolence of another.

87. There is no need for the younger clergy to go to the houses of widows or virgins, except for the sake of a definite visit, and in that case only with the elder clergy, that is, with the bishop, or, if the matter be somewhat important, with the priests. Why should we give room to the world to revile? What need is there for those frequent visits to give ground for rumors? What if one of those women should by chance fall? Why should you undergo the reproach of another's fall? How many even strong men have been led away by their passions? How many are there who have not indeed yielded to sin, but have given ground for suspicion?

88. Why do you not spend the time which you have free from your duties in the church in reading? Why do you not go back again to see Christ? Why do you not address him, and hear his voice? We address him when we pray, we hear him when we read the sacred oracles of God. What have we to do with strange houses? There is one house which holds all. They who need us can come to us. What have we to do with tales and fables? An office to minister at the altar of Christ is what we have received; no duty to make ourselves agreeable to others has been laid upon us.

---

27. Cf. 1 Cor. 12:22ff.
28. Cicero, *On Offices* 2.8.

89. We ought to be humble, gentle, mild, serious, patient. We must keep the mean in all things, so that a calm countenance and quiet speech may show that there is no vice in our lives.

Book 2

24.119. I think, then, that one should strive to win preferment, especially in the church, only by good actions and with a right aim;[29] so that there may be no proud conceit, no idle carelessness, no shameful disposition of mind, no unseemly ambition. A plain simplicity of mind is enough for everything, and commends itself quite sufficiently.

120. When in office, again, it is not right to be harsh and severe, nor may one be too easy; lest on the one hand we should seem to be exercising a despotic power, and on the other to be by no means filling the office we had taken up.

121. We must strive also to win many by kindnesses and duties that we can do, and to preserve the favor already shown us. For they will with good reason forget the benefits of former times if they are now vexed at some great wrong. For it often enough happens that those one has shown favor to and allowed to rise step by step, are driven away, if one decides in some unworthy way to put another before them. But it is seemly for a priest to show such favor in his kindnesses and his decisions as to guard equity, and to show regard to the other clergy as to parents.[30]

122. Those who once stood approved should not now become overbearing, but rather, as mindful of the grace they have received, stand firm in their humility. A priest ought not to be offended if either cleric or attendant or any ecclesiastic should win regard by showing mercy, or by fasting, or by uprightness of life, or by teaching and reading. For the grace of the church is the praise of the teacher. It is a good thing that the work of another should be praised, if only it be done without any desire to boast. For each one should receive praise from the lips of his neighbor, and not from his own mouth, and each one should be commended by the work he has done, not merely by the wishes he had.

123. But if anyone is disobedient to the bishop and wishes to exalt and upraise himself, and to overshadow the bishop's merits by a feigned appearance of learning or humility or mercy, he is wandering from the truth in his pride; for the rule of truth is to do nothing to advance one's own cause whereby another loses ground, nor to use whatever good one has to the disgrace or blame of another.

---

29. On this chapter see Cicero, *On Offices* 2.7–9; 3.21; etc.

30. The vagaries and difficulties of promotion caused, then as now, problems and much discussion. See the annotations to Origen, Hom. 20.4 on Numbers and Hom. 6.1 on Isaiah, p. 35, n. 13.

Book 3

3.15. If, then, anyone wishes to please all, he must strive in everything to do not what is useful for himself, but what is useful for many, as also Paul strove to do. For this is "to be conformed to the image of Christ,"[31] namely, when one does not strive for what is another's, and does not deprive another of something so as to gain it for oneself. For Christ our Lord, though he was in the form of God, emptied himself so as to take on himself human form,[32] which he wished to enrich with the virtue of his works. Will you, then, spoil him whom Christ has put on? Will you strip him whom Christ has clothed? For this is what you are doing when you attempt to increase your own advantage at another's loss.

19. So we see how grave a matter it is to deprive another, with whom we ought rather to suffer, of anything, or to act unfairly or injuriously toward one to whom we ought to give a share in our services. This is a true law of nature, which binds us to show all kindly feeling, so that we should all of us in turn help one another, as parts of one body, and should never think of depriving another of anything, seeing it is against the law of nature even to abstain from giving help. We are born in such a way that limb combines with limb, and one works with another, and all assist each other in mutual service. But if one fails in its duty, the rest are hindered. If, for instance, the hand tears out the eye, has it not hindered the use of its work? If it were to wound the foot, how many actions would it not prevent? But how much worse is it for the whole person to be drawn aside from duty than for one of the members only! If the whole body is injured in one member, so also is the whole community of the human race disturbed in one person.[33] The nature of humankind is injured, as also is the society of the holy church, which rises into one united body, bound together in oneness of faith and love. Christ the Lord, also, who died for all, will grieve that the price of his blood was paid in vain.

4.25. It is clear, then,[34] that all must consider and hold that the advantage of the individual is the same as that of all, and that nothing must be considered advantageous except what is for the general good. For how can one be benefited alone? That which is useless to all is harmful. I certainly cannot think that one who is useless to all can be of use to self. For if there is one law of nature for all, there is also one state of usefulness for all. And we are bound by the law of nature to act for the good of all. It is not,

---

31. Rom. 8:29.
32. Phil. 2:6, 7.
33. A frequent sentiment in Cicero; see *On Offices* 1.44; 2.4.
34. Cicero, *On Offices* 3.6.

therefore, right for one who wishes the interests of another to be considered according to nature, to injure another against the law of nature.

27. Some ask[35] whether a wise person ought in case of a shipwreck to take away a plank from an ignorant sailor? Although it seems better for the common good that a wise person rather than a fool should escape from shipwreck, yet I do not think that a Christian, a just and a wise person, ought to save his own life by the death of another; just as when he meets with an armed robber he cannot return his blows, lest in defending his life he should stain his love toward his neighbor. The verdict on this is plain and clear in the books of the Gospel. "Put up your sword, for every one that takes the sword shall perish with the sword."[36] What robber is more hateful than the persecutor who came to kill Christ? But Christ would not be defended from the wounds of the persecutor, for he willed to heal all by his wounds.

22.131. Preserve then, my children, that friendship you have begun with your intimates, for nothing in the world is more beautiful than that. It is indeed a comfort in this life to have one to whom you can open your heart,[37] with whom you can share confidences, and to whom you can entrust the secrets of your heart. It is a comfort to have a trusty friend by your side, who will rejoice with you in prosperity, sympathize in troubles, encourage in persecution. What good friends those Hebrew children were whom the flames of the fiery furnace did not separate from their love of each other![38] Of them we have already spoken. Holy David says well: "Saul and Jonathan were lovely and pleasant, inseparable in their life, in death they were not divided."[39]

132. This is the fruit of friendship; and so faith[40] may not be put aside for the sake of friendship. One cannot be a friend to someone who has been unfaithful to God. Friendship is the guardian of pity and the teacher of equality, so as to make the superior equal to the inferior, and the inferior to the superior.[41] For there can be no friendship between diverse characters,[42] and so the goodwill of either ought to be mutually suited to the other. Let not authority be wanting to the inferior if the matter demands it, nor humility to the superior. Let one listen to the other as though the other

35. Cicero, *On Offices* 3.23.
36. Matt. 26:52.
37. Cicero, *On Friendship* 6.
38. Dan. 3:16ff.
39. 2 Sam. 1:23.
40. Cicero, *On Offices* 3.10.
41. Cicero, *On Friendship* 19.
42. Cicero, *On Friendship* 14.

were of like position—an equal, and let the other warn and reprove like a friend, not from a desire to show off, but with a deep feeling of love.

133. Let not your warning be harsh, nor your rebuke bitter,[43] for as friendship ought to avoid flattery, so, too, ought it to be free from arrogance. For what is a friend but a partner in love,[44] to whom you unite and attach your soul, and with whom you blend so as to desire from being two to become one; to whom you entrust yourself as to a second self, from whom you fear nothing, and from whom you demand nothing dishonorable for the sake of your own advantage. Friendship is not meant as a source of revenue,[45] but is full of seemliness, full of grace. Friendship is a virtue, not a way of making money. It is produced, not by money, but by esteem; not by the offer of rewards, but by a mutual rivalry in doing kindnesses.

134. Lastly, the friendships of the poor are generally better than those of the rich,[46] and often the rich are without friends, while the poor have many. For true friendship cannot exist where there is lying flattery. Many try fawningly to please the rich, but no one cares to make pretense to a poor person. Whatsoever is stated to a poor person is true, his friendship is free from envy.

138. These things I have left with you, my children, that you may guard them in your minds—you yourselves will prove whether they will be of any advantage. Meanwhile they offer you a large number of examples, for almost all of the examples drawn from our forebears, and also many a word of theirs, are included within these three books; so that, although the language may not be graceful, yet a succession of old-time examples set down in such small compass may offer much instruction.

AUGUSTINE, LETTER 213

"The business which I brought before you yesterday, my beloved, as one in connection with which I wished you to attend, as I see you have done in greater numbers than usual, must be at once disposed of.[47] For while your minds are anxiously preoccupied with it, you would scarcely listen to me if I were to speak of any other subject. We all are mortal, and the day

---

43. Cicero, *On Offices* 1.38.
44. Cicero, *On Friendship* 21.
45. Cicero, *On Friendship* 15.
46. Cicero, *On Friendship* 15.
47. Our text is actually a public record of the announcement of the choice and approval of Eraclius to be Augustine's successor-presumptive and proxy in Hippo. This was not an official, titled position, but it was a common one; see p. 116 on Gregory. On this incident, see P. Brown (1967, ch. 34).

which shall be the last of life on earth is to everyone at all times uncertain; but in infancy there is hope of entering on childhood, and so our hope goes on, looking forward from childhood to youth, from youth to adulthood, and from adulthood to old age: whether these hopes may be realized or not is uncertain, but there is in each case something which may be hoped for. But old age has no other period of this life to look forward to with expectation: how long old age may in any case be prolonged is uncertain, but it is certain that no other age destined to take its place lies beyond. I came to this town—for such was the will of God—when I was in the prime of life. I was young then, but now I am old. I know that churches are wont to be disturbed after the decease of their bishops by ambitious or contentious parties, and I feel it to be my duty to take measures to prevent this community from suffering, in connection with my decease, that which I have often observed and lamented elsewhere. You are aware, my beloved, that I recently visited the church of Milevi;[48] for certain believers, and especially the servants of God there, requested me to come, because some disturbance was apprehended after the death of my brother and fellow bishop Severus, of blessed memory. I went accordingly, and the Lord was in mercy pleased so to help us that they harmoniously accepted as bishop the person designated by their former bishop in his lifetime; for when this designation had become known to them, they willingly acquiesced in the choice which he had made. An omission, however, had occurred by which some were dissatisfied; for brother Severus, believing that it might be sufficient for him to mention to the clergy the name of his successor, did not speak of the matter to the people, which gave rise to dissatisfaction in the minds of some. But why should I say more? By the good pleasure of God, the dissatisfaction was removed, joy took its place in the minds of all, and he was ordained as bishop whom Severus had proposed. To obviate all such occasion of complaint in this case, I now intimate to all here my desire, which I believe to be also the will of God: I wish to have for my successor the presbyter Eraclius."

The people shouted, "To God be thanks! To Christ be praise" (this was repeated twenty-three times). "O Christ, hear us; may Augustine live long!" (repeated sixteen times). "We will have thee as our father, thee as our bishop" (repeated eight times).[49]

---

48. Milevi is about ninety-two miles WSW of Hippo. A common enough situation and solution. Similarly, Sidonius of Clermont was called in to mediate (Ep. 7.9).

49. The crowd's chanting of slogans was the accepted form of expressing public will, for or against an action. While in office, Symmachus, a contemporary pagan aristocrat, was forced to flee Rome briefly because of a riot against his policies. The developing ceremony of acclamation gave considerable power to anyone who could organize and orchestrate a large crowd, e.g., a bishop.

2. *Silence having been obtained, Bishop Augustine said:*

"It is unnecessary for me to say anything in praise of Eraclius; I esteem his wisdom and spare his modesty; it is enough that you know him: and I declare that I desire in regard to him what I know you also to desire, and if I had not known it before, I would have had proof of it today. This, therefore, I desire; this I ask from the Lord our God in prayers, the warmth of which is not abated by the chill of age; this I exhort, admonish, and entreat you also to pray for along with me—that God may confirm that which he has wrought in us[50] by blending and fusing together the minds of all in the peace of Christ. May he who has sent him to me preserve him! preserve him safe, preserve him blameless, that as he gives me joy while I live, he may fill my place when I die.

"The notaries of the church are, as you observe, recording what I say, and recording what you say; both my address and your acclamations are not allowed to fall to the ground. To speak more plainly, we are making up an ecclesiastical record of this day's proceedings; for I wish them to be in this way confirmed so far as pertains to all."

The people shouted thirty-six times, "To God be thanks! To Christ be praise!" "O Christ, hear us; may Augustine live long!" was said thirteen times. "Thee, our father! thee, our bishop!" was said eight times. "He is worthy and just," was said twenty times. "Well deserving, well worthy!" was said five times. "He is worthy and just!" was said six times.

4. *Silence having been obtained, Bishop Augustine said:*

"I approve of that of which you also express your approval; but I do not wish that to be done in regard to him which was done in my own case. What was done many of you know; in fact, all of you, excepting only those who at that time were not born, or had not attained to the years of understanding. When my father and bishop, the aged Valerius, of blessed memory, was still living, I was ordained bishop and occupied the episcopal see along with him, which I did not know to have been forbidden by the Council of Nicaea; and he was equally ignorant of the prohibition. I do not wish to have my son here exposed to the same censure as was incurred in my own case."

The people shouted, saying thirteen times, "To God be thanks! To Christ be praise!"

5. *Silence having been obtained, Bishop Augustine said:*

"He shall be as he now is, a presbyter, meanwhile; but afterwards, at such time as may please God, your bishop. But now I will assuredly begin

---

50. Ps. 68:28.

to do, as the compassion of Christ may enable me, what I have not hitherto done. You know what for several years I would have done, had you permitted me. It was agreed between you and me that no one should intrude on me for five days of each week, that I might discharge the duty in the study of scripture which my brethren and fathers the co-bishops were pleased to assign to me in the two councils of Numidia and Carthage. The agreement was duly recorded, you gave your consent, you signified it by acclamations. The record of your consent and of your acclamations was read aloud to you. For a short time the agreement was observed by you; afterward, it was violated without consideration, and I am not permitted to have leisure for the work which I wish to do: forenoon and afternoon alike, I am involved in the affairs of other people demanding my attention. I now beseech you, and solemnly engage you, for Christ's sake, to suffer me to devolve the burden of this part of my labors on this young man, I mean on Eraclius, the presbyter, whom today I designate in the name of Christ as my successor in the office of bishop."

The people shouted, saying twenty-six times, "We give thanks for your decision."

6. *Silence having been obtained, Bishop Augustine said:*

"I give thanks before the Lord our God for your love and your goodwill; yes, I give thanks to God for these. Wherefore, henceforth, my sisters and brothers, let everything which was wont to be brought by you to me be brought to him. In any case in which he may think my advice necessary, I will not refuse it; far be it from me to withdraw this: nevertheless, let everything be brought to him which used to be brought to me. Let Eraclius himself, if in any case, perchance, he be at a loss as to what should be done, either consult me, or claim an assistant in me, whom he has known as a father. By this arrangement you will, on the one hand, suffer no disadvantage, and I will at length, for the brief space during which God may prolong my life, devote the remainder of my days, be they few or many, not to idleness nor to the indulgence of a love of ease, but, as far as Eraclius kindly gives me leave, to the study of the sacred scriptures: this also will be of service to him, and through him to you likewise. Let no one therefore grudge me this leisure, for I claim it only in order to do important work.

"I see that I have now transacted with you all the business necessary in the matter for which I called you together. The last thing I have to ask is, that as many of you as are able be pleased to subscribe your names to this record. At this point I require a response from you. Let me have it: show your assent by some acclamations."

The people shouted, saying twenty-five times, "Agreed! agreed!" then twenty-eight times, "It is worthy, it is just!" then fourteen times, "Agreed! agreed!" then twenty-five times, "He has long been worthy, he has long been deserving!" then thirteen times, "We give thanks for your decision!" then eighteen times, "O Christ, hear us; preserve Eraclius!"

7. Silence having been obtained, Bishop Augustine said:

"It is well that we are able to transact around his sacrifice those things which belong to God; and in this hour appointed for our supplications, I especially exhort you, beloved, to suspend all your occupations and business, and pour out before the Lord your petitions for this church, and for me, and for the presbyter Eraclius."

JEROME, LETTER 52

1. Again and again you ask me, my dear Nepotian, in your letters from over the sea, to draw for you a few rules of life, showing how one who has renounced the service of the world[51] to become a monk or a clergyman may keep the straight path of Christ, and not be drawn aside into the haunts of vice. As a young man, or rather as a boy, and while I was curbing by the hard life of the desert the first onslaughts of youthful passion, I sent a letter of remonstrance to your reverend uncle, Heliodorus, which, by the tears and complainings with which it was filled, showed him the feelings of the friend whom he had deserted. In it I acted the part suited to my age, and as I was still aglow with the methods and maxims of the rhetoricians, I decked it out a good deal with the flourishes of the schools.[52] Now, however, my head is gray, my brow is furrowed, a dewlap like that of an ox hangs from my chin, and, as Virgil says,

The chilly blood stands still around my heart.[53]

---

51. *Renounced the service*, that is, the *militia*, usually of military service. Nepotian and Heliodorus had both had military careers, as had Pachomius, the organizer of coenobitic monasticism, and other prominent Christians. The first salvo of the Great Persecution was a purge of the army in 299, and there were many soldier martyrs. Ecclesia and Militia shared many aspects, but the relationship was ambivalent, and military service was forbidden by some church authorities. The relationship of the two organizations was complex, and modern study is made difficult by modern tensions, but the study raises relevant questions. One might begin with Harnack (1981), Helgeland (1985), and Swift (1985). See *Ignatius to Polycarp* 6.2, p. 22, and Leo, Ep. 167 Q.12,14, pp. 195f.

52. The "remonstrance" to Heliodorus is Letter 14. *Flourishes of the schools*: see Gregory, *On . . . His Father* 16 and note, p. 124; and Jerome's dream recounted in Letter 22.30.

53. Virgil, *Georgics* 2.484.

Elsewhere he sings:

> Old age bears all, even the mind, away.

And a little further on:

> So many of my songs are gone from me,
> And even my very voice has left me now.[54]

2. But that I may not seem to quote only profane literature, listen to the mystical teaching of the sacred writings. Once David had been a man of war, but at seventy age had chilled him so that nothing would make him warm. A girl is accordingly sought from the coasts of Israel—Abishag the Shunamite—to sleep with the king and warm his aged frame.[55] Does it not seem to you—if you keep to the letter that kills[56]—like some farcical story or some broad jest from an Atellan play?[57] A chilly old man is wrapped up in blankets, and only grows warm in a girl's embrace. Bathsheba was still living, Abigail was still left, and the remainder of those wives and concubines whose names the scripture mentions. Yet they are all rejected as cold, and only in the one young girl's embrace does the old man become warm. Abraham was far older than David; still, so long as Sarah lived he sought no other wife. Isaac counted twice the years of David, yet never felt cold with Rebekah, old though she was. I say nothing of the antediluvians, who, although after nine hundred years their limbs must have been not old merely, but decayed with age, had no recourse to girls' embraces. Moses, the leader of the Israelites, counted one hundred and twenty years, yet sought no change from Zipporah.

3. Who, then, is this Shunamite, this wife and maid, so glowing as to warm the cold, yet so holy as not to arouse passion in him whom she warmed?[58] Let Solomon, wisest of all, tell us of his father's favorite; let the man of peace recount to us the embraces of the man of war.[59] "Get wisdom," he writes, "get understanding: forget it not; neither decline from the words of my mouth. Forsake her not and she shall preserve you: love her and she shall keep you. Wisdom is the principal thing, therefore get wisdom, and with all your getting get understanding. Exalt her and she shall promote you. She shall bring you to honor when you embrace her.

---

54. Virgil, *Eclogues* 9.51, 54–55.

55. 1 Kings 1:1-4.

56. 2 Cor. 3:6.

57. These were popular burlesques with stock characters on scenes from country life or mythology.

58. 1 Kings 1:4.

59. 1 Chron. 28:3; Solomon, from Hebrew *shalom*, peace.

She shall give to your head an ornament of grace: a crown of glory shall she deliver to you."[60]

4. . . . Let Wisdom alone embrace me; let her nestle in my bosom, my Abishag who grows not old. Undefiled truly is she, and a virgin forever; for although she daily conceives and unceasingly brings to the birth, like Mary she remains undeflowered. . . . I know, of course, that from your reverend uncle, Heliodorus, now a bishop of Christ, you have learned and are daily learning all that is holy; and that in him you have before you a rule of life and a pattern of virtue. Take, then, my suggestions for what they are worth, and compare my precepts with his. He will teach you the perfection of a monk, and I shall show you the whole duty of a clergy-person.

5. A clergyperson, then, serving Christ's church, must first understand what his name means; and then, when he realizes this, must endeavor to be that which he is called. For since the Greek word *klēros* means "lot," or "inheritance," the clergy are so called either because they are the lot of the Lord, or else because the Lord himself is their lot and portion. Now, one who in his own person is the Lord's portion, or has the Lord for his portion, must so bear himself as to possess the Lord and to be possessed by him. He who possesses the Lord, and who says with the prophet, "The Lord is my portion,"[61] can hold to nothing beside the Lord. For if he hold to some-thing beside the Lord, the Lord will not be his portion. Suppose, for instance, that one holds to gold or silver, or possessions or inlaid furniture; with such portions as these the Lord will not deign to be his portion. I, if I am the portion of the Lord, and the line of his heritage,[62] receive no portion among the remaining tribes; but, like the priest and the Levite, I live on the tithe,[63] and serving the altar, am supported by its offerings.[64] Having food and raiment, I shall be content with these,[65] and the naked cross I shall follow naked. . . . Beware of all that gives occasion for suspicion; and, to avoid scandal, shun every act that may give color to it. Frequent gifts of handkerchiefs and garters, of facecloths and dishes first tasted by the giver—to say nothing of notes full of fond expressions—of such things as these a holy love knows nothing. Such endearing and alluring expressions as "my honey" and "my darling," "you who are all my charm and my delight," the ridiculous courtesies of lovers and their foolish

---

60. Prov. 4:5-9, with departures from the Vulgate.
61. Pss. 16:5; 73:26.
62. Ps. 16:5, 6.
63. Num. 18:24.
64. 1 Cor. 9:13.
65. 1 Tim. 6:8.

doings, we blush for on the stage and abhor in people of the world. How much more do we loathe them in monks and clerics who adorn the priesthood by their vows while their vows are adorned by the priesthood. I speak thus not because I dread such evils for you or for others of saintly life, but because in all ranks and callings and among both men and women there are found both good and bad and in condemning the bad I commend the good.[66]

6. ... It is the glory of a bishop to make provision for the wants of the poor; but it is the shame of all priests to amass private fortunes.[67] I who was born (suppose) in a poor man's house, in a country cottage, and who could scarcely get of common millet and household bread enough to fill an empty stomach, am now come to disdain the finest wheat flour and honey. I know the several kinds of fish by name. I can tell unerringly on what coast a mussel has been picked. I can distinguish by the flavor the province from which a bird comes. Dainty dishes delight me because their ingredients are scarce and I end by finding pleasure in their ruinous cost.

I hear also of servile attention shown by some toward old men and women when these are childless.[68] They fetch the basin, beset the bed and perform with their own hands the most revolting offices. They anxiously await the advent of the doctor and with trembling lips they ask whether the patient is better. If for a little while the old one shows signs of returning vigor, they are in agonies. They pretend to be delighted, but their covetous hearts undergo secret torture. For they are afraid that their labors may go for nothing and compare an old person with a clinging to life to the patriarch Methuselah. How great a reward might they have with God if their hearts were not set on a temporal prize! With what great exertions do they pursue an empty heritage! Less labor might have purchased for them the pearl of Christ.

7. Read the divine scriptures constantly; never, indeed, let the sacred volume be out of your hand. Learn what you have to teach. "Hold fast the faithful word as you have been taught that you may be able by sound doctrine to exhort and convince the gainsayers. Continue in the things that you have learned and have been assured of, knowing of whom you have

---

66. In his Hom. 35 on Ps. 108(109), Jerome said, "If Judas lost his office of apostle, let priest and bishop be on guard lest they, too, lose their ministry. If an apostle fell, more easily is it possible for a monk to fall."

67. *Private fortunes*: see canon 19 of Elvira, p. 102, and take note of the careers of Gregory Nazianzen's father and Chrysostom.

68. *Servile attention*: a long-established route to wealth was to ingratiate oneself into someone's will. Lucian painted the portraits well: *Dialogues of the Dead* 15(5)–19(9), volume 7 of the Loeb. Several concerns in this letter are found also in Ps.-Clement, *On Virginity* 10, above p. 86.

learned them";[69] and "be ready always to give an answer to everyone that asks you a reason of the hope and faith that are in you."[70] Do not let your deeds belie your words; lest when you speak in church someone may mentally reply "Why do you not practice what you profess? Here is a lover of dainties turned censor! his stomach is full and he reads us a homily on fasting. As well might a robber accuse others of covetousness." In a priest of Christ, mouth, mind, and hand should be at one.[71]

Be obedient to your bishop and welcome him as the parent of your soul. Children love their parents and slaves fear their masters. "If I be a father," God says, "where is my honor? And if I am a master where is my fear?"[72] In your case the bishop combines in himself many titles to your respect. He is at once a monk, a prelate, and an uncle who has before now instructed you in all holy things. This also I say that the bishops should know themselves to be priests, not lords. Let them render to the clergy the honor which is their due that the clergy may offer to them the respect which belongs to bishops. There is a judicious remark of the orator Domitius, "Why should I treat you as leader of the senate, when you do not treat me as a senator?"[73]

We should realize that a bishop and his presbyter are like Aaron and his sons. As there is but one Lord and one temple; so also should there be but one ministry. Let us ever bear in mind the charge which the apostle Peter gives to priests: "Feed the flock of God which is among you, taking the oversight thereof not by constraint but willingly as God would have you; not for filthy lucre but of a ready mind; neither as being lords over God's heritage but being examples to the flock," and that gladly; that "when the chief shepherd shall appear you may receive a crown of glory that fades not away."[74] It is a bad custom which prevails in certain churches for presbyters to be silent when bishops are present on the ground that they would be jealous or impatient hearers. "A wise son makes a glad father";[75] and a bishop should rejoice in the discrimination which has led him to choose such for the priests of Christ.

8. When teaching in church seek to call forth not plaudits but groans. Let the tears of your hearers be your glory. A presbyter's words ought to be seasoned by the reading of scripture. Be not a declaimer or a ranter, one who gabbles without rhyme or reason; but show yourself skilled in the

---

69. Titus 1:9; 2 Tim. 3:14.
70. 1 Pet. 3:15.
71. *Mouth and mind at one*: see Ambrose, 1.18.71–72, above p. 143.
72. Malachi 1:6.
73. Preserved in Cicero, *On the Orator* 3.1.
74. 1 Pet. 5:4.
75. Prov. 10:1.

deep things and versed in the mysteries of God.[76] To mouth your words and by your quickness of utterance astonish the unlettered crowd is a mark of ignorance. Assurance often explains that of which it knows nothing; and when it has convinced others imposes on itself. My teacher, Gregory of Nazianzus, when I once asked him to explain Luke's phrase "sabbaton deuteroprôton,"[77] that is "the second-first Sabbath," playfully evaded my request saying: "I will tell you about it in church, and there, when all the people applaud me, you will be forced against your will to know what you do not know at all. For, if you alone remain silent, everyone will put you down for a fool." There is nothing so easy as by sheer volubility to deceive a common crowd or an uneducated congregation: such most admire what they fail to understand. . . .

9. In dress avoid somber colors as much as bright ones. Showiness and slovenliness are alike to be shunned; for the one savors of vanity and the other of pride. To go about without a linen scarf on is nothing: what is praiseworthy is to be without money to buy one. It is disgraceful and absurd to boast of having neither a napkin nor handkerchief and yet to carry a well-filled purse.

Some bestow a trifle on the poor to receive a larger sum themselves and under the cloak of almsgiving do but seek for riches. Such are almshunters rather than almsgivers. Their methods are those by which birds, beasts, and fishes are taken. A morsel of bait is put on the hook—to land a married lady's purse! The church is committed to the bishop; let him take heed whom he appoints to be his almoner. It is better for me to have no money to give away than shamelessly to beg what I mean to hoard. It is arrogance too to wish to seem more liberal than one who is Christ's bishop. "All things are not open to us all."[78] In the church one is the eye, another is the tongue, another the hand, another the foot, others ears, belly, and so on. Read Paul's epistle to the Corinthians and learn how the one body is made up of different members.[79] The rude and simple person must not suppose himself a saint just because he knows nothing; and one who is educated and eloquent must not measure his saintliness merely by

---

76. See Gregory, *On . . . His Father* 16, p. 124, and Chrysostom, *On the Priesthood* 5.6, 8, p. 179-81.

77. Luke 6:1. *Second-first Sabbath*: this Lukan variant reading, found in a number of good manuscripts, has always puzzled commentators. The adjective is not found anywhere independently of this verse, and it has no clear meaning. (See any good commentary, e.g., Fitzmyer, ad loc., for details.) Gregory, also, did not understand it, but his answer was to *sound* so convincing that it would draw applause. If Jerome alone did not act convinced, he would appear stupid. It takes confidence in one's intelligence to confess that one does not understand (but it often pays off).

78. Virgil, *Eclogues* 8.63.

79. 1 Cor. 12:12-27.

his fluency. Of two imperfect things holy rusticity is better than sinful eloquence.

11. Avoid entertaining persons of the world, especially those whose honors make them swell with pride.[80] You are the priest of Christ—one poor and crucified who lived on the bread of strangers. It is a disgrace to you if the consul's lictors or soldiers keep watch before your door, and if the judge of the province has a better dinner with you than in his own palace. If you plead as an excuse your wish to intercede for the unhappy and the oppressed, I reply that a worldly judge will defer more to a clergyperson who is self-denying than to one who is rich; will pay more regard to your holiness than to your wealth. Or if he is the type who will not hear the clergy on behalf of the distressed except over the bowl, I will readily forgo his aid and will appeal to Christ who can help more effectively and speedily than any judge. Truly "it is better to trust in the Lord than to put confidence in humankind. It is better to trust in the Lord than to put confidence in princes."[81]

Let your breath never smell of wine lest the philosopher's words be said to you: "Instead of offering me a kiss you are giving me a taste of wine." Priests given to wine are both condemned by the apostle[82] and forbidden by the old law. Those who serve the altar, we are told, must drink neither wine nor *shechar*.[83] Now every intoxicating drink is in Hebrew called *shechar* whether it is made of corn or of the juice of apples, whether you distill from the honeycomb a rude kind of mead or make a liquor by squeezing dates or strain a thick syrup from a decoction of corn. Whatever intoxicates and disturbs the balance of the mind, avoid as you would wine. I do not say that we are to condemn what is a creature of God. The Lord himself was called a "wine-bibber" and wine in moderation was allowed to Timothy because of his weak stomach.[84] I only require that drinkers should observe that limit which their age, their health, or their constitution requires. But if without drinking wine at all I am aglow with youth and am inflamed by the heat of my blood and am of a strong and lusty habit of body, I will readily forego the cup in which I cannot but suspect poison. The Greeks have an excellent saying which will perhaps bear translation,

> Fat bellies have no sentiments refined.

12. Lay upon yourself only as much fasting as you can bear, and let your fasts be pure, chaste, simple, moderate, and not superstitious. What good

---

80. On §11, see Ambrose, 1.20.85-86, p. 145.
81. Ps. 118:8, 9.
82. Eph. 5:18; 1 Tim. 3:3, 8.
83. Lev. 10:9; Luke 1:15.
84. Matt. 11:19; 1 Tim. 5:23.

is it to use no oil if you seek after the most troublesome and out-of-the-way kinds of food, dried figs, pepper, nuts, dates, fine flour, honey, pistachios? All the resources of gardening are strained to save us from eating household bread; and to pursue dainties we turn our backs on the kingdom of heaven. There are some, I am told, who reverse the laws of nature and the race; for they neither eat bread nor drink water but imbibe thin decoctions of crushed herbs and beet juice—not from a cup but from a shell. Shame on us that we have no blushes for such follies and that we feel no disgust at such superstition! . . .

14. Beware also of a blabbing tongue and of itching ears.[85] Neither detract from others nor listen to detractors. "You sit," says the psalmist, "and speak against your brother; you slander your own mother's son. These things you have done and I kept silence; you thought wickedly that I was such a one as yourself, but I will reprove you and set them in order before your eyes."[86] Keep your tongue from caviling and watch over your words. Know that in judging others you are passing sentence on yourself and that you are yourself guilty of the faults which you blame in them. . . .

15. It is your duty to visit the sick, to know the homes and children of those who are married, and to guard the secrets of the noble. Make it your object, therefore, to keep your tongue chaste as well as your eyes. Never discuss a woman's figure nor let one house know what is going on in another. Hippocrates,[87] before he will teach his pupils, makes them take an oath and compels them to swear fealty to him. He binds them over to silence, and prescribes for them their language, their gait, their dress, their manners. How much more reason have we to whom the medicine of the soul has been committed to love the houses of all Christians as our own homes. Let them know us as comforters in sorrow rather than as guests in time of mirth. That clergyperson soon becomes an object of contempt who being often asked out to dinner never refuses to go.

16. Let us never seek for presents and rarely accept them when we are asked to do so. For "it is more blessed to give than to receive."[88] Somehow or other the very one who begs leave to offer you a gift holds you the cheaper for your acceptance of it; while, if you refuse it, it is wonderful how much more he will come to respect you. The preacher of continence must not be a maker of marriages. Why does he who reads the apostle's words "It remains that they that have wives be as though they had none"[89]—why does he press a virgin to marry? Why does a priest, who

---

85. On 14, see Ambrose, 1.18.76, p. 144.
86. Ps. 50:20, 21.
87. Hippocratic oath, in the Loeb vol. 1, pp. 291–99.
88. Acts 20:35.
89. 1 Cor. 7:29. *Maker*: i.e., matchmaker. On marriage, see his Ep. 22.20, and annotation to Tertullian *To His Wife*, p. 47.

must be a monogamist,[90] urge a widow to marry again? How can the clergy be managers and stewards of other people's households, when they are bidden to disregard even their own interests? To wrest a thing from a friend is theft but to cheat the church is sacrilege. When you have received money to be doled out to the poor, to be cautious or to hesitate while crowds are starving is to be worse than a robber; and to subtract a portion for yourself is to commit a crime of the deepest dye. I am tortured with hunger, and are you to judge what will satisfy my cravings? Either divide immediately what you have received, or, if you are a timid almoner, send the donor to distribute his own gifts. Your purse ought not to remain full while I am in need. No one can look after what is mine better than I can. He is the best almoner who keeps nothing for himself.[91]

17. . . . I have not inveighed against those who sin: I have but warned them to sin no more. My judgment of myself has been as strict as my judgment of them. When I have wished to remove the mote from my neighbor's eye, I have first cast out the beam in my own.[92] I have calumniated no one. Not a name has been hinted at. My words have not been aimed at individuals and my criticism of shortcomings has been quite general. If anyone wishes to be angry with me he will have first to own that he himself suits my description.

---

90. 1 Tim. 3:2.
91. On liberality, see Dionysius to Soter, pp. 19, 25.
92. Matt. 7:3-5.

9

JOHN CHRYSOSTOM

On the Priesthood

Chrysostom wrote extensively, has been translated extensively, and is extensively relevant. Our selections (1.1, 3–6; 2.4; 3.8–10, 13–17; 5.1–2, 4, 6, 8; 6.1, 4) are from NPNF 1.9, one of six volumes of John in NPNF 1. Among many other possibilities one may note his sermons *In Praise of St. Paul* (Halton, 1963), especially sermon 5; the catechetical homilies (Harkins, 1963); and *On Vainglory* (Laistner, 1951). C. Baur (1959²) is full of information and irrelevancies. On the contemporary Antiochene milieu, important to gauging John, see Liebeschuetz (1972); Wilken (1983) makes illuminating use of the social and rhetorical backgrounds to John's sermons. Laistner, Clark (1982²), and Wilken cover different and sometimes difficult aspects.

John Chrysostom was born in Antioch, about 349, into a Christian family of moderate wealth. His father, Secundus, who had held some senior grade in the military, died while John was an infant. His mother, Anthusa, brought him up carefully, as our selection, I.5, mentions. She, along with Olympias, Macrina, Nonna, Monica, Melania, Paula, Syncletice, and others, form a group whose influence far exceeded their fame, for so many great church fathers candidly admitted their great debts to these church mothers.

John received an excellent education, under Libanius and others, originally directed toward a prominent career in the imperial court. He shifted his focus, however, was baptized in 368, and began study for an ecclesiastical career with Bishop Meletius and the theologian Diodore. Such a career could be as socially advantageous as a civil one and suited very well his education, his

Christian fervor, and his ascetic tendencies. In the 370s, after his mother died and during a period of Arian ascendency, he spent several years in strict ascesis with a monk in the desert. Returning to the city, he entered the diaconate (381) and the priesthood (386). He had special responsibilities for preaching and catechesis, and for the next dozen years, usually preaching several sermons a week, he enjoyed tremendous popularity and influence.

A disastrous honor befell him in 397. The archbishop and first patriarch of Constantinople was Nectarius, a blandly irenic ex-magistrate and the successor to Nazianzen. During his reign, life at court and at the basilica were similarly lax. He died in 397, and the vacancy drew fierce competition. The powerful and intriguing chief minister, Eutropius, however, had other ideas. For motives unknown but probably none too pure, he decided to kidnap Chrysostom from Antioch and install him, even against his wishes, and against the wishes of other powerful people as well.

Once installed, Chrysostom made the "mistake" of doing his job seriously. He attended to the needs of the populace by building hospitals, among other charities, but he attended to the needs of the court and clergy by demanding far stricter moral standards. His problems with the purity of the priesthood stood in contrast to Augustine's. The list of his opponents grew to include both the empress Eudoxia and the ambitious and hardly saintly patriarch of Alexandria, Theophilus. In 404 at the Synod of the Oak, Chrysostom was deposed on false charges and banished. His exile was short-lived, as the *voces populi et dei* (namely, riots and some sort of sign, either an earthquake or the empress's miscarriage) forced his triumphant recall. His reinstatement was also short-lived. John, preaching on the Feast of John the Baptist, began, "Again Herodias raves; again she rages; again she dances; again she asks for the head of John upon a charger."

John spent his three years of exile in two small towns in south central Turkey, Göksun and Afşin, high in the Taurus mountains and exposed to raids by the Isaurians. His loyal friends from Antioch and Constantinople remained in touch, and many of his letters from exile survive. In 407 he died on route to a more remote exile. He ended his life in what amounted to the harsh monastic regimen he had long admired, but not a regimen gained by presumption. "Nevertheless, not as I will, but as thou wilt."

On the Priesthood is a relatively early work, from before 392 at least. John would face later so many of the problems that he described here that often the work seems prophetic; or perhaps the problems were woefully regular. The work is set as a dialogue with his close friend, Basil. No particular Basil can be identified. It is, indeed, rather likely that the general situation and this Basil are fictitious. *Basileios,* which as a word means "kingly," is an apt name for an eager disciple of the Lord.

JOHN CHRYSOSTOM, ON THE PRIESTHOOD

Book 1

1. I had many genuine and true friends, people who understood the laws of friendship and faithfully observed them; but out of this large number there was one who excelled all the rest in his attachment to me, striving to outstrip them as much as they themselves outstripped ordinary acquaintance. He was one of those who were constantly at my side; for we were engaged in the same studies and employed the same teachers. We had the same eagerness and zeal about the studies at which we worked, and a passionate desire produced by the same circumstances was equally strong in both of us. For not only when we were attending school, but after we had left it, when it became necessary to consider what course of life it would be best for us to adopt, we found ourselves to be of the same mind.[1]

3. But when it became our duty to pursue the blessed life of monks, and the true philosophy, our balance was no longer even, but his scale mounted high, while I, still entangled in the lusts of this world, dragged mine down and kept it low, weighting it with those fancies in which youths are apt to indulge. For the future our friendship indeed remained as firm as it was before, but our intercourse was interrupted; for it was impossible for persons who were not interested about the same things to spend much time together. But as soon as I also began to emerge a little from the flood of worldliness, he received me with open arms; yet not even thus could we maintain our former equality: for having got the start of me in time, and having displayed great earnestness, he rose again above my level, and soared to a great height.

4. Being a good man, however, and placing a high value on my friendship, he separated himself from all the rest, and spent the whole of

---

1. This description of friendship has strong classical roots; see E. Clark (1982, ch. 2) and Lucian's *Toxaris* (vol. 5 in the Loeb).

his time with me, which he had desired to do before, but had been prevented as I was saying by my frivolity. . . . He could not bear leaving me even for a moment, and he persistently urged that we should each of us abandon our own home and share a common dwelling—in fact he persuaded me, and the affair was taken in hand.

5. But the continual lamentations of my mother hindered me from granting him the favor, or rather from receiving this boon at his hands. For when she perceived that I was meditating this step, she took me into her own private chamber, and, sitting near me on the bed where she had given birth to me, she shed torrents of tears, to which she added words yet more pitiable than her weeping, in the following lamentable strain: "My child, it was not the will of heaven that I should long enjoy the benefit of your father's virtue. For his death soon followed the pangs which I endured at your birth, leaving you an orphan and me a widow before my time to face all the horrors of widowhood, which only those who have experienced them can fairly understand.

"On this account, even when you were an infant, and had not yet learned to speak, a time when children are the greatest delight to their parents, you did afford me much comfort. Nor indeed can you complain that, although I bore my widowhood bravely, I diminished your patrimony, which I know has been the fate of many who have had the misfortune to be orphans. For, besides keeping the whole of it intact, I spared no expense which was needful to give you an honorable position, spending for this purpose some of my own fortune, and of my marriage dowry. Yet do not think that I say these things by way of reproaching you; only in return for all these benefits I beg one favor: do not plunge me into a second widowhood nor revive the grief which is now laid to rest: wait for my death; it may be in a little while I shall depart. The young indeed look forward to a distant old age; but we who have grown old have nothing but death to wait for. When, then, you shall have committed my body to the ground, and mingled my bones with your father's, embark for a long voyage, and set sail on any sea you care to; then there will be no one to hinder you; but as long as my life lasts, be content to live with me. . . ."

6. These words, and more, my mother spoke to me, and I related them to that noble youth. But he, so far from being disheartened by these speeches, was the more urgent in making the same request as before. Now while we were thus situated, he continually entreating, and I refusing my assent, we were both of us disturbed by a report suddenly reaching us that we were about to be advanced to the dignity of the episcopate. As soon as I heard this rumor I was seized with alarm and perplexity: with alarm lest I should be made captive against my will, and perplexity, inquiring as I

often did whence any such idea concerning us could have entered the minds of these people; for looking to myself I found nothing worthy of such an honor. But that noble youth having come to me privately, and having conferred with me about these things as if with one who was ignorant of the rumor, begged that we might in this instance also as formerly shape our action and our counsels the same way: for he would readily follow me whichever course I might pursue, whether I attempted flight or submitted to be captured. Perceiving then his eagerness, and considering that I should inflict a loss upon the whole body of the church if, owing to my own weakness, I were to deprive the flock of Christ of a young man who was so good and so well qualified for the supervision of large numbers, I abstained from disclosing to him the purpose which I had formed, although I had never before allowed any of my plans to be concealed from him. I now told him that it would be best to postpone our decision concerning this matter to another season, as it was not immediately pressing, and by so doing persuaded him to dismiss it from his thoughts, and at the same time encouraged him to hope that if such a thing should ever happen to us, I should be of the same mind with him.

But after a short time, when one who was to ordain us arrived, I kept myself concealed, but Basil, ignorant of this, was taken away on another pretext, and made to take the yoke, hoping from the promises which I had made to him that I should certainly follow, or rather supposing that he was following me. For some of those who were present, seeing that he resented being seized, deceived him by exclaiming how strange it was that one who was generally reputed to be the more hot tempered (meaning me), had yielded very mildly to the judgment of the church, whereas he, who was reckoned a much wiser and milder kind of person, had shown himself hotheaded and conceited, being unruly, restive, and contradictory. Having yielded to these remonstrances, and afterwards having learned that I had escaped capture, he came to me in deep dejection, sat down near me and tried to speak, but was hindered by distress of mind and inability to express in words the violence to which he had been subjected. No sooner had he opened his mouth than he was prevented from utterance by grief cutting short his words before they could pass his lips. Seeing, then, his tearful and agitated condition, and knowing as I did the cause, I laughed for joy, and, seizing his right hand, I forced a kiss on him, and praised God that my plan had ended so successfully, as I had always prayed it might. But when he saw that I was delighted and beaming with joy, and understood that he had been deceived by me, he was yet more vexed and distressed.

Book 2

4. BASIL: But you yourself—do you not love Christ?

CHRYSOSTOM: I do love him, and shall never cease loving him; but I fear lest I should provoke him whom I love.

BASIL: But what riddle can there be more obscure than this—Christ has commanded him who loves him to tend his sheep, and yet you say that you decline to tend them because you love him who gave this command?

CHRYSOSTOM: My saying is no riddle, but very intelligible and simple, for if I were well qualified to administer this office, as Christ desired it, and then shunned it, my remark might be open to doubt, but since the infirmity of my spirit renders me useless for this ministry, why does my saying deserve to be called in question?

Book 3

8. ... I know my own soul, how feeble and puny it is: I know the magnitude of this ministry, and the great difficulty of the work; for more stormy billows vex the soul of the priest than the gales which disturb the sea.

9. And first of all is that most terrible rock of vainglory,[2] more dangerous than that of the Sirens, of which the fable-mongers tell such marvellous tales: for many were able to sail past that and escape unscathed; but this is to me so dangerous that even now, when no necessity of any kind impels me into that abyss, I am unable to keep clear of the snare: but if anyone were to commit this charge to me, it would be all the same as if he tied my hands behind my back and delivered me to the wild beasts dwelling on that rock to rend me in pieces day by day. Do you ask what those wild beasts are? They are wrath, despondency, envy, strife, slanders, accusations, falsehood, hypocrisy, intrigues, anger against those who have done no harm, pleasure at the indecorous acts of fellow ministers, sorrow at their prosperity, love of praise, desire of honor (which indeed most of all drives the human soul headlong to perdition), doctrines devised to please, servile flatteries, ignoble fawning, contempt of the poor, paying court to the rich, senseless and mischievous honors, favors attended with danger both to those who offer and those who accept them, sordid fear suited only to the basest of slaves, the abolition of plain speaking, a great affectation of humility, but banishment of truth, the suppression of convictions and reproofs, or rather the excessive use of them against the poor, while against those who are invested with power no one dare speak.

For all these wild beasts, and more than these, are bred upon that rock of which I have spoken, and those whom they have once captured are inevitably dragged down into such a depth of servitude that even to please women they often do many things which it is well not to mention. The

---

2. *Vainglory*: see Laistner (1951).

divine law indeed has excluded women from the ministry, but they endeavor to thrust themselves into it; and since they can effect nothing of themselves, they do all through the agency of others; and they have become invested with so much power that they can appoint or eject priests at their will: things in fact are turned upside down, and the proverbial saying may be seen realized—"The ruled lead the rulers": and would that it were men who do this instead of women, who have not received a commission to teach. Why do I say teach? for the blessed Paul did not suffer them even to speak in the church.[3] But I have heard someone say that they have obtained such a large privilege of free speech, as even to rebuke the prelates of the churches, and censure them more severely than masters do their own domestics.

10. And let not anyone suppose that I subject all to the aforesaid charges: for there are some, yea many, who are superior to these entanglements, and exceed in number those who have been caught by them. Nor would I indeed make the priesthood responsible for these evils: far be such madness from me. For people of understanding do not say that the sword is to blame for murder, nor wine for drunkenness, nor strength for outrage, nor courage for foolhardiness, but they lay the blame on those who make an improper use of the gifts which have been bestowed upon them by God, and punish them accordingly. Certainly, at least, the priesthood may justly accuse us if we do not rightly handle it. For it is not itself a cause of the evils already mentioned, but we, as far as lies in our power, have defiled it with so many pollutions by entrusting it to commonplace people.[4] They readily accept what is offered them, without having first acquired a knowledge of their own souls or considered the gravity of the office, and when they have entered on the work, being blinded by inexperience, they overwhelm with innumerable evils the people who have been committed to their care.

This is the very thing which was very nearly happening in my case, had not God speedily delivered me from those dangers, mercifully sparing the church and my own soul. For, tell me, whence do you think such great troubles are generated in the churches? I, for my part, believe the only source of them to be the inconsiderate and random way in which prelates are chosen and appointed. For the head ought to be the strongest part, that it may be able to regulate and control the evil exhalations which arise from the rest of the body below; but when it happens to be weak in itself and

---

3. 1 Cor. 14:34; 1 Tim. 2:12. *Even to rebuke the prelates:* in general, see E. Clark (1982), but notice the particulars of this case. John focuses on the bullying of clergy by some noblewomen. Some, like the empress Eudoxia, were bullies, as also, in fairness, were many men.

4. *Commonplace people:* see Basil, Ep. 54, p. 118.

unable to repel those pestiferous attacks, it becomes feebler itself than it really is, and ruins the rest of the body as well. And to prevent this now coming to pass, God kept me in the position of the feet, which was the rank originally assigned to me. For there are very many other qualities, Basil, besides those already mentioned, which the priest ought to have, but which I do not possess; and, above all, this one: the soul ought to be thoroughly purged from any lust after the office, for if he happens to have a natural inclination for this dignity, as soon as he attains it a stronger flame is kindled, and the one being taken completely captive will endure innumerable evils in order to keep a secure hold upon it, even to the extent of using flattery, or submitting to something base and ignoble, or expending large sums of money.[5] For I will not now speak of the murders with which some have filled the churches, or the desolation which they have brought upon cities in contending for the dignity, lest some persons should think what I say incredible. But I am of opinion one ought to exercise so much caution in the matter, as to shun the burden of the office, and when one has entered upon it, not to wait for the judgment of others should any fault be committed which warrants deposition, but to anticipate it by ejecting oneself from the dignity; for thus one might probably win mercy from God: but to cling to it in defiance of propriety is to deprive oneself of all forgiveness, or rather to kindle the wrath of God, by adding a second error more offensive than the first.

13. And do not be surprised if, in connection with such endurance, I seek another test of fortitude in the soul. For to be indifferent to food and drink and a soft bed, we see is to many no hard task, especially at least to such as are of a rough habit of life and have been brought up in this way from early youth, and to many others also; bodily discipline and custom softening the severity of these laborious practices: but insult, and abuse, and coarse language, and gibes from inferiors, whether wantonly or justly uttered, and rebukes vainly and idly spoken both by rulers and the ruled— this is what few can bear, in fact only one or two here and there; and one may see those, who are strong in the former exercises, so completely upset by these things, as to become more furious than the most savage beasts. Now such persons especially we should exclude from the precincts of the priesthood. For if a prelate did not loathe food, or go barefoot, no harm would be done to the common interests of the church; but a furious temper causes great disasters both to one who possesses it, and to his neighbors. And there is no divine threat against those who fail to do the things referred to, but hell and hellfire are threatened against those who

---

5. *Purged from any lust after the office:* see Origen, p. 35, n. 13. Notice how John's "trick," 1.6, has now absolved Basil of any charge of vainglory.

are angry without a cause.[6] As then the lover of vainglory, when he takes upon him the government of numbers, supplies additional fuel to the fire, so he who alone, or in the company of a few, is unable to control his anger, but readily carried away by it, should he be entrusted with the direction of a whole multitude, like some wild beast goaded on all sides by countless tormentors, would never be able to live in tranquillity himself, and would cause incalculable mischief to those who have been committed to his charge.

14. BASIL: I will not endure this irony of yours any longer: for who knows not how far removed you are from this infirmity?

CHRYSOSTOM: Why then, my good friend, do you wish to bring me near the pyre, and to provoke the wild beast when it is tranquil? Are you not aware that I have achieved this condition, not by any innate virtue, but by my love of retirement? and that when one who is so constituted remains contented alone, or only associates with one or two friends, he is able to escape the fire which arises from this passion, but not if he has plunged into the abyss of all these cares? for then he drags not only himself but many others with him to the brink of destruction, and renders them more indifferent to all consideration for mildness. For the mass of people under government are generally inclined to regard the manners of those who govern as a kind of model type, and to assimilate themselves to them.[7] How then could anyone put a stop to their fury when one is swelling himself with rage? And who amongst the multitude would straightaway desire to become moderate when he sees the ruler irritable? For it is quite impossible for the defects of priests to be concealed, but even trifling ones speedily become manifest. So an athlete, as long as he remains at home, and contends with no one, can dissemble his weakness even if it be very great, but when he strips for the contest he is easily detected. And thus for some who live this private and inactive life, their isolation serves as a veil to hide their defects; but when they have been brought into public they are compelled to divest themselves of this mantle of seclusion, and to lay bare their souls to all through their visible movements. As therefore their right deeds profit many, by provoking them to equal zeal, so their shortcomings make others more indifferent to the practice of virtue, and encourage them to indolence in their endeavors after what is excellent.

Wherefore the priest's soul ought to gleam with beauty on every side, that it may be able to gladden and to enlighten the souls of those who behold it. For the faults of ordinary persons, being committed as it were in

---

6. Matt. 5:22. That one must curb the passion of wrath was a prominent subject of ethical discussion.

7. *To regard . . . as a kind of model:* see Athanasius, p. 70.

the dark, ruin only those who practice them: but the errors of one in a conspicuous position, and known to many, inflict a common injury upon all, rendering those who have fallen more supine in their efforts for good, and driving to desperation those who wish to take heed to themselves. And apart from these things, the faults of insignificant people, even if they are exposed, inflict no injury worth speaking of upon anyone: but they who occupy the highest seat of honor are in the first place plainly visible to all, and if they err in the smallest matters these trifles seem great to others: for all measure the sin, not by the magnitude of the offense, but by the rank of the offender.

Thus the priest ought to be protected on all sides by a kind of adamantine armor, by intense earnestness, and perpetual watchfulness concerning manner of life, lest someone discovering an exposed and neglected spot should inflict a deadly wound, for all who surround him are ready to smite and overthrow him: not enemies only and adversaries, but many even of those who profess friendship.

The souls therefore of those elected to the priesthood ought to be endued with such power as the grace of God bestowed on the bodies of those saints who were cast into the Babylonian furnace.[8] Faggot and pitch and tow are not the fuel of this fire, but things far more dreadful: for it is no material fire to which they are subjected, but the all-devouring flame of envy encompasses them, rising up on every side, and assailing them, and putting their life to a more searching test than the fire then was to the bodies of those young men. When then it finds a little trace of stubble, it speedily fastens upon it; and this unsound part it entirely consumes, but all the rest of the fabric, even if it be brighter than the sunbeams, is scorched and blackened by the smoke. For as long as the life of the priest is well regulated in every direction, it is invulnerable to plots; but if one happens to overlook some trifle, as is natural in a human being traversing the treacherous ocean of this life, no other good deeds are of any avail in enabling him to escape the mouths of his accusers; but that little blunder overshadows all the rest. And all people are ready to pass judgment on the priest as if he were not a being clothed with flesh, or one who inherited a human nature, but like an angel, and emancipated from every species of infirmity.

Just as all fear and flatter a tyrant as long as he is strong, because they cannot put him down, but when they see his affairs going adversely, those who were friends a short time before abandon their hypocritical respect, and suddenly become enemies and antagonists, and having discovered all his weak points, make an attack, and depose him from the government; so

8. Dan. 3.

is it also in the case of priests. Those who honored him and paid court to him a short time before, while he was strong, as soon as they have found some little handle eagerly prepare to depose him, not as a tyrant only, but something far more dreadful than that. And as the tyrant fears his bodyguards, so also does the priest dread most of all his closest fellow ministers. For no others covet his dignity so much, or know his affairs so well as these; and if anything occurs, being near at hand, they perceive it before others, and even if they slander him, can easily command belief, and, by magnifying trifles, take their victim captive. For the apostolic saying is reversed, "Whether one member suffer, all the members suffer with it; or one member be honored, all the members rejoice with it";[9] unless indeed one should be able by great discretion to stand ground against everything.

Are you then sending me forth into so great a warfare? and did you think that my soul would be equal to a contest so various in character and shape? Whence did you learn this, and from whom? If God certified this to you, show me the oracle, and I obey; but if you cannot, and form your judgment from human opinion only, please set yourself free from this delusion. For in what concerns my own affairs it is fairer to trust me than others; inasmuch as "none knows a person's thoughts, save that one's own spirit."[10] That I should have made myself and my electors ridiculous, had I accepted this office, and should with great loss have returned to this condition of life in which I now am, I trust I have now convinced you by these remarks, if not before. For not malice only, but something much stronger—the lust after this dignity—is wont to arm many against one who possesses it. And just as avaricious children are oppressed by the old age of their parents, so some of these, when they see the priestly office held by anyone for a protracted time—since it would be wickedness to destroy him—hasten to depose him from it, being all desirous to take his place, and each expecting that the dignity will be transferred to himself.

15. Would you like me to show you yet another phase of this strife, charged with innumerable dangers? Come, then, and take a peep at the public festivals when it is generally the custom for elections to be made to ecclesiastical dignities, and you will then see the priest assailed with accusations as numerous as the people whom he rules. For all who have the privilege of conferring the honor are then split into many parties; and one can never find the council of elders of one mind with each other, or about the person who has won the prelacy; but each stands apart from the others, one preferring this person, another that. Now the reason is that they

---

9. 1 Cor. 12:26.
10. 1 Cor. 2:11.

do not all look to one thing, which ought to be the only object kept in view, the excellence of the character. Instead other qualifications are alleged as recommending to this honor; for instance, of one it is said, "Let him be elected because he belongs to an illustrious family," of another "because he is possessed of great wealth, and would not need to be supported out of the revenues of the church," of a third "because he has come over from the camp of the adversary." One is eager to give the preference to someone who is on terms of intimacy with himself, another to the one who is related to him by birth, a third to the flatterer, but no one will look to the one who is really qualified, or make some test of his character.

Now I am so far from thinking these things trustworthy criteria of a person's fitness for the priesthood, that even if anyone manifested great piety, which is no small help in the discharge of that office, I should not venture to approve him on that account alone, unless he happened to combine good abilities with piety. For I know many who have exercised perpetual restraint upon themselves, and consumed themselves with fastings, who, as long as they were suffered to be alone, and attend to their own concerns, have been acceptable to God, and day by day have made no small addition to this kind of learning; but as soon as they entered public life, and were compelled to correct the ignorance of the multitude, have, some of them, proved from the outset incompetent for so great a task, and others when forced to persevere in it, have abandoned their former strict way of living, and thus inflicted great injury on themselves without profiting others at all. And if anyone spent the whole time in the lowest rank of the ministry, and reached extreme old age, I would not, merely out of reverence for his years, promote him to the higher dignity; for what if, after arriving at that time of life, he should still remain unfit for the office? And I say this now, not as wishing to dishonor the grey head, nor as laying down a law absolutely to exclude from this authority those who come from the monastic circle (for there are instances of many who issued from that body having shone conspicuously in this dignity); but the point which I am anxious to prove is that if neither piety of itself, nor advanced age, would suffice to show that a person who had obtained the priesthood really deserved it, the reasons formerly alleged would scarcely effect this.

There are also those who bring forward other pretexts yet more absurd; for some are enrolled in the ranks of the clergy so that they will not join the opponents, and others on account of their evil disposition, lest they should do greater mischief if they are overlooked. Could anything be more contrary to right rule than this? that bad persons, laden with iniquity, should be courted on account of those things for which they ought to be punished, and ascend to the priestly dignity on account of things for which they ought to be debarred from the very threshold of the church. Tell me, then, shall we seek any further the cause of God's wrath, when we expose things so holy and awful to be defiled by those who are either wicked or worthless? for when some are entrusted with the administration of things which are not at all suitable to them, and others of things which exceed their natural power, they make the condition of the church like that of Euripus.[11] . . .

And if you would know the causes of this dreadful evil, you will find that they are similar to those which were mentioned before; for they have one root and mother, so to say—namely, envy; but this is manifested in several different forms. For one we are told is to be struck out of the list of candidates because he is young; another because he does not know how to flatter; a third because he has offended such and such a person; a fourth lest such and such a person should be pained at seeing someone whom he has presented rejected, and this one elected instead; a fifth because he is kind and gentle; a sixth because he is formidable to the sinful; a seventh for some other like reason; for they are at no loss to find as many pretexts as they want, and can even make the abundance of wealth an objection when they have no other. Indeed they would be capable of discovering other reasons, as many as they wish, why someone ought not to be brought suddenly to this honor, but gently and gradually. And here I should like to ask the question, "What, then, is the prelate to do, who has to contend with such blasts? How shall he hold his ground against such billows? How shall he repel all these assaults?" . . .

16. Consider,[12] then, what kind of person he ought to be who is to hold out against such a tempest, and to manage skillfully such great hindrances to the common welfare; for he ought to be dignified yet free from arrogance, formidable yet kind, apt to command yet sociable, impartial yet courteous, humble yet not servile, strong yet gentle, in order that he may contend successfully against all these difficulties. And he ought to bring forward with great authority the one who is properly qualified for the office, even if all should oppose him, and with the same authority to reject the one who is not so qualified, even if all should conspire in his favor, and to keep one aim only in view, the building up of the church, in nothing actuated either by enmity or favor.

---

11. Straits in SE Greece, near Chalcis, proverbially violently turbulent.

12. John has moved to discuss the elections over which a bishop presided. See note 48 to Augustine's letter, p. 150.

Well, do you now think that I acted reasonably in declining the ministry of this office? But I have not even yet gone through all my reasons with you; for I have some others still to mention. And do not grow impatient of listening to a friendly and sincere man, who wishes to clear himself from your accusations; for these statements are not only serviceable for the defense which you have to make on my behalf, but they will also prove of no small help for the due administration of the office. For it is necessary for one who is going to enter upon this path of life to investigate all matters thoroughly well, before setting a hand to the ministry. Do you ask why? Because one who knows all things clearly will have this advantage, if no other, that he will not feel strange when these things befall him. Would you like me then to approach the question of superintending widows, first of all, or of the care of virgins, or the difficulty of the judicial function? For in each of these cases there is a different kind of anxiety, and the fear is greater than the anxiety. . . .

Moreover, in the reception of strangers, and the care of the sick, consider how great an expenditure of money is needed, and how much exactness and discernment[13] on the part of those who preside over these matters. For it is often necessary that this expenditure should be even larger than that of which I spoke just now [that is, because of unusual hardship], and that one who presides over it should combine prudence and wisdom with skill in the art of supply, so as to encourage the affluent to emulate and be ungrudging in their gifts, lest while providing for the relief of the sick, he should vex the souls of those who supply their wants. But earnestness and zeal need to be displayed here in a far higher degree; for the sick are difficult creatures to please, and prone to languor; and unless great accuracy and care are used, even a slight oversight is enough to do the patient great mischief.

17. . . . Again, the judicial department of the bishop's office involves innumerable vexations, great consumption of time, and difficulties exceeding those experienced by those who sit to judge secular affairs;[14] for it is a labor to discover exact justice, and when it is found, it is difficult to avoid destroying it. And not only loss of time and difficulty are incurred, but also no small danger. For ere now, some of the weaker folk, when they have plunged into business because they have not secured patronage,

---

13. *Discernment:* which is neither discerning which poor are worthy nor only how to stretch limited funds, but discerning how to increase the giving by the rich.

14. On the civil jurisdiction granted by Constantine, see Nazianzen, *On . . . His Father* 22, p. 126. The important civic, or "secular," roles at both local and imperial levels played by bishops raise difficult issues of church and state.

have made a shipwreck of their faith. This is because many of those who have suffered wrong, no less than those who have inflicted wrong, hate those who do not assist them, and they will not take into account either the intricacy of the matters in question, or the difficulty of the times, or the limits of sacerdotal authority, or anything of that kind; but they are merciless judges, recognizing only one kind of defense—release from the evils which oppress them. And one who is unable to furnish this, although innumerable excuses are alleged, will never escape their condemnation.

And talking of patronage, let me disclose another pretext for fault finding. For if the bishop does not pay a round of visits every day, more even than the idle folk about town, unspeakable offense ensues. For not only the sick, but also the whole, desire to be looked after, not that piety prompts them to this, but rather that in most cases they pretend claims to honor and distinction. And if one should ever happen to visit more constantly one of the richer and more powerful citizens, under the pressure of some necessity, with a view to the common benefit of the church, he is immediately stigmatized with a character for fawning and flattery. But why do I speak of patronage and visiting? For merely from their mode of accosting persons, bishops have to endure such a load of reproaches as to be often oppressed and overwhelmed by despondency; in fact, they have also to undergo a scrutiny of the way in which they use their eyes. For the public rigorously criticize their simplest actions, taking note of the tone of their voice, the cast of their countenance, and the degree of their laughter. He laughed heartily to such a person, one will say, and accosted him with a beaming face, and a clear voice, whereas to me he addressed only a slight and passing remark. And in a large assembly, if he does not turn his eyes in every direction when conversing, the majority declare that his conduct is insulting.

Who, then, unless exceedingly strong, could cope with so many accusers, so as either to avoid being indicted altogether, or, if indicted, to escape? For he must either be without any accusers, or, if this is impossible, purge himself of the accusations which are brought against him; and if this again is not an easy matter, as some delight in making vain and wanton charges, he must make a brave stand against the dejection produced by these complaints. He, indeed, who is justly accused, may easily tolerate the accuser, for there is no bitterer accuser than conscience; wherefore, if we are caught first by this most terrible adversary, we can readily endure the milder ones who are external to us. But he who has no evil thing upon his conscience, when he is subjected to an empty charge, is speedily excited to wrath, and easily sinks into dejection, unless he happens to have practiced beforehand how to put up with the follies of the multitude. For it is utterly impossible for one who is falsely accused without cause, and condemned, to avoid feeling some vexation and annoyance at such great injustice.[15]

And how can one speak of the distress which bishops undergo, whenever it is necessary to cut someone off from the full communion of the church? Would indeed that the evil went no further than distress! but in fact the mischief is not trifling. For there is a fear lest the person, punished beyond deserving, should experience that which was spoken of by the blessed Paul and "be swallowed up by overmuch sorrow."[16] The nicest accuracy, therefore, is required in this matter also, lest what is intended to be profitable should become to him an occasion of greater damage. For whatever sins he may commit after such a method of treatment, the wrath caused by each of them must be shared by the physician who so unskillfully applied his knife to the wound. What severe punishment, then, must be expected by one who has not only to render an account of the offenses which he himself has separately committed, but also incurs extreme danger on account of the sins committed by others? For if we shudder at undergoing judgment for our own misdeeds, believing that we shall not be able to escape the fire of the other world, what must one expect to suffer who has to answer for so many others? To prove the truth of this, listen to the blessed Paul, or rather not to him, but to Christ speaking in him, when he says: "Obey them that have the rule over you, and submit, for they watch for your souls as they that shall give account."[17]

Book 5

1. How great is the skill required for the teacher in contending earnestly for the truth, has been sufficiently set forth by us. But I have to mention one more matter beside this, which is a cause of numberless dangers, though for my own part I should rather say that the thing itself is not the cause, but they who know not how to use it rightly, since it is of itself a help to salvation and to much good besides, whenever you find that earnest and good people have the management of it. What then, do I mean by this? The expenditure of great labor upon the preparation of discourses to be delivered in public. For to begin with, the majority of those who are under the preachers' charge are not minded to behave towards them as towards teachers, but disdaining the part of learners, they assume instead the attitude of those who sit and look on at the public games; and just as the multitude there is separated into parties, and some attach themselves to

---

15. Recall 1 Pet. 2:18-23.
16. 2 Cor. 2:7.
17. Heb. 13:17. Contrast p. 71, n. 17.

one, and some to another, so here also people are divided, and become
the partisans now of this teacher, now of that, listening to them with a view
to favor or spite.[18]

And not only is there this hardship, but another quite as great. For if it
has occurred to any preacher to weave into his sermons any part of other
persons' works, he is exposed to greater disgrace than those who steal
money. Nay, often where he has not even borrowed anything from anyone,
but is only suspected, he has suffered the fate of a thief. And why do I
speak of the works of others when it is not permitted to him to use his own
resources without variety? For the public are accustomed to listen not for
profit, but for pleasure, sitting like critics of tragedies, and of musical
entertainments, and that facility of speech against which we declaimed
just now, in this case becomes desirable, even more than in the case of
barristers, where they are obliged to contend one against the other. A
preacher then should have loftiness of mind, far exceeding my own
littleness of spirit, that he may correct this disorderly and unprofitable
pleasure on the part of the multitude, and be able to lead them over to a
more useful way of hearing, that the people may follow and yield to him,
and that he may not be led away by their own humors, and this it is not
possible to arrive at, except by two means: indifference to their praise, and
the power of preaching well.

2. For if either of these be lacking, the remaining one becomes useless,
owing to its divorce from the other, for if a preacher be indifferent to
praise, and yet cannot produce the doctrine "which is with grace seasoned
with salt,"[19] he becomes despised by the multitude, while he gains nothing from his own nobleness of mind; and if on the other hand he is
successful as a preacher, and is overcome by the thought of applause,
harm is equally done in turn, both to himself and the multitude, because in
the desire for praise he is careful to speak rather with a view to please than
to profit. And as one who neither lets good opinion influence him, nor is
skillful in speaking, does not yield to the pleasure of the multitude, and is
unable to do them any good worth mentioning, because he has nothing to
say, so one who is carried away with desire for praise, though able to
render the multitude better service, rather provides in place of this such
food as will suit their taste, because he purchases thereby the tumult of
acclamation.

---

18. *Discourses to be delivered in public:* See Nazianzen, *On . . . His Father* 16, p. 124.
Separated into parties: there were organized theater claques in Antioch which could
cause considerable public turmoil. The two racing claques, the Blues and the
Greens, centered in Constantinople but not yet active in Antioch, functioned more
like mass political parties.

19. Col. 4:6.

4. To what else ought one then to be indifferent? Slander and envy. The bishop, of course, undergoes some groundless censure, but should neither fear nor tremble at unseasonable evil speaking excessively, nor entirely pass it over; but we ought, though it happen to be false, or to be brought against us by the common herd, to try to extinguish it immediately. For nothing so magnifies both an evil and a good report as the undisciplined mob. For accustomed to hear and to speak without stopping to make inquiry, they repeat at random everything which comes in their way, without any regard to the truth of it. Therefore the bishop ought not to be unconcerned about the multitude, but straightway to nip their evil surmisings in the bud, persuading his accusers, even if they be the most unreasonable of all people, and to omit nothing which is able to dispel an ill-favored report. But if, when we do all this, they who blame us will not be persuaded, thenceforward we should give them no concern. Since if anyone be too quick to be dejected by these accidents, he will not be able at any time to produce anything noble and admirable. For despondency and constant cares are mighty for destroying the powers of the mind, and for reducing it to extreme weakness. Thus then must the priest behave towards those in his charge, as a parent would behave to very young children; and as we are not disturbed either by their insults or their blows or their lamentations, nor even if they laugh and rejoice with us do we take much account of it, so should we neither be puffed up by the promises of these persons nor cast down at their censure, when it comes from them unseasonably. But this is hard, my good friend; and perhaps, I think, even impossible. For I know not whether anyone ever succeeded in the effort not to be pleased when praised, and the one who is pleased at this is likely also to desire to enjoy it, and the one who desires to enjoy it will, of necessity, be altogether vexed and beside himself whenever he misses it. For as they who revel in being rich, when they fall into poverty are grieved, and they who have been used to live luxuriously cannot bear to live shabbily; so, too, they who long for applause, not only when they are blamed without a cause, but when they are not constantly being praised, become, as by some famine, wasted in soul, particularly when they happen themselves to have been used to praise, or if they hear others being praised. . . .

6. You see, my excellent friend, that the person who is powerful in preaching has special need of greater study than others; and besides study, of forbearance also greater than what is needed by all those whom I have already mentioned. For thus are many constantly springing up against him, in a vain and senseless spirit, and, having no fault to find except that he is generally approved of, hate him. He must bear their bitter malice nobly, for

as they are not able to hide this cursed hatred, which they so unreasonably entertain, they both revile and censure and slander in private, and defame in public, and the mind which has begun to be pained and exasperated, on every one of these occasions, will not escape being corrupted by grief. They will not only revenge themselves upon him by their own acts, but will try to do so by means of others, and often having chosen some one of those who are unable to speak a word, will extol him with their praises and admire him beyond his worth.

Some do this through ignorance alone, some through ignorance and envy, in order that they may ruin the reputation of the other, not that they may prove the person to be wonderful who is not so. The noble-minded one has not only to struggle against these, but often against the ignorance of the whole multitude, since it is not possible that all those who come together should consist of learned persons, but the chances are that the larger part of the congregation is composed of unlearned people, and that even the rest, who are clearer-headed than they, fall as far short of being able to criticize sermons as the remainder again fall short of them; so that only one or two are seated there who possess this power. It follows, of necessity, that one who preaches better than others carries away less applause, and possibly goes home without being praised at all, and must be prepared to meet such anomalies nobly, and to pardon those who commit them in ignorance, and to weep for those who acquiesce in them on account of envy as wretched and pitiable creatures, and not to consider that his powers have become less on either of these accounts. For if a person, being a preeminently good painter, and superior to all in his art, sees the portrait which he has drawn with great accuracy held up to ridicule, he ought not to be dejected, and to consider the picture poor, because of the judgment of the ignorant; as he would not consider the drawing that is really poor to be something wonderful and lovely, because of the astonishment of the inartistic.

8. For if one be first carried away with the desire for indiscriminate praise, one will reap no advantage from his labors, or from his power in preaching, for the mind being unable to bear the senseless censures of the multitude is dispirited, and casts aside all earnestness about preaching. Therefore it is especially necessary to be trained to be indifferent to all kinds of praise. For knowing how to preach is not enough for the preservation of that power, if this independence be not added.

If anyone would examine accurately the person who is destitute of this art, it will be found that he needs to be indifferent to praise no less than the other, otherwise he will be forced to do many wrong things in placing himself under the control of popular opinion. For not having the energy to equal those who are famous for the quality of their preaching, he will not refrain from forming ill designs against them, from envying them, and from blaming them without reason, and from many such discreditable practices. He will venture everything, even if it be needful to ruin his own soul, for the sake of bringing down their fame to the level of his own insignificance. And in addition to this, he will leave off his exertions about work; a kind of numbness, as it were, spreading itself over his mind. For much toil, rewarded by scanty praise, is sufficient to cast down one who cannot despise praise, and put him into a deep lethargy, since the farmer also when he spends time over some sorry piece of land, and is forced to till a rock, quickly desists from work, unless he is possessed of much earnestness about the matter, or has a fear of famine impending over him. . . .

Do you not know what a passion for sermons has burst in upon the minds of Christians nowadays? and that they who practice themselves in preaching are in especial honor, not only among the heathen, but among them of the household of the faith? How then could anyone bear such disgrace as to find that all are mute when he is preaching, and think that they are oppressed, and wait for the end of the sermon, as for some release from work; while they listen to another with eagerness though he preach long, and are sorry when he is about to conclude, and almost angry when it is his purpose to be silent. If these matters seem to you to be small, and easily to be despised, it is because of your inexperience. They are truly enough to quench zeal, and to paralyze the powers of the mind, unless one withdraw from all human passions, and study to frame his conduct after the pattern of those incorporeal powers, who are neither pursued by envy, nor by longing for fame, nor by any other morbid feeling. If then there be anyone so constituted as to be able to subdue this wild beast, so difficult to capture, so unconquerable, so fierce—that is to say, public fame—and to cut off its many heads, or rather to forbid their growth altogether, he will easily be able to repel these many violent assaults, and to enjoy a kind of quiet haven of rest. But he who has not freed himself from this monster, involves his soul in struggles of various kinds, and perpetual agitation, and the burden both of despondency and of other passions. But why need I detail the rest of these difficulties, which no one will be able to describe, or to learn unless he has had actual experience of them.[20]

Book 6

1. Our condition here, indeed, is such as you have heard. But our condition hereafter how shall we endure, when we are compelled to give

20. *Withdraw from all human passions:* see Ps.-Basil, Ep. 366, p. 121. *Public fame:* see *Verba Seniorum* 8.2, 19, p. 76, and recall Book 3.17 above, at note 15.

our account for each of those who have been entrusted to us? For our penalty is not limited to shame, but everlasting chastisement awaits us as well. As for the passage, "Obey them that have the rule over you, and submit to them, for they watch in behalf of your souls as they that shall give account";[21] though I have mentioned it once already, yet I will break silence about it now, for the fear of its warning is continually agitating my soul. For if for him who causes one only, and that the least, to stumble, it is profitable that "a great millstone should be hanged about his neck, and that he should be sunk in the depth of the sea";[22] and if they who wound the consciences of the faithful, sin against Christ himself,[23] what then will they one day suffer, what kind of penalty will they pay, who destroy not one only, or two, or three, but so many multitudes? For it is not possible for inexperience to be urged as an excuse, nor to take refuge in ignorance, nor for the plea of necessity or force to be put forward. Yea, if it were possible, one of those under their charge could more easily make use of this refuge for his own sins than bishops in the case of the sins of others. Do you ask why? Because the one who has been appointed to rectify the ignorance of others, and to warn them beforehand of the conflict with the devil which is coming upon them, will not be able to put forward ignorance as an excuse, or to say, "I have never heard the trumpet sound, I did not foresee the conflict." For he is set for that very purpose, says Ezekiel, that he may sound the trumpet for others, and warn them of the dangers at hand. And therefore his chastisement is inevitable, though he that perishes happen to be but one. "For if when the sword comes, the watchman does not sound the trumpet to the people, nor give them a sign, and the sword come and take anyone away, he indeed is taken away on account of his iniquity, but his blood will I require at the watchman's hands."[24]

4. But of those who are subject to the priest, the greater number are hampered with the cares of this life, and this makes them the slower in the performance of spiritual duties. Whence it is necessary for the teacher to sow every day (so to speak), in order that by its frequency at least, the word of doctrine may be able to be grasped by those who hear. For excessive wealth, and an abundance of power, and sloth the offspring of luxury, and many other things beside these, choke the seeds which have been let fall.[25] Often too the thick growth of thorns does not suffer the seed to drop even upon the surface of the soil. Again, excess of trouble, stress of poverty, constant insults, and other such things, the reverse of the forego-

---

21. Heb. 13:17. Contrast its use, pp. 35, 71.
22. Matt. 18:6.
23. 1 Cor. 8:12.
24. Ezek. 33:6; cf. 33:1-20 and 3:16-21.
25. Mark 4:19 = Matt. 13:22.

ing, take the mind away from eagerness about things divine, and not even the smallest part of their sins can become apparent to them. How could they be, since the greater number of these sins they don't recognize by sight?

The priest's relations with the people involve much difficulty. But if any inquire about relations with God, he will find the others to be as nothing, since these require a greater and more thorough earnestness.[26] For one who acts as an ambassador on behalf of the whole city—but why do I say the city? on behalf of the whole world indeed—prays that God would be merciful to the sins of all, not only of the living, but also of the departed. What manner of person ought he to be? For my part I think that the boldness of speech of Moses and Elias is insufficient for such supplication. For as though he were entrusted with the whole world and were himself the father of all, he draws near to God, beseeching that wars may be extinguished everywhere, that tumults may be quelled; asking for peace and plenty, and a swift deliverance from all the ills that beset each one, publicly and privately; and he ought as much to excel in every respect all those on whose behalf he prays, as rulers should excel their subjects.

And whenever he invokes the Holy Spirit, and offers the most dread sacrifice, and constantly handles the common Lord of all, tell me what rank shall we give him? What great purity and what real piety must we demand? For consider what manner of hands they ought to be which minister in these things, and of what kind the tongue which utters such words. Ought not the soul which receives so great a spirit to be purer and holier than anything in the world? At such a time angels stand by the priest; and the whole sanctuary, and the space round about the altar, is filled with the powers of heaven, in honor of him who lies thereon. For this, indeed, is capable of being proved from the very rites which are being then celebrated. I myself, moreover, have heard someone once relate that a certain aged, venerable man, accustomed to see revelations, used to tell him that he, being thought worthy of a vision of this kind, at such a time saw, on a sudden, so far as was possible for him, a multitude of angels, clothed in shining robes and encircling the altar and bending down, as one might see soldiers in the presence of their king, and for my part I believe it. Moreover another told me, without learning it from someone

---

26. *Relations with God:* the following examples refer to the words and actions of the priest in the liturgy. Concerning the angels, recall Isa. 6:1-4, the Sanctus, which is used in Jewish, Greek, and Latin liturgies, and is always introduced as something sung by both angels and people.

We have seen discussion of the relative need of holiness of clergy and laity in Cyprian, Ep. 67.3, pp. 62f., a complex of issues which so exercised the Latin church, but which was accepted more naively and calmly in the East.

else, but as being himself thought worthy to be both an ear and eye witness of it, that, in the case of those who are about to depart hence, if they happen to be partakers of the mysteries, with a pure conscience, when they are about to breathe their last, angels keep guard over them for the sake of what they have received, and bear them hence. And do you not yet tremble to introduce a soul into so sacred a mystery of this kind, and to advance to the dignity of the priesthood, one robed in filthy raiment, whom Christ has shut out from the rest of the band of guests?[27] The soul of the priest should shine like a light beaming over the whole world. But mine has so great darkness overhanging it, because of my evil conscience, as to be always cast down and never able to look up with confidence to its Lord. Priests are the salt of the earth.[28] But who would easily put up with my lack of understanding, and my inexperience in all things, but you, who have been wont to love me beyond measure.

For the priest ought not only to be thus pure as one who has been dignified with so high a ministry, but very discreet, and skilled in many matters, and to be as well versed in the affairs of this life as they who are engaged in the world, and yet to be free from all cares more than the recluses who occupy the mountains. Since he must mix with men who have wives, and who bring up children, who possess servants, and are surrounded with wealth, and fill public positions, and are persons of influence, he too should be many-sided. I say many-sided, not unreal, nor yet fawning and hypocritical, but full of much freedom and assurance, and knowing how to adapt profitably, where the circumstances of the case require it, and to be both kind and severe. It is not possible to treat all those under one's charge on one plan, since neither is it proper for physicians to apply one course of treatment to all their sick, nor for a pilot to know but one way of contending with the winds. For, indeed, continual storms beset this ship of ours, and these storms do not assail from without only, but take their rise from within,[29] and there is need of much condescension and circumspection. All these different matters have one end in view, the glory of God, and the edifying of the church.

---

27. Matt. 22:13.
28. Matt. 5:13.
29. *Take their rise from within:* a common understanding; see Cyprian, Ep. 11.1.2, p. 56.

10

FOUNDATIONS OF
THE MIDDLE AGES

Leo the Great
Letters 4.1, 3–6; 19.1; 106.1–2, 6; 167.1–3

These letters are from NPNF 2.12, which is a collection of Leo's letters and sermons. From 167.3 we have taken Questions 2, 4–15. The most modern English life is Jalland (1941); otherwise, see DiBerardino (1986).

Virtually nothing is known of Leo's life before his election, and relatively little after it. It is guessed that he was born at the end of the fourth century, and his excellent Latin style but ignorance of Greek show a Western upbringing of some substance. Of his writings, only collections of letters and sermons remain.

We hear of Leo, before his election, actively opposing Pelagianism and involved in mediation between hostile generals. This pattern of stalwart defense of Orthodoxy and political mediation marked his career. He played the major Western role in the christological controversies leading to the Council of Chalcedon and opposed Pelagianism and Manichaeism as well. In the years following 451, he also took part in the successful imperial delegation to Attila the Hun and gained some concessions for Rome from the invading Vandal general Gaiseric.

Leo is known for establishing further the primacy of the Roman See. He involved himself in various Western disputes, and his support was solicited by some Eastern bishops (although ignored by others). In the West, however, the political situation was falling apart: the rapid growth of the Arian Vandal kingdom was matched, after 455, by a series of hapless Western Roman emperors. Leo's work in extending papal influence and codifying orthodox belief and moral practice was aimed at preventing chaos and anarchy. The situation was moving toward the watershed period of Gregory the Great's episcopate.

On this period of nascent Europe, further relevant reading is in Salvian of Marseille's *On the Governance of God*, especially books 3–4; Bishop Sidonius of Clermont's letters, especially book 7, number 9; and Eugippius's *Life of Severin*, especially ch. 17. On the generation before Gregory, the sermons of Caesarius of Arles (died 542), especially 78 and 230, are interesting; on the generation after, consult Braulio of Saragossa (died 651), especially Ep. 5, 13, 21, 35, 36. Sidonius is translated in the Loeb series, and the others in the Fathers of the Church.

Gregory the Great
The Book of Pastoral Rule 1.1–3, 5, 6, 11; 2.1, 8;
3. Prologue, 1, 25, 40; 4

These portions are taken from Davis (1950), in ACW. *The Pastoral Rule* along with a large selection of Gregory's letters is found in NPNF 2.12–13. Besides Richards's biography (1980), one should consult Evans (1986) and especially Straw (1988).

Gregory the Great, our final author, was a transitional figure: the last patristic bishop of Rome and the first medieval pope. His heritage was fully Greco-Roman, but the world he helped so much to shape was clearly European.

Born of a Roman senatorial family around 540, Gregory, as prefect of Rome ca. 573, showed his aptitude for effective and disinterested administration in accordance with the highest traditions of Roman public service. He was soon drawn, however, to the contemplative life: he distributed his wealth to support the poor, founded seven monasteries, and entered one as a monk, Saint Andrew's, which was set up in the family's Roman estate.

Gregory was too skilled to be left in the tranquility he desired. He was soon made a deacon of Rome; then in about 578 he was sent to Constantinople as the pope's ambassador. This experience formed the basis for his relationship to imperial authority. Constantinople's luxury shocked him, and its weaknesses and intense self-interest cautioned him. By 585 he had returned to Rome as abbot of St. Andrew's. In 590, after much soul searching, and in the midst of the plague and the Lombard invasion, he was elected pope. He served, "servant of the servants of God," as he called himself, until his death in 604.

Gregory was Europe's greatest reformer, perhaps excepting Luther. Not only did he deal vigorously with the staggering problems at hand, but through his voluminous writings he laid the foundations on which medieval institutions and culture were built. All his various works share a common thread: an attention to the needs of the common Christian believer, the united needs of body and spirit.

His political activities aimed to pacify and organize the fragmented European scene. Gregory settled a peace with the Lombards, independently of the nearly impotent imperial court, and set up other treaties and local governments, which helped relieve the populace from the long-suffered ravages of war and anarchy. His reorganization of papal property and clergy and of monasticism released great wealth for greatly needed relief of the poor and established important central controls over the despotic power of the local nobilities.

Gregory's theology was a simplified Augustinianism, with a measure of pseudo-Dionysius's thought. It emphasized, as did his biblical exegesis, moral and practical aspects. Popular religious expression in Europe for the next millennium was shaped primarily by the elements assembled in his work: his reforms of church prayer and music, initiating the development towards Gregorian chant; his appreciative treatment and organization of angelology, hagiography, and the veneration of relics; and his mission strategy. A notable example of the last was his commissioning the prior of St. Andrew's, Augustine of Canterbury, to refound the church in England.

LEO THE GREAT, SELECT LETTERS

Letter 4.1, 3–6

Leo, bishop of the city of Rome, to all the bishops appointed in Campania, Picenum, Etruria,[1] and all the provinces, greeting in the Lord.

1. As the peaceful settlement of the churches causes us satisfaction, so are we saddened with no slight sorrow whenever we learn that anything

---

1. Regions to the south, northeast, and northwest, respectively, of Rome.

has been taken for granted or done contrary to the ordinances of the canons and the discipline of the church; and if we do not repress such things with the vigilance we ought, we cannot excuse ourselves to God who intended us to be watchmen,[2] for permitting the pure body of the church, which we ought to keep clean from every stain, to be defiled by contact with wicked schemers, since the framework of the members loses its harmony by such dissimulation.

3. Again, when each one's respectability of birth and conduct has been established, what sort of person should be associated with the ministry of the sacred altar we have learnt both from the teaching of the Apostle and the divine precepts and the regulations of the canons, from which we find very many of the faithful have turned aside and quite gone out of the way. For it is well known that the husbands of widows have attained to the priesthood; certain others, too, who have had several wives and have led a life given up to all licentiousness, have had all facilities put in their way, and been admitted to the sacred order. This is contrary to that utterance of the blessed Apostle, in which he proclaims and says to such, "the husband of one wife,"[3] and contrary to that precept of the ancient law which says by way of caution: "Let the priest take a virgin to wife, not a widow, not a divorced woman."[4] All such persons, therefore, who have been admitted we order to be put out of their offices in the church and from the title of priest by the authority of the Apostolic See; for they will have no claim to that for which they were not eligible, on account of the obstacle in question. We specially claim for ourselves the duty of settling this, that if any of these irregularities have been committed, they may be corrected and may not be allowed to occur again, and that no excuse may arise from ignorance, although it has never been allowed a priest to be ignorant of what has been laid down by the rules of the canons.

4. This point, too, we have thought must not be passed over, that certain possessed with the love of base gain lay out their money at interest, and wish to enrich themselves as usurers. For we are grieved that this is practiced not only by those who belong to the clergy, but also by laity who desire to be called Christians. And we decree that those who have been convicted be punished sharply, that all occasion of sinning be removed.

5. The following warning, also, we have thought fit to give, that no cleric should attempt to make money in another's name anymore than in his own: for it is unbecoming to shield one's crime under another's gains. Nay, we ought to look at and aim at only that usury whereby what we bestow in

2. Cf. Ezek. 3:17.
3. 1 Tim. 3:2.
4. Lev. 21:13, 14.

mercy here we may recover from the Lord, who will restore a thousandfold what will last forever.

6. This admonition of ours, therefore, proclaims that if any of our clergy endeavor to contravene these rules and dare to do what is forbidden by them, he may know that he is liable to deposition from office, and that he will not be a sharer in our communion who refuses to be a sharer of our discipline.[5]

Letter 19.1

Leo, bishop, to Dorus his well-beloved brother.

1. We grieve that the judgment, which we hoped to entertain of you, has been frustrated by our ascertaining that you have done things which by their blameworthy novelty infringe the whole system of church discipline: although you know full well with what care we wish the provisions of the canons to be kept through all the churches of the Lord, and the priests of all the peoples to consider it their especial duty to prevent the violation of the rules of the holy constitutions by any extravagances. We are surprised, therefore, that you who ought to have been a strict observer of the injunctions of the Apostolic See have acted so carelessly, or rather so contumaciously, as to show yourself not a guardian, but a breaker of the laws handed on to you. For from the report of your presbyter, Paul, which is subjoined, we have learnt that the order of the presbyterate has been thrown into confusion by strange intrigues and vile collusion; in such a way that one has been hastily and prematurely promoted, and others passed over whose advancement was recommended by their age, and who were charged with no fault. But if the eagerness of an intriguer or the ignorant zeal of supporters demanded that which custom never allowed, viz. that a beginner should be preferred to veterans, and a mere child to those of years, it was your duty by diligence and teaching to check the improper desires of the petitioners with all reasonable authority; lest he whom you advanced hastily to the priestly rank should enter on his office to the detriment of those with whom he associated and become demoralized by the growth within him, not of the virtue of humility, but of the vice of conceit. For you were not unaware that the Lord had said that "he that humble himself shall be exalted: but he that exalt himself shall be humbled,"[6] and also had said, "But seek from little to increase, and from the greater to be less."[7] For both actions are out of order and out of place;

---

5. On usury, still obtaining, see canon 20 of Elvira, p. 102.
6. Luke 14:11; 18:14.
7. Matt. 20:28 (Codex D).

and all the fruit of their labors is lost, all the measure of their deserts is rendered void, if the gaining of dignity is proportioned to the amount of flattery used: so that the eagerness to be eminent belittles not only the aspirer himself, but also him that connives at him. But if, as is asserted, the first and second presbyter were so agreeable to Epicarpius being put over their heads as to demand his being honored to their own disgrace, that which they wished ought not to have been granted them when they were voluntarily degrading themselves: because it would have been worthier of you to oppose than to yield to such a pitiable wish. Moreover, their base and cowardly submission could not be to the prejudice of others whose consciences were good and who had done nothing to offend God's grace; so that, whatever the transaction was whereby they gave up their precedence to another, they could not lower the dignity of those that came next to them, nor because they had placed the last above themselves, could he take precedence of the rest.[8]

Letter 106.1–2, 6

Leo, the bishop, to Anatolius, the bishop.

1. Now that the light of gospel truth has been manifested, as we wished, through God's grace, and the night of most pestilential error has been dispelled from the universal church, we are unspeakably glad in the Lord, because the difficult charge entrusted to us has been brought to the desired conclusion, even as the text of your letter announces, so that, according to the Apostle's teaching, "we all speak the same thing, and that there be no schisms among us: but that we be perfect in the same mind and in the same knowledge."[9] In devotion to which work we commend you, beloved, for taking part: for thus you benefited those who needed correction by your activity, and purged yourself from all complicity with the transgressors. For when your predecessor Flavian, of happy memory, was deposed for his defense of catholic truth, not unjustly it was believed

---

8. The problems resemble Basil's in canon 10, p. 107; on wrong zeal and wrong reticence, see Origen, Hom. 20.4 on Numbers; 6.1 on Isaiah, p. 35, n. 13.

9. 1 Cor. 1:10. Leo wrote his famous Tome at the request of Flavian, patriarch of Constantinople, whose successor was this Anatolius. The "gospel light" refers to the Council of Chalcedon, which accepted the Tome, but the Council also caused the disorder mentioned below. Its canon 28 gave the See of Constantinople equal honor to Rome's, because it was the New Rome. Nicaea's canon 6 honored Rome, then Alexandria, then Antioch, since Constantinople had not yet been built. (Nicaea became regularly called the Council of the 318 Holy Fathers, alluding to Abraham's contingent, Gen. 14:14, although it appears that there were not so many bishops there. "The anathemas of the 318 Holy Fathers" became a popular element of curse formulas.)

that your ordainers seemed to have consecrated one like themselves, contrary to the provision of the holy canons. But God's mercy was present in this, directing and confirming you, that you might make good use of bad beginnings, and show that you were promoted not by human judgment, but by God's loving-kindness: and this may be accepted as true, on condition that you lose not the grace of this divine gift by another cause of offense. For the catholic, and especially the Lord's priest, must not only be entangled in no error, but also be corrupted by no covetousness; for, as says the holy scripture, "Go not after your lusts, and decline from your desire."[10] Many enticements of this world, many vanities must be resisted, that the perfection of true self-discipline may be attained: the first blemish of which is pride, the beginning of transgression and the origin of sin. For the mind greedy of power knows not either how to abstain from things forbidden nor to enjoy things permitted, so long as transgressions go unpunished and run into undisciplined and wicked excesses, and wrong doings are multiplied, which were only endured in our zeal for the restoration of the faith and love of harmony.

2. I grieve, beloved, that you have fallen into this too, that you should try to break down the most sacred constitutions of the Nicene canons: as if this opportunity had expressly offered itself to you for the See of Alexandria to lose its privilege of second place, and the church of Antioch to forego its right to being third in dignity.... Let no synodal councils flatter themselves upon the size of their assemblies, and let not any number of priests, however much larger, dare either to compare or to prefer themselves to those 318 bishops, seeing that the Synod of Nicaea is hallowed by God....

6. In thus writing to you, brother, I exhort and admonish you in the Lord, laying aside all ambitious desires to cherish rather a spirit of love and to adorn yourself to your profit with the virtues of love, according to the Apostle's teaching. For love "is patient and kind, and envies not, acts not iniquitously, is not puffed up, is not ambitious, seeks not its own."[11] Hence if love seeks not its own, how greatly does one sin who covets another's? From which I desire you to keep yourself altogether, and to remember that sentence which says, "Hold what you have, that no other take your crown."[12] For if you seek what is not permitted, you will deprive yourself by your own action and judgment of the peace of the universal church. Our brother and fellow bishop Lucian and our son Basil, the deacon,

10. Ben Sira 18:30.
11. 1 Cor. 13:4, 5.
12. Rev. 3:11.

attended to your injunctions with all the zeal they possessed, but justice
refused to give effect to their pleadings.

Letter 167.1–3

Leo, the bishop, to Rusticus, bishop of Gallia Narbonensis.

1. Your letter, brother, . . . I have gladly received; the number of different
matters it contains makes it indeed lengthy, but not so tedious to me on a
patient perusal that any point should be passed over, amid the cares that
press upon me from all sides. . . . We gather that Sabinian and Leo,
presbyters, lacked confidence in your action. . . . What form or what
measure of justice you ought to mete out to them I leave to your own
discretion, advising you, however, with the exhortation of love that to the
healing of the sick you ought to apply spiritual medicine, and that remembering the scripture which says "be not over just,"[13] you should act with
mildness toward these who in zeal for chastity seem to have exceeded the
limits of vengeance, lest the devil, who deceived the adulterers, should
triumph over the avengers of the adultery.

2. But I am surprised, beloved, that you are so disturbed by opposition
in consequence of offenses, from whatever cause arising, as to say you
would rather be relieved of the labors of your bishopric, and live in
quietness and ease than continue in the office committed to you. But since
the Lord says, "Blessed is he who shall persevere unto the end,"[14] whence
shall come this blessed perseverance, except from the strength of patience? For as the Apostle proclaims, "All who would live godly in Christ
shall suffer persecution."[15] And it is not only to be reckoned persecution,
when sword or fire or other active means are used against the Christian
religion; for the direct persecution is often inflicted by nonconformity of
practice and persistent disobedience and the barbs of ill-natured tongues;
and since all the members of the church are always liable to these attacks,
and no portion of the faithful are free from temptation, so that a life neither
of ease nor of labor is devoid of danger, who shall guide the ship amidst
the waves of the sea if the helmsman quit his post? Who shall guard the
sheep from the treachery of wolves if the shepherd be not on the watch?
Who, lastly, shall resist the thieves and robbers if love of quietude draw
away the guard that is set to keep the outlook from the strictness of the
watch? One must abide, therefore, in the office committed to him and in
the task undertaken.[16] Justice must be steadfastly upheld and mercy

---

13. Eccles. 7:16.
14. Matt. 24:13.
15. 2 Tim. 3:12.
16. See Origen, Hom. 20.4 on Numbers and 6.1 on Isaiah, p. 35, n. 13.

lovingly extended. Not individuals, but their sins must be hated. The proud must be rebuked, the weak must be borne with; and those sins which require severer chastisement must be dealt with in the spirit not of vindictiveness but of desire to heal. And if a fiercer storm of tribulation fall upon us, let us not be terror stricken as if we had to overcome the disaster in our own strength, since both our counsel and our strength is Christ, and through him we can do all things, without him nothing, who, to confirm the preachers of the gospel and the ministers of the mysteries, says, "Lo, I am with you all the days even to the consummation of the age."[17] And again he says, "These things I have spoken unto you that in me you may have peace. In this world you shall have tribulation, but be of good cheer because I have overcome the world."[18] The promises, which are as plain as they can be, we ought not to let any causes of offense to weaken, lest we should seem ungrateful to God for making us his chosen vessels, since God's assistance is powerful as his promises are true.

3. On those points of inquiry, beloved, which your archdeacon has brought me separately written out, it would be easier to arrive at conclusions on each point face to face, if you could grant us the advantage of your presence. For since some questions seem to exceed the limits of ordinary diligence, I perceive that they are better suited to conversation than to writing: for as there are certain things which can in no wise be controverted, so there are many things which require to be modified either by considerations of age or by the necessities of the case; always provided that we remember in things which are doubtful or obscure, that must be followed which is found to be neither contrary to the commands of the gospel nor opposed to the decrees of the holy Fathers.

QUESTION 2. Concerning a presbyter or deacon, who on his crime being known asks for public penance, whether it is to be granted by laying on of hands?

REPLY. It is contrary to the custom of the church that they who have been dedicated to the dignity of the presbyterate or the rank of the diaconate, should receive the remedy of penitence by laying on of hands for any crime; which doubtless descends from the apostles' tradition, according to what is written, "If a priest shall have sinned, who shall pray for him?"[19] And hence such persons when they have lapsed in order to obtain God's mercy must seek private retirement, where their atonement may be profitable as well as adequate.

---

17. Matt. 28:20.
18. John 16:33.
19. 1 Sam. 2:25.

QUESTION 4.[20] Concerning a presbyter or deacon who has given his unmarried daughter in marriage to a man who already had a woman joined to him, by whom he had also had children.

REPLY. Not every woman that is joined to a man is his wife, even as every child is not his parent's heir. But the marriage bond is legitimate between the freeborn and between equals: this was laid down by the Lord long before the Roman law had its beginning. And so a wife is different from a concubine, even as a bondwoman from a free woman. For which reason also the Apostle in order to show the difference of these persons quotes from Genesis, where it is said to Abraham, "Cast out the bondwoman and her son: for the son of the bondwoman shall not be heir with my son Isaac."[21] And hence, since the marriage tie was from the beginning so constituted as apart from the joining of the sexes to symbolize the mystic union of Christ and his church, it is undoubted that that woman has no part in matrimony, in whose case it is shown that the mystery of marriage has not taken place. Accordingly a clergyperson of any rank who has given a daughter in marriage to a man that has a concubine, must not be considered to have given her to a married man, unless perchance the other woman should appear to have become free, to have been legitimately dowered and to have been honored by public nuptials.

QUESTION 5. Concerning young women who have married men that have concubines.

REPLY. Those who are joined to husbands by their fathers' will are free from blame, if the women whom their husbands had were not in wedlock.

QUESTION 6. Concerning those who leave the women by whom they have children and take wives.

REPLY. Seeing that the wife is different from the concubine, to turn a bondwoman from one's couch and take a wife whose free birth is assured, is not bigamy but an honorable proceeding.

QUESTION 7. Concerning those who in sickness accept terms of penitence, and when they have recovered, refuse to keep them.

REPLY. Such persons' neglect is to be blamed but not finally to be abandoned, in order that they may be incited by frequent exhortations to carry out faithfully what under stress of need they asked for. For no one is

---

20. Questions 4–6 deal with problems springing from the social dislocation of the period, but they also show the power of social norms, such as class, to determine the shape of decisions.

21. Gen. 21:10.

to be despaired of so long as he remain in this body, because sometimes what the diffidence of age puts off is accomplished by maturer counsels.

QUESTION 8. Concerning those who on their deathbed promise repentance and die before receiving communion.

REPLY. Their cause is reserved for the judgment of God, in whose hand it was that their death was put off until the very time of communion. But we cannot be in communion with those, when dead, with whom when alive we were not in communion.

QUESTION 9. Concerning those who under pressure of great pain ask for penance to be granted them, and when the presbyter has come to give what they seek, if the pain has abated somewhat, make excuses and refuse to accept what is offered.

REPLY. This tergiversation cannot proceed from contempt of the remedy but from fear of falling into worse sin. Hence the penance which is put off, when it is more earnestly sought must not be denied in order that the wounded soul may in whatever way attain to the healing of absolution.[22]

QUESTION 10. Concerning those who have professed repentance, if they begin to go to law in the forum.

REPLY. To demand just debts is indeed one thing and to think nothing of one's own property from the perfection of love is another. But one who craves pardon for unlawful doings ought to abstain even from many things that are lawful, as says the Apostle, "All things are lawful for me, but all things are not expedient."[23] Hence, if the penitent has a matter which perchance he ought not to neglect, it is better for him to have recourse to the judgment of the church than of the forum.

QUESTION 11. Concerning those who during or after penance transact business.

REPLY. The nature of their gains either excuses or condemns the trafficker, because there is an honorable and a base kind of profit. Notwithstanding, it is more expedient for the penitent to suffer loss than to be involved in the risks of trafficking, because it is hard for sin not to come into transactions between buyer and seller.

QUESTION 12. Concerning those who return to military service after doing penance.

---

22. Tergiversation is equivocation. Leo will credit the coy penitent with the better of the two possible motives, and so try to assure healing.

23. 1 Cor. 6:12. The Forum was the civil court, but church courts had jurisdiction as well, and Leo urges that they be used instead.

Reply. It is altogether contrary to the rules of the church to return to military service in the world after doing penance, as the Apostle says, "No soldier in God's service entangles himself in the affairs of the world."[24] Hence one is not free from the snares of the devil who wishes to entangle himself in the military service of the world.

Question 13. Concerning those who after penance take wives or join themselves to concubines.

Reply. If a young man under fear of death or the dangers of captivity has done penance, and afterwards fearing to fall into youthful incontinence has chosen to marry a wife lest he should be guilty of fornication, he seems to have committed a pardonable act, so long as he has known no woman whatever save his wife. Yet herein we lay down no rule, but express an opinion as to what is less objectionable. For according to a true view of the matter nothing better suits him who has done penance than continued chastity both of mind and body.[25]

Question 14. Concerning monks who take to military service or to marriage.

Reply. The monk's vow being undertaken of his own will or wish cannot be given up without sin. For that which one has vowed to God, he ought also to pay. Hence he who abandons his profession of a single life and betakes himself to military service or to marriage, must make atonement and clear himself publicly, because although such service may be innocent and the married state honorable, it is transgression to have forsaken the higher choice.

Question 15. Concerning young women who have worn the religious habit for some time but have not been dedicated, if they afterwards marry.

Reply. Young women, who without being forced by their parents' command but of their own free will have taken the vow and habit of virginity, if afterwards they choose wedlock, act wrongly, even though they have not received dedication: of which they would doubtless not have been defrauded, if they had abided by their vow.

---

24. 2 Tim. 2:4. On soldiery in questions 12 and 14, see Jerome, Ep. 52.1, p. 153.
25. The place of marriage remains ambivalent; see Tertullian, p. 47.

GREGORY THE GREAT,
THE BOOK OF PASTORAL RULE[26]

Part 1
(1–3, 5, 6, 11)

1. No one ventures to teach any art without having learned it after deep thought. With what rashness, then, would the pastoral office be undertaken by the unfit, seeing that the government of souls is the art of arts! For who does not realize that the wounds of the mind are more hidden than the internal wounds of the body? Yet, although those who have no knowledge of the powers of drugs shrink from giving themselves out as physicians of the flesh, people who are utterly ignorant of spiritual precepts are often not afraid of professing themselves to be physicians of the heart, and though, by divine ordinance, those now in the highest positions are disposed to show a regard for religion, some there are who aspire to glory and esteem by an outward show of authority within the holy church. They crave to appear as teachers and covet ascendancy over others, and, as the truth attests: "They seek the first salutations in the market place, the first places at feasts, and the first chairs in the synagogues."[27]

These persons are all the more unfitted to administer worthily what they have undertaken, the office of pastoral care, in that they have attained to the tutorship of humility by vanity alone.

2. Further, there are some who investigate spiritual precepts with shrewd diligence, but in the life they live trample on what they have penetrated by their understanding. They hasten to teach what they have learned, not by practice, but by study, and belie in their conduct what they teach by words. Hence it is that when the pastor walks through steep places, the flock following comes to a precipice. Therefore, the Lord complains through the prophet of the contemptible knowledge of pastors, saying: "When you drank the clearest water, you troubled the rest with your feet. And my sheep were fed with that which you had trodden with your feet, and they drank what your feet had troubled."[28] Evidently, the pastors drink water that is most clear, when with a right understanding they imbibe the streams of truth, whereas to foul the water with the feet is to corrupt the

---

26. Gregory Nazianzen's Oration 2, *In Defense of His Flight* (see NPNF 2.7.204ff.) was a major inspiration to Gregory, as it was also for Chrysostom's *On the Priesthood* (see p. 164). It is interesting to study how Chrysostom and Gregory took up and reformulated Nazianzen's work. How did their presuppositions and goals differ?

On the weightiness and dangers of office, and the dictum that one fitted by God must take it up, see Origen, above p. 35, n.13.

27. Matt. 23:6ff.

28. Ezek. 34:18.

studies of holy meditation by an evil life. The sheep, of course, drink of the water befouled by those feet, when the subjects do not follow the instruction which they hear, but imitate only the wicked examples which they see. While they thirst for the things said, but are perverted by the things done, they imbibe mud with their draught as if they drank from polluted fountains of water. Consequently, too, it is written by the prophet: "Bad priests are a snare of ruin to my people."[29]

Hence again, the Lord says by the prophet concerning the priests: "They were a stumbling block of iniquity to the house of Israel."[30] For no one does more harm in the church than one who, having the title or rank of holiness, acts evilly. No one presumes to take to task such a delinquent, and the offense, serving as an example, has far-reaching consequences, when the sinner is honored out of respect paid to rank. Yet everyone who is unworthy would flee from the burden of such great guilt if with the attentive ear of the heart he pondered on that saying: "He that shall scandalize one of these little ones that believe in me, it were better for him that a millstone should be hanged about his neck, and that he should be drowned in the depth of the sea."[31] By the millstone is symbolized the laborious round of worldly life, and by the depth of the sea final damnation is referred to. Therefore, if one vested with the appearance of holiness destroys others by word or example, it certainly were better that his earthly deeds, performed in a worldly guise, should press him to death, rather than that his sacred offices should have pointed him out to others for sinful imitation; surely, the punishment of hell would prove less severe if he fell alone.

3. We have briefly said this much to show how great is the burden of government, lest one who is unfit for it should profane that sacred office, and through a desire of eminence should undertake a preeminence that leads to perdition. For that reason, James, with parental concern, utters the prohibition, saying: "Be not many masters, my brethren."[32] Wherefore, even the Mediator between God and humankind, who excels in knowledge and understanding even the celestial spirits and who reigns in heaven from eternity, shrank from receiving an earthly kingdom. For it is written: "Jesus, therefore, when he knew that they would come to take him by force and make him king, fled again into the mountain himself alone."[33]

5. There are those who are gifted with virtues in a high degree and who are exalted by great endowments for the training of others; who are

---

29. Hos. 5:1 and 9:8. See p. 70 on imitation.
30. Ezek. 44:12.
31. Matt. 18:6; see also Luke 17:1ff.
32. James 3:1; cf. Matt. 23:8, 10.
33. John 6:15.

unspotted in their zeal for chastity, strong in the vigor of their abstinence, replete with feasts of knowledge, humble in their long-suffering patience, erect in the fortitude of authority, gentle in the grace of loving-kindness, strict and unbending in justice. Such, indeed, in declining to undertake supreme rule when invited to do so, deprive themselves, for the most part, of the gifts which they have received not for their own sakes only, but for the sake of others also.

When these regard their own personal advantage, not that of others, they lose such advantages in wishing to retain them for themselves. If, then, the care of feeding is a testimony of love, one who, abounding in virtues, refuses to feed the flock of God, is convicted of having no love for the Supreme Shepherd.

6. There are some also who flee from this burden only out of humility: they do not wish to be preferred to those others to whom they think they are inferior. Their humility is, indeed, genuine in God's eyes, provided it is accompanied by the other virtues, and when it is not obstinate in declining to undertake what is enjoined to be profitably undertaken. For no one is genuinely humble, who understands that the decision of the Supreme Will is for him to take leadership, and yet refuses that leadership. But when the supreme rule is imposed, and provided that he is already endowed with those gifts whereby others can benefit, he ought, in submission to God's dispositions and removed from the vice of obstinacy, to flee from it in his heart and obey, though to obey is contrary to his inclination.

11. Therefore, everyone should wisely assess oneself, lest one dare to take on the role of government, while vice still reigns in him to his condemnation; one who is debased by his own guilt must not intercede for the faults of others.

Wherefore, the voice from on high said to Moses: "Say to Aaron: Whosoever of thy seed throughout their families hath a blemish shall not offer bread to the Lord God. Neither shall he approach to minister to him." It is immediately added: "If he be blind, if he be lame, if he has a little, or a great and crooked nose, if his foot or if his hand be broken, if he be crookbacked, or blear-eyed, or have a pearl in his eye, or a continual scab, or a dry scurf in his body, or a rupture."[34]

Now, that person is blind who is ignorant of the light of heavenly contemplation; who, oppressed by the darkness of the present life, does not behold the light to come as he does not love it, and, therefore, does not

---

34. Lev. 21:17-20. This list of diseases follows the Vulgate. Interpreting such lists through moral allegory was an ancient practice, its first great exponent being Philo. Notice how useful it is in organizing a discussion of moral types. See Nazianzen, *On . . . His Father* 24, p. 127.

know whither to direct the steps of his conduct. Hence, the prophetess Anna said: "He will keep the feet of his saints, and the wicked shall be silent in darkness."[35]

One is lame who does, indeed, see the way he should go, but through infirmity of purpose is unable to follow persistently the way of life which he sees. Because his unstable habit cannot rise to the estate of virtue, he is not strong enough to make his conduct follow in the direction of his desires. Consequently, St. Paul says: "Lift up the hands which hang down, and the feeble knees, and make straight steps with your feet, that no one halting, may go out of the way, but rather be healed."[36]

One with a little nose is that person who is incapable of discernment, for by the nose we discern sweet odors from stench. Rightly, then, the nose symbolizes discernment, whereby we elect virtue and reject sin. Therefore, too, it is said in praise of the bride: "Your nose is like the tower of Lebanon."[37] For, certainly, holy church perceives by its discernment what temptations proceed from various causes, and, as from an eminence, detects the oncoming wars of vice.

But there are some who, disliking to be considered dull, often busy themselves with a variety of inquisitions, more than is needful, and fall into error by their excessive subtlety. Therefore, here the addition: "A great and crooked nose." Evidently, a great and crooked nose is immoderate subtlety in making distinctions; when this develops inordinately, it distorts the correctness of its own functioning.

Again, one has a fractured foot or hand when wholly unable to walk in the way of God and entirely bereft of all share in good deeds. In this one is not like the lame person who can share in good deeds, at least with difficulty; one is bereft of them altogether.

The crookbacked is one who is weighed down by the burden of earthly cares, so that he never looks up to the things that are above, but is wholly intent on what is underfoot in the lowest sphere. If at any time he hears something good about the heavenly fatherland, he is so weighed down by the burden of evil habit that he does not raise up the face of his heart; he just cannot lift up the cast of his thought, being kept bowed down by habitual earthly solicitude. This is the kind of whom the psalmist says: "I have been bowed down and humbled exceedingly."[38] Their fault is also reprobated by the truth in person, saying: "And that seed which fell among thorns, are they who have heard the Word, and going their way, are

---

35. 1 Sam. 2:9.
36. Heb. 12:12ff.; Isa. 35:3; Prov. 4:26.
37. Song of Songs 7:4.
38. Ps. 38:6.

choked with the cares and riches and pleasures of this life, and yield no fruit."[39]

The blear-eyed is one whose natural disposition does, indeed, shine forth unto the knowledge of truth, but is obscured by carnal works. For in the blear-eyed the pupils are sound, but owing to a flux of serous matter the eyelids become weak and swollen and are often worn away by the flow, so that the keenness of the pupils is impaired. And there are those whose perception is weakened by the works of a carnal life—those who were capable of a nice discrimination of what was right, which, however, is obscured by the habit of evil deeds.

The blear-eyed is, then, one whose sense was naturally keen, but whose depraved way of life has confounded it. To such it was well said through the angel: "Anoint your eye with eye salve, that you may see."[40] For we anoint our eyes with salve for seeing when we assist the eye of our understanding with the medicaments of good works, so that we may perceive the brightness of the true light.

But that person has a white film over his eyes, who is prevented from perceiving the light of truth owing to blindness, induced by the arrogant assumption of wisdom or righteousness. For the pupil of the eye, if black, can see, but if it has a white film, it sees nothing; and, obviously, when one understands that he is foolish and a sinner, his faculty of thought grasps the knowledge of the interior light. But if he attributes to himself the radiance of righteousness or wisdom, he shuts himself off from the light of supernal knowledge; and in proportion to his arrogant self-exaltation, he futilely endeavors to penetrate the bright light of truth—as is said of some: "For professing themselves to be wise, they became fools."[41]

One is "permanently scabrous" when constantly dominated by wantonness of the flesh. For in a case of scabies the internal heat is drawn to the skin, a condition that rightly symbolizes lechery. Thus, when the temptation in the heart issues forth into action, then it can be said that the interior heat issues forth as scabies on the skin; and to the visible injury of the body corresponds the fact that as pleasure is not repressed in the thought, it gains the mastery in act. Hence, Paul was anxious to cleanse, as it were, this itch of the skin, when he said: "Let no temptation take hold on you, but such as is human"[42]—as though he wished to make plain: "It is, indeed, human to suffer temptation in the heart, but it is diabolical, when in the struggle with temptation one is overcome and does its bidding."

---

39. Luke 8:14.
40. Rev. 3:18.
41. Rom. 1:22.
42. 1 Cor. 10:13.

Further, one has pustular disease of the skin if his mind is ravaged by avarice, which, if not restrained in small matters, grows immeasurably. The pustular disease itself invades the body without causing pain, and spreads in the infected without resulting in annoyance, while disfiguring the comeliness of the members. So, too, avarice, while affording the mind of its victim apparent delight, ulcerates it. While filling its thoughts with the acquisition of one thing after another, it kindles enmities, but gives no pain with the wounds it inflicts, because it promises to the fevered mind abundance as the wages of sin. And the comeliness of the members is lost, because this sin results also in the marring of other fair virtues. Indeed, the whole body, as it were, is befouled, since the mind is overthrown by all vices, as St. Paul testified in saying: "Covetousness is the root of all evil."[43]

The ruptured person is he who, though not actually given to baseness, is yet weighed down by it beyond measure by the constant thought of it; though not carried away by evil deeds, his mind is ravished with the pleasure of lechery, without any stings of repugnance. As to the blemish of rupture, it is due to the descent of the internal fluids to the genitals, which in consequence produces a troublesome and unseemly swelling. A person, then, is ruptured when he allows all his thoughts to run on lascivious matters, and thus carries in his heart a load of turpitude; and though he does not actually engage in deeds of shame, his mind cannot disengage itself from them. At the same time he lacks the strength to raise himself to the overt exercise of good deeds, because a shameful hidden burden weighs him down.

Whosoever, then, is subject to any of the aforesaid defects, is forbidden to offer loaves of bread to the Lord. The reason is obvious: one who is still ravaged by his own sins cannot expiate the sins of others.

And now, since we have briefly shown how one who is worthy should undertake pastoral ruling, and how the unworthy should fear to undertake it, we shall explain how one who has worthily undertaken the office ought to live in the exercise of it.

Part 2
(1, 8)

1. The conduct of a prelate should so far surpass the conduct of the people as the life of a pastor sets him apart from the flock. For one who is so regarded that the people are called his flock must carefully consider how necessary it is for him to maintain a life of rectitude. It is necessary, therefore, that one should be pure in thought, exemplary in conduct, discreet in keeping silence, profitable in speech, in sympathy a near

---

43. 1 Tim. 6:10.

neighbor to everyone, in contemplation exalted above all others, a humble companion to those who lead good lives, erect in zeal for righteousness against the vices of sinners. One must not be remiss in the care for the inner life by preoccupation with the external; nor must one, in solicitude for what is internal, fail to give attention to the external.[44]

8. At the same time it is also necessary that a ruler should be studiously vigilant that he be not actuated by the desire of pleasing others; that, while seriously penetrating the inner life, and with provident care supplying the things that are external, he does not seek to be loved by his subjects more than he seeks truth; or that while relying on his good actions and giving himself the appearance of a stranger to the world, his self-love does not render him a stranger to his Maker.

For that person is an enemy to his redeemer who on the strength of the good works he performs, desires to be loved by the church, rather than by him. Indeed, a servant is guilty of adulterous thought if he craves to please the eyes of the bride when the bridegroom sends gifts to her by him. In truth, when this self-love captures a ruler's mind, it sometimes rushes him into inordinate laxity, sometimes into asperity. For from love of himself, the ruler's mind is diverted into laxity when he sees his subjects sinning and does not dare to correct them, lest their love of him grow weak; indeed, sometimes when he should have reproved their faults, he glosses them over with adulation.

This attitude the rulers show to those, of course, from whom they fear they can be retarded in the pursuit of temporal glory. Indeed, persons who in their estimation can do nothing against them, they constantly hound with bitter and harsh reproof. They never admonish them gently, but, forgetful of pastoral meekness, terrify them in the exercise of their right to govern. The divine word rightly reproves such rulers by the prophet, saying: "But you ruled over them with rigor and with a high hand."[45] These love themselves more than their Maker, and brag as they take measures against their subjects. They have no thought for what they should do, but only for the power that is theirs. They do not fear the judgment to come. They glory impiously in their temporal power, it pleases them to do freely what is wrong, and without any opposition from their subjects.

---

44. *Prelate's rectitude:* that those who lead Christians ought to be able to lead by example as well is obvious enough and an oft stated thought; but here the potentially dangerous track continues which was begun in Cyprian's time (see above, p. 63, n. 71): an ecclesiology so based on priestly holiness that there evolves a two-level church, with priests being the first-class Christians. Gregory would, of course, prescribe a large dose of humility.

45. Ezek. 34:4.

One, therefore, who sets himself to act evilly and yet wishes others to be silent, is a witness against himself, for he wishes himself to be loved more than the truth, which he does not wish to be defended against himself. There is, of course, no one who so lives as not sometimes to sin; but he wishes truth to be loved more than himself, who wills to be spared by no one against the truth.

It is also to be observed that good rulers should wish to please people, but so as to draw their neighbors to the love of truth by the fair esteem they have of their rulers, not that these long to be loved themselves, but wish that this love should be a road, as it were, whereby they lead the hearts of the hearers to the love of the Creator. It is difficult for one who is not loved, however well he preaches, to find a sympathetic hearing. Wherefore, one who rules ought to aim at being loved, that he may be listened to, and yet not seek to be loved on his own account, lest he be discovered to rebel in the tyranny of his thought against him whom he ostensibly serves in his office.

This is well suggested by Paul, when he reveals to us the secrets of his endeavor, saying: " ... As I also in all things please all people"; though again he says: "If I yet pleased people, I should not be the servant of Christ."[46] Thus Paul pleases and does not please, because, in wishing to please he sought not to please men, but that through him truth might please men.

Part 3
(Prologue, 1, 25, 40)

PROLOGUE. We have shown, then, what the character of the pastor should be: let us now set forth his manner of teaching. Well, as long before us Gregory of Nazianzus of revered memory has taught, one and the same exhortation is not suited to all, because they are not compassed by the same quality of character. Often, for instance, what is profitable to some, harms others. Thus, too, herbs which nourish some animals, kill others; gentle hissing that calms horses, excites young puppies; medicine that alleviates one disease, aggravates another; and bread such as strengthens the life of robust adults, destroys that of little children.

Wherefore, the discourse of a teacher should be adapted to the character of the hearers, so as to be suited to the individual in his respective needs, and yet never deviate from the art of general edification. For what else are the minds of attentive hearers but, if I may say so, the taut strings of a harp, which the skillful harpist plays with a variety of strokes, that he may not produce a discordant melody? And it is for this reason that the strings

---

46. Gal. 1:10.

give forth a harmonious melody, because they are not plucked with the same kind of stroke, though plucked with the one plectrum. Hence, too, every teacher, in order to edify all in the one virtue of charity, must touch the hearts of all hearers by using one and the same doctrine, but not by giving to all one and the same exhortation.

1. In giving admonition we must distinguish between:
   men and women;
   the young and the old;
   the poor and the rich;
   the joyful and the sad;
   subjects and superiors;
   slaves and masters;
   the wise of this world and the dull;
   the impudent and the timid;
   the insolent and the fainthearted;
   the impatient and the patient;
   the kindly and the envious;
   the sincere and the insincere;
   the hale and the sick;
   those who fear afflictions and, therefore, live innocently, and those so hardened in evil as to be impervious to the correction of affliction;
   the taciturn and the loquacious;
   the slothful and the hasty;
   the meek and the choleric;
   the humble and the haughty;
   the obstinate and the fickle;
   the gluttonous and the abstemious;
   those who mercifully give of their own, and those addicted to thieving;
   those who do not steal yet do not give of their own, and those who give of their own yet do not desist from despoiling others;
   those living in discord and those living in peace;
   sowers of discord and peacemakers;
   those who do not understand correctly the words of the holy law and those who do, but utter them without humility;
   those who, though capable of preaching worthily, yet are afraid to do so from excessive humility, and those whose unfitness or age debars them from preaching, yet who are impelled thereto by their hastiness;

those who prosper in their pursuit of temporal things, and those
who desire, indeed, the things of the world yet are wearied out
by suffering and adversity;

those who are bound in wedlock and those who are free from the
ties of wedlock;   ·

those who have had carnal intercourse and those who have had no
such experience;

those who grieve for sins of deed and those who grieve for sins of
thought only;

those who grieve for their sins yet do not abandon them, and those
who abandon their sins yet do not grieve for them;

those who even approve of their misdeeds and those who confess
their sins yet do not shun them;

those who are overcome by sudden concupiscence, and those
who deliberately put on the fetters of sin;

those who commit only small sins but commit them frequently,
and those who guard themselves against small sins yet sometimes sink into grave ones;

those who do not even begin to do good, and those who begin but
do not finish;

those who do evil secretly and good openly, and those who hide
the good they do, yet allow themselves to be thought ill of
because of some things they do in public.

25. Those who can preach worthily, but fear to do so from excessive
humility, are to be admonished in one way, and in another, those who are
debarred from it by their unfitness or age, and yet are impelled thereto by
their hastiness. Those who can preach with good results, but shrink from
doing so from inordinate humilty, are to be admonished to infer from a
consideration of what is a small matter, how greatly they are at fault in
matters of greater moment. Thus, if they were to hide from their indigent
neighbors money which they themselves have, they would, without doubt,
show themselves to be abettors of distress. Let them, then, consider in
what great guilt they are implicated, because by withholding the word of
preaching from sinners, they are hiding the medicine of life from souls that
are dying.

Wherefore, a wise person said well: "Wisdom that is hid, and treasure
that is not seen, what profit is there in them both?"[47] If a famine were
wasting away the people, and these same people kept their corn hidden
away, they would, undoubtedly, be the authors of death. Consequently, let

47. Ben Sira 20:30.

them consider what punishment is to be meted out to those who do not minister the bread of grace which they themselves have received, when souls are perishing from hunger for the Word. Wherefore, too, it is well said by Solomon: "He who hoards corn shall be cursed among the people."[48] To hoard corn is to retain with oneself the words of sacred preaching. Among the people any such is cursed, since, for the fault of mere silence, one is condemned in the punishment of the many who could have been corrected.

40. But at this juncture we are brought back in the zeal of our charity to what we have already said, namely, that every preacher should make himself heard rather by deeds than by words, and that by a righteous way of life should imprint footsteps for people to tread in, rather than show them by word the way to go. For that cock,[49] too, which the Lord in his figure of speech took as a symbol of the good preacher, when he is preparing to crow, first shakes his wings, and beating himself with them, makes himself more alert. So, it is obviously necessary that they who give utterance to words of holy preaching, should first be awake in the earnest practice of good deeds, lest, being themselves slack in performing them, they stir up others by words only. Let them first rouse themselves up by lofty deeds, and then make others solicitous to live good lives. Let them first smite themselves with the wings of their thoughts. Let them carefully examine themselves and discover in what respects they are idling and lagging, and make amends by severe penance. Then, and only then, let them set in order the lives of others by their words. They should first take heed to punish their own sins by tears, and then declare what deserves punishment in others; and before they utter words of exhortation, they should proclaim in their deeds all that they are about to say.

Part 4

Now, seeing that often when a sermon is delivered with due propriety and with a fruitful message, the mind of the speaker is exalted by joy over his performance, he must take care to torment himself with painful misgivings: in restoring others to health by healing their wounds, he must not disregard his own health and develop tumors of pride. Let him not, while helping his neighbors, neglect himself; let him not, while lifting up others, fall himself. In many instances, indeed, the greatness of certain people's virtues has been an occasion of their perdition, in that they have felt inordinately secure in the assurance of their strength, and they died suddenly because of their negligence. For as virtue struggles against vice,

---

48. Prov. 11:26.
49. Cf. Job 38:36, Vulgate.

the mind, as it were, exhilarated by this virtue, flatters itself; and it comes to pass that the soul of one actually engaged upon doing good casts aside all anxiety and circumspection, and rests secure in its self-confidence. In this state of inertia the cunning Seducer enumerates all that the person has done well, and aggrandizes him with conceited thoughts about his pre-eminence over all others.

Whence it happens that in the eyes of the just Judge the consciousness of virtue is a pitfall for the soul. In calling to mind what it has done, in exalting itself before itself, it falls in the presence of the Author of humility. Wherefore, it is said to the soul that is proud: "Whom do you excel in beauty? Go down and sleep with the uncircumcised";[50] which means in plain words: "Since you exalt yourself because of the beauty of your virtues, it is this your beauty that is hurrying you on to your ruin." Hence, under the figure of Jerusalem, the soul which vaunts its virtue is reproved, when it is said: "You were perfect through my beauty, which I had put upon you, says the Lord, but trusting in your beauty, you played the harlot because of your renown."[51] The mind is lifted up in the confidence of its beauty, when with blithe self-assurance it glories over its virtues. But through this same confidence it is led on to play the harlot: that is, when by its thoughts the mind robs and deceives itself, evil spirits seduce and corrupt it with numerous vices. Note, too, that it is said: "You played the harlot because of your renown"—meaning that when the soul has no regard for the Supernal Ruler, it at once seeks its own praise and begins to arrogate to itself all the good it has received for its mission as a herald of the Giver. Its desire is to spread the glory of its esteem, and its one concern is to impress all with its admirable qualities. Therefore, it plays the harlot because of its renown, when, forsaking the wedlock of its lawful bed, it prostitutes itself to the corrupting spirit in its lust for praise. Hence David says: "He delivered their strength into captivity, and their beauty into the hands of the enemy."[52] Virtue is, indeed, delivered into captivity, and beauty into the hands of the foe, when the ancient Enemy lords it over the deceived soul for its elation in well-doing.

Often this elation in virtue in a measure tempts the minds even of the elect, though it does not quite overcome them. In this case when the mind is lifted up, it is deserted, and deserted, it is recalled to fear. It is for this reason that David says again: "In my abundance I said: I shall never be moved." But because in the assurance of his virtue he became conceited, he presently added what he had endured: "You turned away your face

50. Ezek. 32:19.
51. Ezek. 16:14.
52. Ps. 78:61.

from me, and I became troubled";[53] which is as if he were saying plainly: "I believed myself strong in my virtues, but when I was deserted, I came to realize how great my weakness was." Wherefore, he says again: "I have sworn and am determined to keep the judgments of your justice." But because it was beyond his power to continue to observe his oath, he at once, on being troubled, discovered his weakness. Therefore, he betook himself at once to the help of prayer, saying: "I have been humbled, O Lord, exceedingly. Quicken me according to your word."[54]

Sometimes, too, divine guidance recalls to the mind the recollection of its infirmity before advancing it by gifts, lest it pride itself on the virtues it has received. Wherefore, the prophet Ezekiel, as often as he is led to the contemplation of heavenly things, is first called "son of man,"[55] as though the Lord plainly admonished him, saying: "That you may not proudly lift up your heart because of what you are to see, consider carefully what you are. When you penetrate the sublimest things, remember that you are mortal; for when you are enraptured above yourself, you will be recalled in anxiety to yourself by the curb of your infirmity."

Hence, it is necessary that when a wealth of virtues flatters us, the eye of the soul should turn its gaze on its infirmities, and for its own good it should prostrate itself. It should look to the good not that it has done, but that which it has neglected to do, so that while the heart becomes contrite in recalling its weakness, it may be the more solidly established in the eyes of the Author of humility. For Almighty God perfects in great measure the minds of those who rule, but leaves them partially imperfect, for this reason, that when they are resplendent with extraordinary attainments, they may grieve with disgust for their imperfections, and, least of all, exalt themselves for great things, when they have to labor and struggle against very small matters. And as they are not able to overcome the very little things, they should not presume to pride themselves on the great things they accomplish.

See, my good friend, compelled by the urgency of your remonstrances with me, I have tried to show what a pastor should be like. I, miserable painter that I am, have painted the portrait of an ideal pastor; and here I have been directing others to the shore of perfection, I, who am still tossed about on the waves of sin. But in the shipwreck of this life, sustain me, I beseech you, with the plank of your prayers, so that, as my weight is sinking me down, you may uplift me with your meritorious hand.

---

53. Ps. 30:7.
54. Ps. 119:107.
55. Ezek. 2:1, 3, 6, 8; 3:1, 3, 4, etc.

BIBLIOGRAPHY

Adams, Jeremy du Q. *The Populus of Augustine and Jerome: A Study in the Patristic Sense of Community.* New Haven: Yale University Press, 1971.

Ayer, Joseph C. *A Source Book for Ancient Church History.* New York: Charles Scribner's Sons, 1913.

Barnes, Timothy. *Tertullian: A Historical and Literary Study.* Oxford: Clarendon Press, 1985[2].

Baur, Chrysostomus. *John Chrysostom and His Time.* London: Sands & Co., 1959[2].

Beard, Mary, and John North, eds. *Pagan Priests: Religion and Power in the Ancient World.* Ithaca, N.Y.: Cornell University Press, 1989.

Best, Ernest. *Paul and His Converts.* Edinburgh: T. & T. Clark, 1988.

Beyenka, Mary. *St. Ambrosius: Letters.* FoC 26. New York: Fathers of the Church, 1968[2].

Bobertz, Charles. *Cyprian of Carthage as Patron: A Social Historical Study of the Role of Bishop in the Ancient Christian Community of North Africa.* Ph.D. diss., Yale University, 1988.

Bolkestein, Hendrik. *Wohltätigkeit und Armenpflege im vorchristlichen Altertum.* Utrecht: A. Oosthoek Verlag, 1939.

Bradshaw, Paul. *Liturgical Presidency in the Early Church.* Bramcote, England: Grove Books, 1983.

Brock, Sebastian, and Susan Harvey. *Holy Women of the Syrian Orient.* Berkeley: University of California Press, 1987.

Brown, Peter. *Augustine of Hippo.* Berkeley: University of California Press, 1967.

———. "The Rise and Function of the Holy Man in Late Antiquity." *Journal of Roman Studies* 61 (1971): 80–101.

———. *The Making of Late Antiquity.* Cambridge: Harvard University Press, 1978.

———. "The Notion of Virginity in the Early Church." Chap. 17, pp. 427–443 in *Christian Spirituality: Origins to the Twelfth Century,* edited by Bernard McGinn and John Meyendorff. New York: Crossroad, 1985.

———. *The Body and Society: Men, Women, and Sexual Renunciation in Early Christianity.* New York: Columbia University Press, 1988.

Brown, Raymond. *The Community of the Beloved Disciple: The Life, Loves, and Hates of an Individual Church in New Testament Times.* New York: Paulist Press, 1979.

Brown, Raymond, and John Meier. *Antioch and Rome.* New York: Paulist Press, 1983.

Browning, Don. *The Moral Context of Pastoral Care.* Philadelphia: Westminster Press, 1976.

Budge, E. Wallis. *The Book of Paradise.* London: Chatto and Windus, 1904.

———. *The Wit and Wisdom of the Christian Fathers of Egypt.* Oxford: Oxford University Press, 1934.

Campenhausen, Hans von. *The Fathers of the Greek Church.* Translated by Stanley Godman. New York: Pantheon, 1959.

———. *The Fathers of the Latin Church.* Translated by Manfred Hoffmann. London: A. & C. Black, 1964.

Chabot, J. *Synodicon Orientale.* Paris: Imprimerie Nationale, 1902.

Chadwick, Henry. *Early Christian Thought and the Classical Tradition.* New York: Oxford University Press, 1966.

———. *The Early Church.* Harmondsworth, England: Penguin, 1967.

———. *Origen: Contra Celsum.* London: Cambridge University Press, 1979².

Chadwick, Owen. *Western Asceticism.* Philadelphia: Westminster Press, 1958.

———. *John Cassian.* London: Cambridge University Press, 1968².

Chitty, Derwas. *The Desert a City.* London: Basil Blackwell, 1966. Reprint. Crestwood, N.Y.: St. Vladimir's Press, 1977.

Clark, Elizabeth. "John Chrysostom and the *Subintroductae.*" *Church History* 46 (1977): 171–185.

———. *Jerome, Chrysostom and Friends.* Lewiston, N.Y.: Edwin Mellen Press, 1982².

Clark, Mary T. *Augustine of Hippo: Selected Writings.* Classics of Western Spirituality. New York: Paulist Press, 1984.

Clarke, Graeme W. *The Letters of St. Cyprian of Carthage.* New York: Newman Press, vol. 1–2 (ACW 43–44), 1984; vol. 3 (ACW 46), 1986; vol. 4 (ACW 47), 1989.

Clarke, William K. L. *Ascetical Works of Saint Basil.* London: SPCK, 1925.

Clebsch, William, and Charles Jaekle. *Pastoral Care in Historical Perspective.* Englewood Cliffs, N.J.: Prentice-Hall, 1964. Reprint. New York: Jason Aronson, 1983.

Collins, John J. *Between Athens and Jerusalem: Jewish Identity in the Hellenistic Diaspora.* New York: Crossroad, 1986.

Collins, John N. *Diakonia: The Sources and Their Interpretation.* Oxford: Oxford University Press, 1990.

Comby, Jean. *How to Read Church History,* vol. 1. New York: Crossroad, 1985.

Constantelos, Demetrios. *Byzantine Philanthropy and Social Welfare.* New Brunswick, N.J.: Rutgers University Press, 1968.

_____. "Basil the Great's Social Thought and Involvement." *Greek Orthodox Theological Review* 26 (1981): 81–86.

Cornell, Tim, and John Matthews. *Atlas of the Roman World.* New York: Facts on File, Inc., 1983.

Cross, Frank L., and Elizabeth Livingstone, eds. *The Oxford Dictionary of the Christian Church.* London: Oxford University Press, 1974[2].

Crouzel, Henri. *Origen: The Life and Thought of the First Great Theologian.* Translated by A. S. Worrall. San Francisco: Harper & Row, 1989.

Daniélou, Jean. *Origen.* London: Sheed and Ward, 1955.

Davis, Henry. *St. Gregory the Great: Pastoral Care.* Westminster, Md.: Newman Press, 1950.

Dawes, Elizabeth, and Norman Baynes. *Three Byzantine Saints.* Oxford: Basil Blackwell, 1948.

Deferrari, Roy J. *Saint Basil: The Letters,* 4 vols. Loeb Classical Library. Cambridge: Harvard University Press, 1926–34.

DiBerardino, Angelo. *Patrology.* Westminster, Md.: Christian Classics, 1986. (Published uniformly with Quasten vols. 1–3, Italian ed. 1978).

Evans, G. *The Thought of Gregory the Great.* Cambridge: Cambridge University Press, 1986.

Evans, Robert. *One and Holy: The Church in Latin Patristic Thought.* London: SPCK, 1972.

Ewald, Marie. *The Homilies of St. Jerome.* FoC 48, 57. Washington, D.C.: Catholic University of America Press, 1964, 1966.

Faivre, Alexandre. *The Emergence of the Laity in the Early Church.* Translated by David Smith. New York: Paulist Press, 1990.

Fedwick, Paul. *The Church and the Charisma of Leadership in Basil of Caesarea.* Toronto: Pontifical Institute of Mediaeval Studies, 1979.

Fedwick, Paul, ed. *Basil of Caesarea: Christian, Humanist, Ascetic. A Sixteen-Hundredth Anniversary Symposium.* Toronto: Pontifical Institute of Mediaeval Studies, 1981.

Ferguson, Everett, et al., eds., *Encyclopedia of Early Christianity.* New York: Garland, 1990.

Frend, William H. C. *The Donatist Church.* Oxford: Clarendon Press, 1971[2].

_____. "Athanasius as an Egyptian Church Leader in the Fourth Century." Chap. 16 in *Religion Popular and Unpopular.* London: Variorum, 1976.

_____. *The Rise of Christianity.* Philadelphia: Fortress Press, 1984.

Garrett, Susan. *The Demise of the Devil: Magic and the Demonic in Luke's Writings.* Minneapolis: Fortress Press, 1989.

Gaudemet, Jean. *Les sources du droit de l'église en occident du IIe au VIIe siècle.* Paris: Éditions du Cerf, 1985.

Geanakoplos, Dino. *Byzantium.* Chicago: University of Chicago Press, 1984.

Greer, Rowan. *Broken Lights and Mended Lives.* University Park: Pennsylvania State University Press, 1986.

_____. *The Fear of Freedom: A Study of Miracles in the Roman Imperial Church.* University Park: Pennsylvania State University Press, 1989.

Greer, Rowan, trans. *Origen.* Classics of Western Spirituality. New York: Paulist Press, 1979.

Gregg, Robert. *Athanasius: The Life of Anthony and the Letter of Marcellinus.* Classics of Western Spirituality. New York: Paulist Press, 1980.

_____. *Consolation Philosophy: Greek and Christian Paideia in Basil and the Two Gregories.* Cambridge, Mass.: Philadelphia Patristics Foundation, 1975.

Hagendahl, Harald. *Latin Fathers and the Classics: A Study on the Apologists, Jerome, and Other Christian Writers.* Göteborg: Elanders, 1958.

_____. *Augustine and the Latin Classics.* Göteborg: Universitet, 1967.

_____. "Jerome and the Latin Classics." *Vetus Christianus* 28 (1974): 216–227.

Halton, Thomas. *John Chrysostom: In Praise of St. Paul.* Boston: Daughters of St. Paul, 1963.

Halton, Thomas, gen. ed. *Message of the Fathers of the Church,* 22 vols. Wilmington, Del.: Michael Glazier.

Hands, Arthur Robinson. *Charities and Social Aid in Greece and Rome.* London: Thames & Hudson, 1968.

Harkins, Paul. *St. John Chrysostom: Baptismal Instructions.* Westminster, Md.: Newman Press, 1963.

Harnack, Adolf von. *Militia Christi.* Translated with an introduction by D. Gracie. Philadelphia: Fortress Press, 1981.

Helgeland, J., et al. *Christians and the Military: The Early Experience.* Philadelphia: Fortress Press, 1985.

Hennecke, Edgar, and Wilhelm Schneemelcher. *New Testament Apocrypha,* 2 vols. Philadelphia: Westminster Press, 1963–65.

Herford, R. Travers. *The Ethics of the Talmud: Sayings of the Fathers.* Cincinnati: Jewish Institute of Religion, 1945³. Reprint. New York: Schocken Books, 1962.

Hickey, Anne. *Women of the Roman Aristocracy as Christian Monastics.* Ann Arbor: University of Michigan Press, 1987.

Hinchliff, Peter. *Cyprian of Carthage.* London: Chapman, 1974.

Homes-Dudden, Frederick. *The Life and Times of St. Ambrose.* Oxford: Clarendon Press, 1935.

Hunter, David G., ed. *Preaching in the Patristic Age.* New York: Paulist Press, 1989.

Jaeger, Werner. *Early Christianity and Greek Paideia.* Cambridge: Harvard University Press, 1961.

Jalland, Trevor. *The Life and Times of St. Leo the Great.* London: SPCK, 1941.

Jones, A. H. M. *The Later Roman Empire 284–604: A Social, Economic, and Administrative Survey.* Oxford: Basil Blackwell, 1964.

Jones, Cheslyn, et al., eds. *The Study of Liturgy.* New York: Oxford University Press, 1978.

Jones, F. Stanley. "The Pseudo-Clementines: A History of Research." *Second Century* 2 (1982): 1–33, 63–96.

Kelly, J. N. D. *Jerome: His Life, Writings and Controversies.* New York: Harper & Row, 1975.

Kevane, Eugene. *Augustine the Educator: A Study in the Fundamentals of Christian Formation.* Westminster, Md.: Newman Press, 1964.

Kidd, B. J. *Documents Illustrative of the History of the Church,* 3 vols. London: SPCK, 1920–41.

Kraft, Robert, and George Nickelsburg. *Early Judaism and Its Modern Interpreters.* Atlanta: Scholars Press, 1986.

Kruse, Colin G. *New Testament Models for Ministry, Jesus and Paul.* New York: Nelson, 1985.

Lacy, J., et al. *Early Christian Biographies.* FoC 15. New York: Fathers of the Church, 1952.

Laistner, Max L. W. *Christianity and Pagan Culture in the Later Roman Empire.* Ithaca: Cornell University Press, 1951.

Lake, Kirsopp. *Apostolic Fathers.* Cambridge: Harvard University Press, 1912.

Lane Fox, Robin. *Pagans and Christians.* New York: Knopf, 1987.

Liebeschuetz, J. H. W. G. *Antioch: City and Imperial Administration in the Late Roman Empire.* Oxford: Clarendon Press, 1972.

Lietzmann, Hans. *A History of the Early Church,* 4 vols. London: Lutterworth, 1949–51.

Luibheid, Colm, trans. *John Cassian: Conferences.* Classics of Western Spirituality. New York: Paulist Press, 1985.

MacMullen, Ramsey. *Paganism in the Roman Empire.* New Haven: Yale University Press, 1981.

———. *Christianizing the Roman Empire.* New Haven: Yale University Press, 1984.

Malherbe, Abraham. *Social Aspects of Early Christianity.* Philadelphia: Fortress Press, 1983².

———. *Moral Exhortation: A Greco-Roman Sourcebook.* Library of Early Christianity. Philadelphia: Westminster Press, 1986.

———. *Paul and the Thessalonians.* Philadelphia: Fortress Press, 1987.

Malone, E. *The Monk and the Martyr.* Washington, D.C.: Catholic University of America Press, 1950.

Marrou, Henri. *Saint Augustine and His Influence through the Ages.* New York: Harper Torchbooks, 1957.

McCullough, W. Stewart. *A Short History of Syriac Christianity to the Rise of Islam.* Chico, Calif.: Scholars Press, 1982.

McNeill, John T. *A History of the Cure of Souls*. New York: Harper & Row, 1951.

Meeks, Wayne. *The First Urban Christians*. New Haven: Yale University Press, 1983.

_____. *The Moral World of the First Christians*. Library of Early Christianity. Philadelphia: Westminster Press, 1986.

_____. "The Polyphonic Ethics of the Apostle Paul." *Annual of the Society of Christian Ethics* (1988): 17–29.

Meeks, Wayne, and Robert Wilken. *Jews and Christians in Antioch*. Missoula, Mont.: Scholars Press, 1978.

Meijoring, E. *Orthodoxy and Platonism in Athanasius: Synthesis or Antithesis?* Leiden: E. J. Brill, 1968.

Merton, Thomas. *The Wisdom of the Desert*. New York: New Directions, 1970.

Moltmann-Wendel, Elizabeth. *The Women around Jesus*. New York: Crossroad, 1987.

Monachino, Vincenzo. *S. Ambrogio e la cura pastorale a Milano nel sec. IV*. Milan: Centro Ambrosiano di Documentazione e Studi Religiosi, 1973.

Murray, Robert. *Symbols of Church and Kingdom*. London: Cambridge University Press, 1975.

Nickelsburg, George, and Michael Stone. *Faith and Piety in Early Judaism: Texts and Documents*. Philadelphia: Fortress Press, 1983.

Norris, Richard A. *Christological Controversies*. Philadelphia: Fortress Press, 1980.

Oden, Thomas. *Pastoral Theology: Essentials of Ministry*. San Francisco: Harper & Row, 1983.

Pellegrino, Michael, and Audrey Fellowes. *"We Are Your Servants": Augustine's Homilies on Ministry*. Villanova, Pa.: Augustinian Press, 1986.

Poschmann, Bernhard. *Paenitentia Secunda*. Bonn: P. Hanstein, 1940.

Quasten, Johannes. *Patrology*. Utrecht: Spectrum, 1950–60. Reprint. Westminster, Md.: Christian Classics, 1983.

Ramsey, Boniface. *Beginning to Read the Fathers*. New York: Paulist Press, 1985.

Richards, Jeffrey. *Consul of God: The Life and Times of Gregory the Great*. London: Routledge and Kegan Paul, 1980.

Roberts, Alexander, and James Donaldson, eds. *The Ante-Nicene Fathers*. (ANF) Grand Rapids, Mich.: Wm. B. Eerdmans, 1950 (with frequent reprints).

Rousseau, Philip. *Ascetics, Authority and the Church in the Age of Jerome and Cassian*. London: Oxford University Press, 1978.

Ruether, Rosemary Radford. *Gregory of Nazianzus: Rhetor and Philosopher*. Oxford: Clarendon Press, 1969.

Schaff, Philip, ed. *A Select Library of Nicene and Post-Nicene Fathers of the Christian Church*. NPNF, Series 1 (14 vols.), 2 (14 vols.). Grand Rapids: Wm. B. Eerdmans, 1956. Often reprinted.

Schoedel, William. *Ignatius of Antioch*. Philadelphia: Fortress Press, 1985.

Stanniforth, Maxwell, trans. *Apostolic Fathers*. New York: Penguin Books, 1968, 1987².

Straw, Carole. *Gregory the Great: Perfection in Imperfection*. Berkeley: University of California Press, 1988.

Swift, L. J. *The Early Fathers on War and Military Service*. Wilmington, Del.: Michael Glazier, 1985.

Talbert, Charles. *Perspectives on First Peter*. Macon, Ga.: Mercer University Press, 1986.

Thurston, Bonnie Bowman. *The Widows: A Women's Ministry in the Early Church*. Philadelphia: Fortress Press, 1989.

Tollinton, Richard. *Selections from the Commentaries and Homilies of Origen*. London: SPCK, 1929.

van Loveren, A. E. D. "Once Again: 'The Monk and the Martyr': St. Anthony and St. Macrina." *Studia Patristica* 17.2 (1982): 528–538.

Vasey, Vincent. *The Social Ideas in the Works of St. Ambrose: A Study on de Nabuthe*. Rome: Institutum Patristicum Augustinianum, 1982.

Volz, Carl A. *Pastoral Life and Practice in the Early Church*. Minneapolis: Augsburg Publishing House, 1990.

Vööbus, Arthur. *The Synodicon in the West Syrian Tradition*. Corpus Scriptorum Christianorum Orientalium, vol. 368. Louvain: CSCO, 1975.

Waddell, Helen, ed. *The Desert Fathers*. London: Constable, 1936. Reprint. Ann Arbor: University of Michigan Press, 1957.

Wagner, Monica. *Saint Basil: Ascetical Works*. FoC 9. New York: Fathers of the Church, 1950.

Walker, G. S. M. *The Churchmanship of St. Cyprian*. Ecumenical Studies in History ix. London: Lutterworth Press, 1968.

Walker, Williston, Richard Norris, et al. *A History of the Christian Church*. New York: Charles Scribner's Sons, 1985⁴.

Ward, Benedicta. *The Sayings of the Desert Fathers: The Alphabetical Collection*. London: Mowbrays, 1981.

Wengst, Klaus. *Humility-Solidarity of the Humiliated: The Transformation of an Attitude*. Minneapolis: Fortress Press, 1989.

Wilken, Robert. *John Chrysostom and the Jews: Rhetoric and Reality in the Late Fourth Century*. Berkeley: University of California Press, 1983.

Winston, David. *Philo of Alexandria*. Classics of Western Spirituality. New York: Paulist Press, 1981.

Zlotnick, Dov. *The Tractate "Mourning" (Semaḥot): Regulations Relating to Death, Burial, and Mourning*. Yale Judaica Series 17. New Haven: Yale University Press, 1966.

Zucker, Lois. *S. Ambrosii de Tobia: A Commentary, with Introduction and Translation*. Washington, D.C.: Catholic University of America Press, 1933.

MAP INDEX

Adiabene (north-east Iraq): 36°-37°N 43°-45°E. Chapter 5.
Afşin (Arabissus): 38°12′N 36°54′E. Chapter 9.
Alexandria: 31°13′N 29°55′E. Chapters 2, 4.
Ancyra: 39°55′N 32°50′E. Chapters 3, 6.
Antioch: 36°12′N 36°10′E. Chapters 1, 6, 9.
Aquileia: 45°47′N 13°22′E. Chapter 8.
Arles 43°41′N 4°38′E. Chapter 2.
Asturica: 42°27′N 6°04′W. Chapter 3.
Athens: 38°00′N 23°44′E. Chapters 2, 7.
Caesarea, Cappadocia (Mazaca): 38°42′N 35°28′E. Chapters 6, 7.
Caesarea Maritima: 32°30′N 34°54′E. Chapter 2.
Campania: 40°-41°30′N 14°-16°E. Chapter 10.
Carthage: 36°54′N 10°16′E. Chapter 3.
Chalcedon: 40°59′N 29°02′E. Chapters 6, 9.
Chalcis, Euboea: 38°28′N 23°36′E. Chapter 9.
Clermont (Augustonemetum): 45°47′N 3°05′E. Chapters 2, 10.
Constantinople (Byzantium, Istanbul): 41°02′N 28°57′E. Chapters 7, 9, 10.
Corinth: 37°56′N 22°55′E. Chapter 1.
Ctesiphon: 33°06′N 44°36′E. Chapter 7.
Elvira (Illiberis): 37°17′N 3°53′W. Chapter 6.
Emerita (modern Merida): 38°55′N 6°20′W. Chapter 3.
Ephesus: 37°55′N 27°19′E. Chapter 1.
Etruria (roughly modern Tuscany): 41°30′-44°30′N 10°-12°E. Chapter 10.
Gangra (Germanicopolis): 40°35′N 33°37′E. Chapter 6.
Göksun (Cucusus): 38°03′N 36°25′E. Chapter 9.
Hippo Regius: 36°55′N 7°47′E. Chapter 8.
Laodicea: 37°46′N 29°02′E. Chapter 6.
Legio (modern Leon): 42°34′N 5°34′W. Chapter 3.
Lyon (Lugdunum): 45°46′N 4°50′E. Chapter 1.
Magnesia (ad Meandrum): 37°46′N 27°29′E. Chapter 1.
Marseille (Massilia): 43°18′N 5°22′E. Chapters 4, 10.
Milan (Mediolanum): 45°28′N 9°12′E. Chapter 8.
Nazianzus: 38°16′N 34°23′E. Chapters 7, 9, 10.
Nicaea (modern Iznik): 40°27′N 29°43′E. Chapters 4, 6.
Nyssa: 38°51′N 34°00′E. Chapter 7.
Philadelphia (modern Alaşehir): 38°22′N 28°32′E. Chapter 1.
Picenum (roughly modern Marche): 43°-44°N 12°-14°E. Chapter 10.
Rimini (Ariminum): 44°03′N 12°34′E. Chapter 7.
Rome: 41°53′N 12°30′E. Chapters 1, 3, 8, 10.
Saragossa (Caesaraugusta): 41°39′N 0°54′W. Chapters 2, 10.
Smyrna (modern Izmir): 38°25′N 27°10′E. Chapter 1.
Thagaste: 36°14′N 8°00′E. Chapter 8.
Tralles (modern Aydin): 37°52′N 27°50′E. Chapter 1.
Trier (Augusta Treverorum): 49°45′N 6°39′E. Chapter 8.

Selected approximate mileage: Hippo to Carthage: 148; Marseille to Milan: 244; Milan to Rome: 297; Chalcedon to Antioch: 480; Antioch to Caesarea: 264.

217

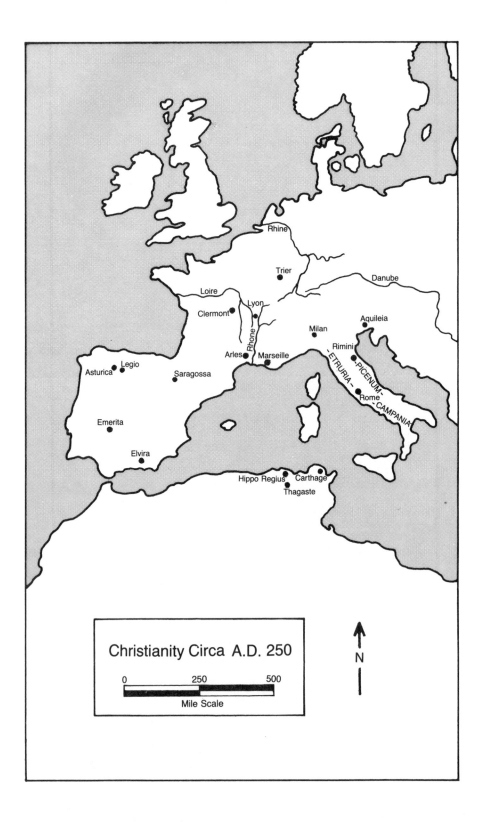

Rhine

Trier

Danube

Loire

Lyon

Clermont

Rhone

Aquileia

Milan

Rimini

- ETRURIA -

- PICENUM -

Arles Marseille

Asturica Legio

Saragossa

Rome

- CAMPANIA -

Emerita

Elvira

Hippo Regius Carthage

Thagaste

Christianity Circa A.D. 250

0   250   500

Mile Scale

N

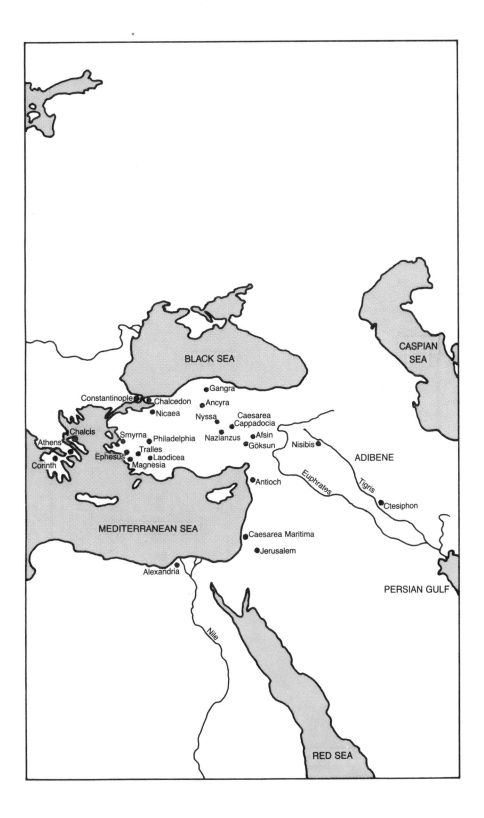

INDEX OF
SCRIPTURAL REFERENCES

The index of scripture citations and allusions is largely taken from our sources, with corrections and additions. It reflects, therefore, to a degree, the different criteria of those sources. "Allusions" can range from the obvious to vague or conflated remembrances, and it is instructive to examine how different authors make use of scripture and scripture-like language.

INDEX OF
NONSCRIPTURAL REFERENCES

POST-BIBLICAL JEWISH LITERATURE

CLASSICAL AUTHORS

EARLY CHRISTIAN LITERATURE
Bold indicates author with text.